Beyond Spirit Tailings

Haunted Houses

All houses wherein men have lived and died
Are haunted houses. Through the open doors
The harmless phantoms on their errands glide,
With feet that make no sound upon the floors.

We meet them at the door-way, on the stair,
Along the passages they come and go,
Impalpable impressions on the air,
A sense of something moving to and fro.

Henry Wadsworth Longfellow

BEYOND SPIRIT TAILINGS

MONTANA'S MYSTERIES, GHOSTS, AND HAUNTED PLACES

ELLEN BAUMLER

Montana Historical Society Press
Helena, Montana

Cover: Kuehn children's tombstone, Benton Avenue Cemetery.
COURTESY KATIE BAUMLER 2004

Back Cover: "Spirited Victorian Charmer" after renovations.
COURTESY KATIE BAUMLER 2004

Cover and Book Design by UpperWest Creative Services
Typeset in Sabon
Printed by Creasey Printing Services
Copyright © 2005 by Montana Historical Society Press
P.O. Box 201201, Helena, MT 59620-1201

Distributed by the Globe Pequot Press, 246 Goose Lane,
Guilford, Connecticut 06437 (800) 243-0495
05 06 07 08 09 10 10 9 8 7 6 5 4 3 2 1
ISBN 0-9721522-4-5
Printed in Canada

Library of Congress Cataloging-in-Publication Data

Baumler, Ellen.
     Beyond spirit tailings : Montana's mysteries, ghosts, and haunted
places / Ellen Baumler.-- 1st ed.
               p. cm.
     Includes index.
     ISBN 0-9721522-4-5 (pbk. : alk. paper)
1.   Ghosts--Montana. 2.   Haunted places--Montana.   I. Title.
     BF1472.U6B376 2005
     133.1'09786--dc22
                                        2004031028

For Vivian Paladin (1918-2002), mentor and friend, who cared deeply about bringing Montana's past to the public and passionately believed that history, when rightly told, is much more remarkable than fiction.

TABLE OF CONTENTS

LIST OF ILLUSTRATIONS

ACKNOWLEDGEMENTS

Many generous and enthusiastic people had a role in the preparation of this book. The creation of *Beyond Spirit Tailings* depended upon all those who contributed their stories, their expertise, and their enthusiasm for a subject sometimes controversial. Family, friends, colleagues at the Montana Historical Society, and audiences from third graders to senior citizens across the state have patiently listened to my stories and offered suggestions making them that much better. It has been a pleasure and a privilege to work with each of the many contributors mentioned on the following pages who have allowed me to share their experiences. Thanks to many others who asked and answered questions and offered their opinions. As in my first book of Montana ghost tales, *Spirit Tailings*, the staff of the Publications Program has believed in this project and contributed in many ways. Jon Axline, historian at the Montana Department of Transportation, graciously read versions of the stories and offered comments on the final manuscript. Designer Bob Smith joined the team, adding his talents and boundless creativity to the project. And finally, without the support of my husband, Mark, and daughter, Katie, who give their undivided attention (most of the time) to my endless stream of stories and revisions, I could not have completed this book.

Ellen Baumler
Helena, Montana
2004

BEGINNINGS

The scene remains etched in my mind. We sat around a picnic table with smoke from the fire stinging our eyes and its pungent fragrance permeating our clothing. So much time had passed, here in the midst of the old beer garden, since brewer Henry Gilbert had served his draughts to the thirsty miners of Alder Gulch. Gilbert's false-fronted brewery loomed behind us as the evening chill crept in over the darkening shadows. The rambling house where Henry and Margaret Gilbert raised fifteen children stood nearby, long uninhabited, its gray weathered boards decaying leisurely. Huge and ancient cottonwood trees, their roots watered by the swift-flowing creek, sheltered this little hollow by the bank. Massive branches swayed above us, leaves rustling in the summer breeze.

The fire popped and the stream rushed past. It was easy to imagine miners of long ago squatting on the banks, searching for golden treasure. My audience of adolescent history-buff campers quietly listened to my scary tales as I did my best to give them nightmares to remember. I had exhausted my Virginia City repertoire, at least for the evening, and they professed to be suitably scared. They were not yet ready to give up the fire and head back to their rooms at the Fairweather Inn, a place whose haunted reputation we had just spent some time discussing. So we began to swap stories. During a pause in the lively conversation, one gangly young man spoke up. In a low and serious voice, the young man shared, with some difficulty, an experience that even now in recollection haunts me.

He and his family had been through a tragedy that left permanent scars. A few years before, he told me, his family home in the tiny community of Geraldine, Montana, had burned to the ground, and his little sister died in the flames. Despite the tragedy, the family rebuilt the house on the same site, and began again. With a steady gaze, the young man ignored the other kids giggling and joking around him. He turned to face me, looked me in the eye, and said, "Sometimes late at night, when I am up alone watching TV in the living room, I can feel my sister's presence. I know she is there watching me. Sometimes, I can even see her footprints in the carpet as she walks across the room."

When it comes to ghosts and other unexplained phenomena, proof is a very personal thing. Unless the experience is spectacular, most of us tend to disregard it. We have all have had some brush at some time with something eerie, something scary, or something so uncanny it defies rational explanation. A rush of déjà vu, the sound of footsteps in an empty room, a misplaced or moved object—these subtle things we usually do not dwell upon, but they, as much as our day-to-day routines—help shape our views of the world. When these little events become intertwined with oral traditions or family histories, they influence us when we hear them repeated. My mother, for example, had her own wonderful stories of our family's exploits. She gave little thought to the unexplained (at least, that I know of), but she did have one eerie story that was my favorite. Her matter-of-fact telling is probably what made the incident so dramatic and so believable to a ten-year-old. The story went something like this:

In the early spring of 1941, Jeanne Popham (my mother), Edward M "Bud" Boddington (my father), and his best friend, P. V. "Plez" Miller were freshmen at the University of Kansas at Lawrence. One Saturday night, they visited a local fortuneteller. She advertised herself as "Madam Arkle," a misspelling, said my mother, of the word "oracle." The three friends did not believe Madam Arkle could predict the future, but they went to the creepy house on the edge of town on a dare. They knocked at the door and it opened a crack to reveal a wizened (my mother's word) old woman. She motioned them inside and they stood there uncomfortably.

"Cross my palm with silver," she said, "whatever you have, and I will tell you a few things." They dug into their pockets and covered Madam's open palm with change.

She carefully studied the hand of each young man; Jeanne did not interest her. Finally she looked at Plez, "You have a motorcycle, yes?" He nodded. "Your parents don't know you have it, do they?" Plez shook his head. "Get rid of it," said she, "before you have a wreck." The other two giggled, but Plez was ill at ease. A few months later, he found himself lying in a cornfield, the wheels of his wrecked motorcycle spinning.

Madam Arkle revealed a number of other minor things that came to pass, but one detail came back to haunt all three of them. As the fortuneteller peered into the palms of each young man, she seemed troubled. "I can't understand it," she mused. "When I look at the palms of you two young men, all I can see is blue. Blue above, blue below. *Blue joins blue.* It must be water or sky, but it doesn't make any sense."

The three laughed all the way home, making light of Madam Arkle's predictions. But later that year, on December 7, the attack on Pearl Harbor brought an abrupt end to college for Plez and Bud. They joined the Navy, went to flight school, and months later, both were carrier-based Navy pilots flying F6-F Hellcats in the South Pacific, where *blue joins blue.*

After the war, the two friends returned to graduate from the University of Kansas and settled in the greater Kansas City area. My dad, a cowboy at heart, became an attorney like his father before him and practiced law for forty years in Kansas City. Plez was the longtime president of a Kansas City, Missouri, bank. He and his wife Alice were my godparents. Throughout his life, my dad talked about the war at every opportunity, but neither he nor Plez ever talked about Madam Arkle and her predictions. My dad, however, did acknowledge discomfort over my mother's accurate telling.

Spirit Tailings, published in 2002, was in a way a result of the Madam Arkle story that so influenced me. This second book is a continuation and to some extent, a further exploration, into Montana ghosts, spirits, history, and mysteries. The stories span communities from Polson to Billings and Havre to Hamilton. Some would argue that such an endeavor is an eccentricity for a professional historian—and perhaps they are right—but I am convinced that such stories, and the histories behind them, shape our sense of family, our sense of place, and our understanding of community. *Spirit Tailings* opened the floodgates to many more new stories that have streamed in from Montanans across the state. They cover a wide range of unique experiences.

Ken Walton, for example, is one of the many willing folks who shared interesting experiences. He is of Chickasaw descent and has been around American Indian religions all his life. Once, he told me, he met a guy who practiced Eckankar, a New Age religion based on ancient Hindu philosophy in which teletransportation, the art of transporting oneself to places without physically going there, is an important aspect. Ken had a casual conversation with the man about this practice, and then they parted and each went his own way. That night Ken's wife awakened to find a bald-headed man standing at the foot of the bed. She thought it was a dream and went back to sleep. The next morning she told her husband about the dream, saying that it had been very real, not like a dream at all. Then she described the man, and her description matched the man with whom Ken had conversed the day before.

Some time later, Ken ran into this man again. The man said, "So, remember our last conversation?" Ken acknowledged that he recalled it well. "Good," said the man. "And that night, did your wife have a visitor at the foot of her bed?"

Stories almost always come in unexpected ways. When I shared "Count Your Blessings" in *Spirit Tailings* with a colleague, she suddenly realized a friend had briefly rented Annabelle Richards' house, the home featured in the story. The colleague told me how her friend's young daughter had a room off the landing where Annabelle had heard ghostly men coming up the stairs. The mother had removed the doorknob so that the child could not lock herself in the room. One night the little girl awoke from a sound sleep to see her cat, usually asleep at her side, staring at the doorknob. The cat was staring so hard and its eyes were so big that the little girl became frightened. She followed the cat's gaze to the doorknob and what she saw gave her nightmares for years to come. A finger was sticking out of the hole where the doorknob had been. And it was pointing directly at her.

In Virginia City, ghost sightings and supernatural events continue to surface. At the Bonanza Inn, the former Catholic Hospital in Virginia City, a Montana Historical Society volunteer told me of a scary overnight stay in notorious Room 1. She had brought a green nightlight with her to plug into the bathroom. She awoke in the middle of the night to what she first thought was a dream. It looked like a hazy green alien was standing at the foot of her bed. Then she remembered that she had plugged in the green nightlight, and realized that she was not asleep. She could make out the form of a man, watching her. The green light illuminated the room, and defined the outline of the figure, except that the light was coming *through* him. As she stared at the apparition, it dissolved, leaving her to wonder what she had seen. A history camp counselor had a similar experience, awaking to find a man in a hat at the foot of her bed staring at her. As she looked at him, he faded away. Another Bonanza Inn episode occurred during extensive renovations in the building. One of the many workers was staying there overnight. Each room features prison-issue bunk beds consisting of an iron frame with open springs holding a plastic-covered mattress. All night long he said he could feel something under the bed plucking at the springs.

Vicki Smith is a vivacious, charming veteran of the Virginia City Players—Montana's first professional acting company, founded in the late 1940s. She and her former husband, Harry, were involved in the opera house during its early years. Vicki had gone to the theater to critique a variety show rehearsal at the request of a friend. The rehearsal was underway, and Vicki quietly entered the deserted theater and took one of the roomy aisle seats. As she sat there quietly, Vicki heard a "*whoosh*" in the seat next to her, like someone had just sat down on a whoopee cushion. She could see a depression in the empty seat, and she felt a presence there. As she sat next to him or her, she wondered what she should do. Then suddenly, whoever it was got up, the seat returned to normal, and the incident was over.

The late Barbara Brook also had an experience in the opera house. Vicki's daughter, Leisa, was debuting as a Player. Since her mom and dad were veterans of the stage, Vicki asked her friend to pick up a bouquet of flowers for her daughter on opening night. Barbara took the flowers to the opera house and upon entering the building, heard beautiful, lilting music. She was drawn to the voice and went into the theater to see who was rehearsing. There was no one on stage, but she could hear the singer distinctly. The words were in a foreign language, and she sang at a volume just low enough that the words were unintelligible. Barbara peered into the wings but saw no one. It was very eerie. She never discovered the identity of the phantom singer, but others over the years also claim to have heard the singer.

There are so many stories about Helena that I could never tell them all. Kate Axline, for example, is now in middle school, but until she was in fifth grade, she and her family lived in a spooky old house on Eighth Avenue. Kate has never been afraid of the dark, and with a black belt in tae kwon do, she can take care of herself. But she remembers from the time she was very small that there was something weird about the house. Kate did not know this at the time, but at least one owner died in the house. He was an old-time cowboy who worked the rodeo circuit in the 1890s, retired in 1921, and died in the house ten years later. His wife lived there for another forty years. A neighbor remembers that she was tall, slim, motherly, and she liked cats, a good thing, since the Axlines have five.

Kate insisted the door to her room stay open at night, and she had a hard time falling asleep. As she was about to drift off, she often sensed someone standing by her bedside playing with her hair, which understandably gave her the creeps. One of the family's cats always slept in her room, maybe to protect her, or maybe because the spirit of the cowboy's wife who liked cats was there and the cats liked the slim, motherly woman. Kate's sister Kira could never fall asleep in that room. She always went to sleep elsewhere and had to be moved to her bed. In their new house, none of the cats sleeps in the girls' rooms and Kira falls asleep in her own bed with no problem.

Kate's mom sometimes smelled cigar smoke in the house, but no one in the family smoked. Then there was something about the dark, dim basement. Kate's dad never much liked being down there. Coming down the steps one day, he saw something dark hunched on the floor. He stared at it, thinking it was one of the family's cats. It looked like a cat, and it slunk away like a cat, but it was not one of theirs. The family cats were all accounted for upstairs. After that, he didn't like the house much anymore and he didn't like the basement. Hauntings do not have to be horrific to be real. Kate saw no screaming skulls or ghostly apparitions. But still, she and other family members are sure that there was something there.

Marbles are an important theme in *Spirit Tailings*. Old marbles that turn up in odd places are reminders that the past is still part of the present. The Axlines found many old clay marbles buried in the dirt and lying on the ground in their backyard, little leavings from another time. Owners of old houses often have stories about marbles. One day at a book signing, a lady struck up a conversation telling me she had tried to persuade her neighbor to read my book. She told the neighbor that finding marbles in old houses might be evidence of ghostly inhabitants. The unconvinced neighbor said, "Marbles? Hell, I find 'em all the time in my house. I have a whole jar of 'em." The lady said she now sees the house next door and its occupant in a whole new light. Marbles figure here in "The Fruit of the Hangman's Tree."

People sometimes think I have answers for them. A lady called the Montana Historical Society library, frantic to discover what might have occurred on her property to explain a terrifying experience. She told me that she and her husband had just finished building a new home in a heavily wooded area of Jefferson County. After the family moved in, they began to hear children playing outside. They did not think much about it at first, but soon realized that, except for themselves and their four-year-old son, there were no near neighbors with children. Then one day her husband saw two oddly dressed little boys playing around the house. He went out to talk to them, but they scampered away and disappeared down a ravine. The couple became concerned when the boys did not come out and called the neighbors to see if they had children visiting. The answer was no. My caller had grown increasingly concerned about her son "seeing something" and becoming afraid of the house. Then she told me what had so frightened her. She had awakened early that morning to find the two little boys her husband described standing at the foot of her bed.

Don Pogreba tells of several experiences he had at Carroll College, one of which I have included in "School Spirit." Another story has to do with Helena High School. Don is sure that there is a woman there whose presence haunts the building after dark. He teaches English, coaches debate, and like most teachers puts in long hours after class. The building late at night is in total darkness. He has a key to the east back door by the cafeteria, but his classroom is way down one main hallway at the west end of the school. One icy winter night, well after midnight, Don remembered he had forgotten some tests he had promised to grade. He felt badly about it, so he came back to school, entering through the back door by the cafeteria. It was not cold in the heated hallway, but he felt cold as the door shut behind him. A clock way down the long wide hallway, past the library, began to tick. He had been in the building at night before, but he had never heard the clock. This night it was loud. Tick. Tick. Tick. It seemed to get louder. Something just didn't feel right, and the hair on his arms was standing straight up.

Don finally reached his room on the west side of the building. As he passed the clock, the ticking stopped and it was dead silent in the dark, empty school. Don got to his room, retrieved the tests, came back into the hallway, and the clock started to tick again. Tick. Tick. Tick. At the end of the hallway he saw it. A wisp of something disappeared around the corner. A woman's skirt? At that moment he knew it was a woman, and she was angry. He could feel the tension like knots in a cord. He began to hurry, then race down the hall toward the door. He was frightened, running to get out. OUT! He pushed the heavy door open and as it gave way, a terrible shriek made his heart leap to his throat. A cat had huddled against the warmth of the door, startling both of them out of their wits. When he thought about it later, he remembered that it was not cold in the school hallway but he felt a bone-chilling cold and felt this woman's anger. In a place like Helena High School, where so many students and teachers have come and gone, it is impossible to say who the spirit might be, but Don is certain that late at night, her anger spills through the hallway. And more recently, when he made a trip at eleven one night, there in the dark he not only felt this woman's presence, he also smelled her perfume—an old lady's perfume.

In the neighborhood in Shelby where Don grew up, about a block away from his grandmother's home, there was a house where a reclusive woman lived. The kids all talked about her, how she was always waiting for someone who never came for her. No matter when you walked past that house, the woman was always there, sitting in the same window, staring out. You could see her head, and feel her eyes, watching. When she died, people said that she was still sitting in that window, waiting, watching. You could walk past and see her in the window. When Don was a youngster, he and the other neighborhood kids were really scared of that house. Most of us have those kinds of places we remember as kids, places we were scared of. This free rein of imagination is one of those things that makes being a kid exciting.

Jeff Bickenheuser, for example, grew up in Harlem, Montana, where he had a scare in the old Harlem Hotel, one of the old buildings built to serve the railroad. Parents around town had forbidden their children to play in these decaying relics, so, of course, kids such as Jeff availed themselves of every opportunity to sneak into them. One summer evening well before dark, he and his friend Jesse snuck into the old hotel that stood on the north side of town. The two-story building had narrow hallways down the center with rooms on either side. At the end of the first floor hallway was a tight stairway leading to the second-floor rooms. Jeff and Jesse climbed the stairs and moved down the second-floor hallway, peering into the empty rooms on either side. As they got to the last room at the end of the hall, they saw that it was not empty. Sitting in the room was an old-fashioned wooden wheelchair, the kind with a caned seat. As the boys stared at it, they realized it was moving slowly toward them. There was no squeaking, no sound, and it scared them. They backed partway down the hall, turned, and bounded down the stairs; the only sound was their own heavy footsteps as they ran. Jeff remembers hitting the front doorway and stumbling outside. Looking back into the silent building and down the deserted first-floor hall, the memory of what he saw where he and Jesse had been not seconds before still gives him chills. There at the bottom of the stairway was the wheelchair.

Havre has many such haunted places, and Debbie and Vince Woodwick lived in one of them in the mid-1970s. Several times when Debbie was alone in the house, she felt that she was not alone, that someone was behind her. The dog felt it, too, and she seemed to follow something that wasn't there, growling weirdly. The strangest event of all involved a picture of Bear Paw Lake in Beaver Creek Park that Vince had taken and had enlarged. It was hanging on the living room wall near a wide doorway that led into the dining room. Debbie came home one day to find the picture on the floor, on the other side of the wall in the dining room, propped against the wall behind a chair. Research into the history of the home revealed that the only son of the longtime owner had committed suicide at Beaver Creek Park in 1963. Local rumor had it that he put a curse on the house before he died. And finally, Vince loved the workbench he found in the basement until a physician told him what it was: a marble morgue slab.

Traumatic events cannot help but leave a historic impression on a place, often forming one of the foundations upon which a community builds its common heritage. Many friends and strangers have generously shared these kinds of experiences, and as before, I have searched out the threads and carefully researched the history behind each. "The Hoo Doo Block," "A Ghost within a Ghost," "The Adams Hotel," "The Legacy of the Grant-Kohrs Ranch," and "Stranger at the Door" provide careful historical contexts important for understanding the time period and the incident's impact on the individual or community.

Some stories are so persistent that they are more properly "urban legends" such as the ones about Carroll College in "School Spirit." What is interesting about these stories is that so many students have experienced similar incidents. That lends credence to the tales, particularly when they can be tied to factual events, places, or people as in the "Bishop of All Outdoors," "Laura's Canaries," and "Remnants of a Copper King."

While *Spirit Tailings* explored the supernatural, this book goes a step further in considering some of Montana's unsolved mysteries. "Montana's Nessie," the creature that may be lurking in Flathead Lake is one. Another, "Speaking with Artifacts," introduces George McMullen, a man with an interesting approach to learning about the past. His story touches on some of the questions that spark debate about Henry Plummer and Thomas Francis Meagher. "The Sleeping Buffalo" examines the power of an ancient object revered by generations of native people. The brutal murder told in "Celestia Alice Earp" involves not a haunting but a mysterious and unexplained discovery; the story about Thomas Walsh examines the mysterious circumstances surrounding his death; and "The Hanging of Peter Pelkey" explores the phenomenon of "ghost lights." "Spirited Victorian Charmer" investigates a nationally famous haunted house.

Experience is one thing, but it is never my intention to persuade or convince readers of the existence of ghosts. Rather, my aim is to write history with a twist, history that transcends the heavily studied fields of politics and battlefields and brings the past to the present. The stories in this collection illustrate time and again how explanations for current events can often be found in the shared experiences of yesteryear. In this way, history sparks the imagination and thereby becomes relevant beyond the classroom. No matter where we grew up or what our backgrounds might be, the unexplained and the mysterious intertwined with the past touch a universal chord and make an emotional connection—fear, doubt, or wonder—timeless and familiar.

In pursuit of historical facts at the root of supernatural stories, I have had my own share of adventures. Fire ants viciously attacked me as I photographed ruins at Fort Assinniboine. A woman in an upstairs window bared her upper torso as I told stories in the pouring rain to a large crowd at the Original Governor's Mansion in Helena. Skeptics have ridiculed me (albeit politely), and intuitive guests in my home have insisted that my bedroom closet is a portal to something evil. Despite all this, I remain steadfast in my pursuit of the unexplained and look forward to these adventures. I still live in, and love, my historic home and the spirits therein.

Spirit Tailings brought Montana's colorful historical tapestry to a new audience, especially younger readers who might otherwise not choose to read history outside the classroom. Whether you are a believer or a skeptic of ghosts, spirits, and "things that go bump in the night," homegrown mysteries and tales of the unexplained are important to our culture and help define our community heritage. They are stories worth telling, preserving, and handing down to our children. Decide for yourself what you want to believe; belief is incidental. But when people ask me why I don't try writing a novel, my answer is simple: the truth is much more remarkable than anything I could conjure up.

THE SLEEPING BUFFALO

The outlined shapes of the small buffalo herd upon a wind-swept ridge overlooking the Milk River rose sharply against the blue sky. The five warriors stalking them were hungry and weary from their travels. They halted a distance away and chose two of the young men to approach the animals. The pair began to move toward the figures lying peacefully along the ridge top. Quietly they crept closer to the small herd. They moved closer still, but the buffalo remained motionless. When the great beasts were within easy range of their arrows, the young men lay flat on the earth. After some time, not even one of the buffalo so much as flicked a tail. The young men were perplexed and motioned the three waiting warriors to join them. The five hunters together cautiously approached the herd. When they reached the ridge top, they discovered not buffalo, but gray boulders. The largest one in the center of the group resembled a bull lying down.

Through countless generations the stories of Sleeping Buffalo Rock have been handed down among the tribes of Montana and western Canada. The Blackfeet, Assiniboine, Gros Ventre, Chippewa, Cree, and the more distant Crow and Northern Cheyenne all know of the Sleeping Buffalo through oral traditions. Each tribe has its own stories about how the great boulder and its smaller companions fooled hunters.

Montana's State Historic Preservation Office in Helena, with the cooperation of tribal elders, researched the significance of the Sleeping Buffalo Rock. Staff interviewed members of the various tribes, collected accounts about the venerable object, and in the early 1990s Chere Jiusto wove this information into an eloquent nomination to the National Register of Historic Places. The Sleeping Buffalo Rock earned listing in 1996. It is an unusual and significant nomination because it was prepared with, and required the aid and consensus of, Montana's tribes. The venerated object illustrates the importance of the buffalo to the culture of Montana's native people and how traditional practices even today emphasize a reverence for this animal once essential to the survival of the Plains Indian. Respectful hands made the incised markings in the gray, weatherworn granite ages ago. Horns, eyes, backbone, and ribs further define the great bull while other decorative markings honor its sacred power. Incised markings likewise adorn the smaller Medicine Rock, reportedly collected from a site north of the stone buffalo herd. Multiple carvings of animal hoof prints and other symbols illustrate the Medicine Rock's solemn religious significance.

Some tribal elders tell of experiencing the power of the Sleeping Buffalo firsthand. Leslie Fourstar, the last surviving speaker of the Assiniboine language on the Fort Peck Reservation, told how his stillborn daughter—lifeless for nearly half an hour—began to breathe after he invoked the power of "Rock Buffalo." Century-old ethnographic accounts of the Gros Ventre include references to a large buffalo stone. Its horns, hump, ribs and upper body lay above ground, but the Gros Ventre believed that the rest of it was underground. The late Bill Tallbull, cultural and spiritual leader of the Northern Cheyenne, speculated that the hole where the Sleeping Buffalo Rock originated was a buffalo wallow. The healing power of the rock itself stemmed from this wallow. Tallbull expressed his reverence for the Sleeping Buffalo Rock this way, "With a stone this big, there is lots of power. The power of the prairie was the buffalo."

Buster Yellow Kidney, elder and spiritual leader of the Blackfeet who visited the Sleeping Buffalo with his grandfather, explained that belief in it was so powerful among his people that warring clans came and camped together near the ridge top for days at a time. They kept peace out of respect for the holiness of the area. People of the plains, from time immemorial, passed beneath the lonely ridge overlooking the river. There the wide river narrowed to allow the people on their journeys to or from the north to cross with ease. The place below the ridge along the river was known as the Cree Crossing.

Canadian Indians at Waterton Park, Alberta, tell a tale that parallels the more recent history of Montana's Sleeping Buffalo Rock. Road construction crews encountered a large boulder blocking the route of a new highway. Using poles for leverage, workmen rolled the rock out of the way and down a steep embankment. The next day when the crew returned to the work site, they found to their amazement the boulder back in its original place, sitting right in the middle of the road. They related their difficulties to a medicine man who began to pray. When his prayer was finished, he told the men, "That rock is sacred. It doesn't want to be moved. Let it sit where you found it."

In 1932 Montana's Sleeping Buffalo Rock above the ancient Cree Crossing was separated from its other ridge top companions and moved to Trafton Park along old U.S. Highway 2 in Malta. Locals tell a number of stories about the rock's stay in the park. Like the sacred rock near Waterton Park in Alberta, the Sleeping Buffalo Rock would somehow move during the night. Sometimes it turned to face the opposite direction, and sometimes it moved locations altogether around the perimeter of the park as if it were looking for a way to get out.

Other stories tell how the restless Sleeping Buffalo could be heard bellowing and making noises in the night. Townsfolk of Malta found these sounds unsettling. One night a city patrolman heard the bellowing and thought perhaps it was indeed coming from the Buffalo Rock. He and another patrolman approached the rock in Trafton Park, and both heard it bellow again. After that incident, the Sleeping Buffalo was again moved several times. During this time of transition, visitors honored the Sleeping Buffalo by putting pennies in a small depression on his great stone back. These small offerings replaced the beads and trinkets reverent Indian people offered to the great Sleeping Buffalo in times past. In 1987, along with the smaller Medicine Rock, the Sleeping Buffalo was moved to its current resting place at the junction of Montana 243 and US 2. The tradition of leaving small offerings to the scared buffalo, rooted in the murky past, continues to the present day. Both tribal and non-tribal travelers along the highway stop to pay homage.

Despite this homage, the separation of the Sleeping Buffalo Rock from its ancient resting place above the Cree Crossing remains a painful event for some. Bill Tallbull expressed his belief that the ridge above Cree Crossing was like a church and the Sleeping Buffalo an altar: "When the buffalo was moved, it was like taking the altar from the church." These revered objects are now more accessible to tribal and non-tribal visitors who stop to pay their respects, but they are also more vulnerable. Education of the public is the key to their preservation. According to the National Register nomination, " ... tribal groups on the Northern Plains continue to trace an uninterrupted affiliation with their aboriginal territories and a continuance of the cultural fabric." As in ancient times, visitors who pay homage to the sacred rocks and leave their personal offerings believe that the power has not diminished. Sleeping Buffalo Rock provides a link to the ancestral peoples of the high plains and the long ago time when the power of the prairie was the buffalo." Chippewa-Cree elder Pat Chief Stick further explained, "These rocks are sacred, just like our old people." And like older people who let you know when they are not content, the Sleeping Buffalo Rock did just that in Trafton Park. Today under its little shelter, the ancient bull seems to like its present home. At least, there have been no more reports of its bellowing.

Sources

Chere Jiusto prepared the National Register nomination, filed at the State Historic Preservation Office, for the Sleeping Buffalo Rock. The document provided much of the information for this story. Firsthand accounts of the power of the Sleeping Buffalo can be found in the WPA Writers' Program *Land of Nakoda: The Story of the Assiniboine Indians.*

THE FRUIT OF THE HANGMAN'S TREE

It is a distinctive house, a *brooding* kind of house, perched high at the top of a rise on Hillsdale Street in South-Central Helena; this house has its secrets. Although the surrounding neighborhood is not Helena's oldest residential area, a few homes along the streets date to the 1870s, and others to the 1880s and 1890s. Before there was any residential development, this part of town was well outside the earliest settlement areas and played a significant role in the early history of the gold camp at Last Chance Gulch. In this vicinity between 1865 and 1870 at least ten men were hanged.

The first five years quickly passed into legend as the booming gold camp grew from settlement to town. By the 1880s, the territorial capital had moved from Virginia City to Helena. Montana's future was as bright as a newly minted silver dollar when the railroad brought waves of newcomers seeking their fortunes. And the railroad brought George Appleton, an imaginative and enthusiastic carpenter eager to make his mark. He was twenty-four when he began to put his creativity to work building whimsical houses in Helena from pattern book plans. Within several years he left his stamp on dozens of homes. But Appleton may have had more on his mind than building houses. Legend has it that while he built homes on speculation or for property owners, he also first mined the property, carefully sifting through the dirt excavated for foundations and cellars. Neighbors say he carried out this work by the light of the moon, taking any gold he could find. This gold, mind you, did not rightly belong to him. Appleton's hunger for other people's gold was known among old-timers and the legend persists especially in the neighborhood along Hillsdale.

After a decade, Appleton had left his mark on the community. Some two hundred houses and other landmarks—the National Biscuit Company's factory, Broadwater's fabulous Natatorium, and the windmill at Forestvale Cemetery—enriched the local streetscapes. Appleton moved on to greener pastures, first to Colorado, then to Washington, and finally he went back to the East coast.

Others took over his clandestine hobby. In the house Appleton built on Hillsdale, someone had been digging in the basement. Records show that the house dates to the mid-1880s when Appleton had sixteen dwellings under construction in the neighborhood at roughly the same time. At the turn of the twentieth century, well-known Helena photographer William Taylor and his wife, Carrie, bought the house. Throughout Taylor's long career, as he documented families and places with shutter, lens, and expert eye, the house sheltered his family. On Christmas Eve in 1931, as Taylor worked at his downtown studio, a paralyzing stroke ended his career. Friends moved him to his home on Hillsdale where Carrie nursed him as best she could. He lingered for several days and died on December 27 at the age of seventy-eight. To help make ends meet Carrie divided her home into a space for herself and an apartment from which she collected rents. Some years later, others bought the property and over the decades a succession of occupants left their imprints on the house. What went on in the house behind closed doors over the course of a century may, or may not, have influenced the home's developing personality.

Herb Dawson bought the property in 1990. Herb is a motorcycle-riding gun enthusiast who is not easily intimidated. He is also a talented architect with a long career in historic preservation behind him. Herb's specialty is helping owners of historic homes and buildings rehabilitate them. He bought the house on Hillsdale because he thought it would be the perfect place to put his skills to work. The house had seen neglect and needed his expertise. Herb, a levelheaded preservationist with a good eye for architectural potential, had carefully considered the pros and cons of buying the old Taylor home. He knew the house was in bad shape but the price was right, and he had the skills to do most of the work himself. Besides, he reasoned, the house *needed* him.

Despite its dilapidated condition, it was a lovely home with handsome features and interesting architecture, Appleton's trademark. It had a wonderful bay window in the dining room, and a curious stained glass window in the parlor. The window was solid red glass, and it would bathe the front rooms with the oddest red light in the morning sun. Herb, who has toured more historic buildings in a year than most people have in a lifetime, to this day has never seen anything like it. Herb could see that beyond the peeling paint and shabby stained wallpaper, the house had potential.

After he struck a deal with the seller, Herb waited to sign the papers. But the longer he waited, the more anxious he became about the house. He had a bad feeling about it; nothing he could put his finger on, but a bad feeling just the same. He went to the final closing and put his signature on the papers. He could not imagine why he was having these negative feelings about the house, but he actually dreaded moving in.

It was not like Herb to be apprehensive. He told himself that this was ridiculous. He should be excited about the project. Nevertheless, the seed of unease was firmly planted, and it was with some effort on moving day in 1990 that he determined to shove his trepidation aside. Herb set to work on the house even before he had unpacked from the move, tearing out parts that needed replacing and stripping layers of old wallpaper from the walls. As he worked around the place, getting used to its nooks and crannies and old house noises, he began to notice something odd. He kept finding marbles—marbles like kids used to trade and shoot. These were old marbles, though, of different colors and sizes. He didn't think much about it, but he began to pick them up. Pretty soon he had a small collection of them. Nothing to worry about, just darn strange and that was all.

One day Herb was stripping wallpaper in the upstairs hallway foyer. He laboriously peeled off the layers. Each successive pattern reflected a specific time period. Some of the choices were charming, and some were a decorator's nightmare. Then he peeled back a final layer, and down low on the wall near the baseboard, Herb found something curious. A message, scrawled in pencil, noting the name of the paperhanger and the date, November 12, 1911, probably the same time the back room was added downstairs. "How cool," thought Herb, "some long-dead paperhanger thought to sign and date his handiwork." Then it struck him. "This can't be," thought Herb, and he backed off and thought a moment. "How could this be? *Today is November 12.*" The hair stood up on the back of his neck.

The basement was dim and uninviting, and clammy. Spiders seemed to like it, however, as the dank spaces crawled with them. And Herb found a dead cat—for some reason, the house attracted cats like a magnet. They were always coming around. He also found something else in the basement. A miner's pick with a personal brand on it and piles of tailings revealed that either someone over the last century knew about Appleton's clandestine diggings or they were digging for some other reason. There was also evidence of diggings under and around the front porch. Herb had heard the neighbors talk about Appleton and his gold. Herb's house was not the only one in the neighborhood where owners had continued Appleton's work, digging in the soft earth of the basement. Someone who knew about Appleton probably began this industry in Herb's basement, secretly digging for gold. Or maybe they were digging for something else. Who could say? Others likely continued the operation, looking for whatever those before might have missed, or tried to cover up. Herb had heard stories about the previous occupant whose several husbands had continued the digging. She got mad at one of them for spending so much time down there with his shovel. Digging became an obsession. He threatened to kill her and bury her there. She, according to her son, pulled a gun on the unfortunate husband. Did the house get to them, too?

Herb thought about the diggings in his basement as he tried to sleep at night. The house was not conducive to sleep. The possibilities of what might lie below gave him the creeps. The house was noisy, too, with bangs and footsteps that Herb tried hard to blame on the twelve stray cats that had taken up residence with him. Strange the way those cats came around and wouldn't leave.

Then there was the back bedroom off the kitchen. It was a one-story addition, and Herb says that it had a "strange oppressive atmosphere." Maps show that it was added to the house prior to 1930; Herb estimates its construction around 1911. To enter the back addition, one had to pass through what had once been a closet on the original rear wall of the house. It was architecturally and functionally weird, according to Herb. It is likely that in 1931, Carrie Taylor nursed her debilitated husband through his last days in this bedroom rather than upstairs. Not only that, but off the bedroom addition was a small bathroom. It had a narrow footed tub. In all his years working in historic preservation, Herb had never seen such an extraordinarily narrow tub and it put him in mind of a coffin. He went out of his way to avoid it. During the first year Herb owned the house, he had a frequent boarder who slept in the downstairs bedroom. She never slept well in the room. Noises kept her awake, things she couldn't quite identify. She thought she heard people walking around outside when there wasn't anyone there. She felt objects flying around her head as she lay in bed at night. And she heard whispering in the dark.

After a year of bachelorhood in the house, Herb brought his bride to live there. They had been married less than an hour when Herb carried her over the threshold. She was not thrilled to note that Herb had unfinished projects all over the house and things were in disarray. But the newlyweds had other things to think about. Moments after they had entered the house, the couple stood in the kitchen near the back bedroom talking. Without warning a heavy section of the ceiling plaster suddenly crashed to the floor in a cloud of dust and debris, narrowly missing Herb's new wife. It was an inauspicious beginning. Herb wondered at the time if the house did not like her.

As the months passed, Herb's health deteriorated. He couldn't sleep; he was nervous and depressed. And he was not getting along with his wife. He thought she was unreasonable. They had heated arguments. It seemed that she said one thing and did another. She was sick much of the time with unspecified maladies and terrible headaches. She was a trained nurse, and her training told her that something wasn't right. So she had her blood tested to see if she had elevated levels of lead. Nothing was physically wrong. Away from the house she was better.

As Herb worked on the house, he made several interesting discoveries, including personal items belonging to William Taylor stuffed in the slot where the parlor's pocket doors opened to fit into the wall. Herb often stayed up late stripping woodwork and sanding floors with his wife closeted upstairs in their bedroom. One night, as he was working on the parlor wall near the steam radiator, he turned his back to do some small task. When he turned back to the radiator, he saw it glinting in the light. Another marble like the ones he had been finding on the porch. No reason for it, no explanation, but there it was, like a disembodied eye staring at him. The marble Herb found that night by the radiator was the first of many to appear in the same place over the next few years. He found them upstairs as well, and eventually collected some forty marbles.

As the months went by, the arguments between Herb and his wife got worse. Herb's house projects grew in number, but none was even near completion. The entire house was torn apart, with half-finished projects everywhere. One night as Herb worked at stripping the living room baseboards, he sat facing the steam radiator where a number of the marbles in his collection had appeared. This evening, though, there had been no marbles and Herb was feeling good about his work. He worked among the various tools and supplies strewn about. A table knife lay discarded on the mantle across the room. Herb concentrated on the baseboards around the steam heater. He worked away, sanding the old wood trim, thinking how much better it would look when all the paint was gone and the old wood could breathe. It was nice when the house was quiet and he was left to his thoughts. The creaky floors and stairway always told him when his wife was on her way down to try to persuade him to come to bed. There was no sneaking around in such a house, and Herb knew that this night she had given up long ago and was upstairs asleep.

Whap! Something hit a nearby bucket with such force that it overturned. There had been no creaks to announce an intruder, and there was no one in the room. Even if he had not heard creaking, there would have been no opportunity for an intruder to get past Herb to reach the mantle and cross the room again to escape. Herb was still alone downstairs, but whatever had come flying had been thrown with force. Maybe something somehow had fallen and knocked the bucket over? But when Herb looked, nothing was out of place except the table knife. It had been on the other side of the room just moments before. Now it lay on the floor next to the overturned bucket. In retrospect, Herb said that in his years in the house the only thing that really spooked him was that knife being thrown across the room.

After months of tension, Herb's marriage ended. Financial difficulties and legal troubles began—all while he lived in the house. Finally Herb put the house on the market and sold it at the first opportunity. He had finished none of the projects he had started. When he locked the door behind him for the last time, Herb was relieved. New owners could have it!

Herb began to recover his health. He slept at night, and he wasn't anxious anymore. He could never discover what made the house so oppressive, but there was no question that the house was an unhappy place, and its attitude rubbed off on its occupants. The house taught Herb to follow his instincts. "I am much more tuned into the vibes of a house now," he says, "and if it doesn't 'feel' right, I go the opposite direction."

Some years after Herb left, while I was researching China Mary for "The Hoo Doo Block," a clipping from the *Helena Daily Independent,* April 20, 1900, long buried in a file at the Montana Historical Society, surfaced. The article suggests a possible reason for the discontent not only in Herb's house, but also in the neighborhood. It has nothing to do with former occupants of the house. Herb had been aware that before residential development of the neighborhood, miners had stripped the area of trees. A short distance to the west of Herb's house, a lone Ponderosa pine once stood near where today there is a four-way intersection. Herb knew that this tree had served a gruesome purpose, both legal and not, and that likely not all of the men hanged upon that dead pine tree deserved so harsh a punishment.

Few modern Helenans, however, know the details of any of these hangings unless they have combed the sources for tidbits of information. John Keene was the first human fruit the tree bore; he was hanged on June 7, 1865, for the murder of Harry "Ed" Slater whom Keene claimed had threatened him. According to witnesses, Keene saw Slater sitting in front of a Bridge Street saloon, asleep in a drunken stupor. He put a pistol to Slater's head, fired, and Slater fell over dead. Keene was soon arrested. A miner's court swiftly organized and the trial took place outside the cabin of newly appointed Sheriff George J. Wood. A crowd of approximately four hundred men observed the proceedings conducted in the open-air courtroom. Stephen Reynolds

The hangings of Joseph Wilson and Arthur Compton on April 30, 1870, were the last executions on Helena's hangman's tree
COURTESY MONTANA HISTORICAL SOCIETY PHOTOGRAPHIC ARCHIVES 948-123

served as the judge, and the jury, chosen from among the crowd, sat on piles of A. M. Holter's lumber, stacked nearby in preparation for a building soon to be erected. No one could be found to corroborate Keene's claims that Slater had sworn to kill him. How hard the men present looked for witnesses is open to question. One hundred men guarded the makeshift jail through the night, and the jury returned a guilty verdict the following morning.

A huge crowd, including a surprising number of women spectators, swarmed behind the wagon as it proceeded under heavy guard out to Dry Gulch east of the settlement. Cornelius Hedges recalled many years later, " ... there was a big pine tree with a convenient limb extending out at one side. That tree seemed to have been specially prepared by providence for just such an occasion. . . ." The wagon came to rest beneath the limb. John X. Beidler, an experienced member of Virginia City's vigilance committee and a man with a sadistic streak, adjusted the rope around Keene's neck. Given a last request, Keene asked for a drink of whiskey. It was very odd that not a drop was found among the crowd and so a messenger was dispatched. Once procured, Keene drank every last drop and called out, "Well, boys, let her rip." The driver whipped the team, the wagon gave a forward lurch, a dozen men at the other end of the rope yanked, and Keene was left dangling. Friends took his body a few rods away and buried him on the hill.

The tree died shortly after its first few uses, but it continued to bear gruesome fruit. The last hanging, the double execution of Arthur Compton and Joe Wilson, who were guilty of the attempted murder of a local rancher, occurred in 1870. Among the ten men known to have met their fates on the hangman's tree, some were tried under miner's court or territorial law, and some were lynched.

A few years after the hangings of Compton and Wilson, the Reverend W. H. Shippen, a Methodist Episcopal minister, purchased the property where the hangman's tree stood. After heavy flooding exposed the tree's roots, he became concerned that the old dead tree, leaning on his barn, would fall over and kill his horse. So in 1875 the reverend had it chopped down. To his amazement, people flocked to the site to cut a souvenir sliver from the famous old relic.

A generation later, homeowners in the neighborhood had all but forgotten that the hangman's tree once stood only yards from their homes (near the northwest corner of Blake and Highland streets). Then in April 1900 John Norley's pick uncovered the bones of an arm while digging a foundation for an addition at the back of the Highland Street home of Robert Sturrock. Digging deeper, Norley discovered the remains of a pine box and leg bones encased in trousers. Sturrock's backyard and that of Herb's house on Hillsdale are nearly adjacent. The coroner, Dr. Ben Brooke, Jr., whose father had been present at the hanging of Keene, identified the body as Keene's and took possession of the skull. According to some reports, Keene had suffered a broken nose, and this detail helped identify the corpse. (In a strange coincidence, the Brookes are Herb Dawson's distant ancestors.)

Some years later in the spring of 1923 the Montana Historical Society, then housed in the basement of the Montana State Capitol, opened a new exhibit in its permanent gallery highlighting vigilante history. Included in this exhibit was the skull of John Keene, his name written in permanent ink across the frontal bone. Dr. Ben Brooke, Jr., made the donation. Historical Society secretary James U. Sanders, son of the famous vigilante prosecutor Wilbur F. Sanders, personally placed the skull in the exhibit case. The public expressed shock at this display. In a tragic and bizarre twist a few weeks later on April 17, 1923, Sanders was struck by a car on a Helena street and died of his injuries.

These grim events tied to the vigilantes' ghastly and violent legacy hold us even today. Charleen Spalding, whose meticulous cemetery research has added greatly to this little-known subject, has found that although interment records are sporadic during Helena's first years, some burials in both the Catholic Cemetery on Oakes (today's Robinson Park) and the City Cemetery (where Central School is today) were officially documented in the mid-1860s. There are, however, no burial locations on record for the first five men executed on the tree in 1865. Wouldn't those hanged, whether guilty as accused or not, their lives cut short in such a horrible, sudden, violent end, find rest in peace a dictum impossible to follow?

Herb is not the only homeowner to experience odd events in his home. Stories about this neighborhood abound. One concerns Charleen's aunt and uncle, Harry and Freda Moore, who lived across the street from Robert Sturrock whose back yard yielded the body of John Keene. Harry and his father built the house in the 1930s and they, like the former owners of Herb's house, were compelled to dig in their basement. When they dug the foundation, they never mentioned finding anything out of the ordinary, but they kept digging in the basement for years afterward. Like Kevin Bacon's character in the horror movie, *Stir of Echoes,* perhaps they were obsessed with the digging. If they found any gold, it was not enough to make them rich. However, after the Moores were long dead, a relative discovered an antique bronze Chinese dragon vase, carved oriental sconces, and an authentic shillelagh or cudgel, buried in the soft dirt of the basement crawl-space. To whom they belonged remains a mystery. Could they have been items buried with some early-day resident on the lonely hilltop?

After more than twenty years at home in the neighborhood, in 1961, Freda died of cancer. Six months later, Harry remarried. But he soon became ill, stricken with an undiagnosed malady that put him in and out of the hospital. This pattern continued throughout most of his second marriage. At home he was sick, in the hospital he was better. Then Harry died suddenly while he and his second wife, Ida, were on a trip to Alabama on January 14, 1972.

Ida had her husband cremated immediately and she returned to live in the house alone. According to Charleen, Harry's family felt that Ida's behavior was odd. First of all, the marriage was quite sudden, and Ida disposed of all of Freda's belongings, giving them to the Salvation Army. Freda's family resented this hasty disposal of her earthly possessions and when Harry died, it was no surprise that they questioned the cause of his death.

Ida disregarded the accusations, but soon reportedly told her family and friends that she was hearing noises in the house. She said she heard a rocking chair, rocking back and forth, and other creaks, footsteps, and thumping noises in the attic. She thought it was Freda, come back looking for her belongings, demanding retribution for her disposing of them. Six months after Harry died, Ida was visiting family in Rapid City, South Dakota, while her kitchen was being painted. She was caught in a flash flood and drowned on June 9, 1972. Many years later in the late 1990s, Charleen interviewed the current homeowner and asked him about the noises in the attic. He expressed neither surprise at the question nor a denial that there were noises, but simply said, *"I don't pay any attention to them."*

Sources

Scattered sources about the Helena hangings include a Montana News Insert in the *Forsyth Independent,* May 5, 1939; the *Coffee Creek Herald,* May 2, 1923; *Helena Independent,* April 23, 1900; and the *Montana Record Herald,* July 12, 1939. The *Helena Daily Independent,* April 20, 1900 carried the story of the discovery of Keene's skull. The Montana Historical Society Research Center Library vertical files, both biographical and subject, include these clippings and many others as well. Sanborn-Perris Fire Insurance Maps of Helena (1884, 1888, 1890, 1892) provide valuable details of the neighborhood, and deed records, unearthed by Charleen Spalding, allow identification of Reverend Shippen's property, by lot and block numbers, where the hangman's tree stood.

THE HOO DOO BLOCK

John X. Beidler, a vigilante and pioneer lawman who bragged about the hangings over which he had presided, claimed to have pursued and seen to the execution of some thirty members of Henry Plummer's gang. Beidler ended up at Last Chance Gulch where he served as Deputy U.S. Marshall into the 1880s. He was in this position by 1867 and already the town had a violent history behind it. Gold dust was the currency, and the town was full of rough characters waiting to help themselves to other people's fortunes. Beidler had plenty to do.

Like most mining camps, Helena had a vibrant, but isolated, Chinese community that settled at the south end of the gulch. Late one night, someone strangled "China Mary," a well-known prostitute and one of a few Asian women among the male-dominated population. Locals knew that she had been saving gold—nuggets and dust—and possessed a small fortune worth about $1500 she kept in her cabin. According to the newspapers, her "consort" (possibly a polite term for pimp), discovered her warm but lifeless body on the floor, strangled with a pair of drawers tied tightly around her neck.

As Beidler asked questions and gathered information about the crime, he strongly suspected one Bill Hynson (also known as Hensel, Hanson, or Henson) of the murder. Hynson fit the description of the man Mary's consort saw with her just before her death. Beidler arrested Hynson on an unrelated charge hoping he could gather enough evidence to prove guilt. But the evidence was not forthcoming and Beidler had no choice but to order his release. Hynson made his way up to Fort Benton where he was quite at home among the rough characters who lounged in the dusty streets and along the levee. While Virginia City and Helena were wild frontier gold camps, Fort Benton was a trade center, but it matched the camps in violence and notoriety.

Fort Benton—named for Senator Thomas Hart Benton of Missouri, a promoter of the American Fur Company—had its origins as a fur trading post, founded in 1846, and became famous in the 1860s as the last steamboat port along the Missouri River. It thus was a fur trading post long before the discovery along Grasshopper Creek touched off the first Montana gold rush in 1862. The town, today a National Historic Landmark, claims the longest continuous occupation of any settlement in Montana. As the gold camps boomed, steamboats loaded with goods from the States docked at Fort Benton's levee. Freighters then carried everything from grand pianos to crystal glasses and canned goods overland to the settlements of Virginia City, Helena, Deer Lodge, Missoula, and Bozeman in Montana and to Calgary and Edmonton north across the Canadian line. Along what today is called the Old Forts Trail, Fort Benton was also the key military supply route for Fort Assinniboine in Montana and Forts Walsh and Battleford in Saskatchewan, Canada. From June to September eight-mule teams, ten-horse teams, and twenty-yoke oxen teams waited patiently for their burdens of freight to all points of the compass.

Buffalo hides, pelts, and skins of all kinds piled as high as two-story houses awaited loading, bound for domestic and European markets. Fort Benton was the end of the line for gamblers, gold-seekers, speculators, big-game hunters, fugitives, and settlers who came to Montana Territory via the muddy Missouri. As the center of the river trade from the United States and British Columbia, Fort Benton saw more than its share of border warfare. The vast fortunes of T. C. Power, I G. Baker, and the Conrad brothers were made in merchandizing and freighting at Fort Benton. Although in size it was but a village, its importance in territorial commerce aptly earned it the nickname "Chicago of the Plains."

Hynson's arrival at Fort Benton came a year after the famous Civil War general Thomas Francis Meagher, who was Montana's appointed territorial secretary, and twice acting governor, stumbled—or was pushed—from the deck of the steamer G. A. Thompson into the murky Missouri and was never seen again. The town's volatile reputation suited Hynson where he first worked in a livery. After a time Hynson took up the post of night watchman, unofficially appointing himself. City officials allowed him to do the job because there was no one in the position. Hynson, a rough character, in a strange manner scripted his own death. A series of thefts reported by men who had been imprudent in their consumption of liquor cast suspicions on Hynson. Although accounts vary, all agree that locals observed Hynson keeping company with inebriated saloon patrons whose funds came up short. The local vigilance committee—that Hynson, ironically, took some credit for organizing—planned a trap to catch the perpetrator. The men planted a "drunken" patron with heavy pockets in the local saloon.

The "plant" pretended to pass out and observed Hynson helping himself to his pockets. The next day, August 18, 1868, the committee informed Hynson that the perpetrator had been discovered. Deputy Marshall Beidler was in town and the vigilantes announced that they intended to have a hanging. Hynson, unaware that he had been observed, volunteered to supply the rope and directed "Nigger Henry" Mills, an old time American Fur Company employee, to dig the grave. Hynson promised Mills that in due time he would supply the corpse.

Beidler, a cruel man well versed in the art of hanging, took the rope Hynson offered him and without hesitation—as he had done on previous occasions—took up the noose and placed it over the doomed man's neck. Without so much as a word of protest, Hynson's life was quickly snuffed. When the men removed his body from the gallows two days later, they found a letter from Hynson's mother in his pocket that read:

> My Dear Son, —I write to relieve my great anxiety, for I am in great trouble on your account. Your father had a dream about you. He dreamed that he had a letter from your lawyer, who said that your case was hopeless. God grant that it may prove only a dream! I, your poor, broken-hearted mother, am in suspense on your account. For God's sake, come home.

The site of Hynson's execution varies among surviving accounts of the incident, but W. S. Stocking, who was a resident of Fort Benton at the time of the hanging, claims the makeshift gallows stood on Block 25 of the original Fort Benton townsite. Main and Franklin streets to the east and west and Bond and Benton streets to the north and south were its boundaries. Hynson's hanging, one of three known hangings conducted by vigilantes in Fort Benton, triggered what some believe was a source of evil for several generations to come.

For example, John Morgan was one of the community's most hardened characters. He arrived in Fort Benton as head of a militia group sent by General Thomas Francis Meagher to punish marauding Blackfeet in 1865 and 1866. He was sheriff by default at the time of Hynson's hanging, Asa Sample—the first officially elected sheriff—having resigned. Historian Joel Overholser in *Fort Benton: World's Innermost Port* cites an example that paints a vivid picture of Morgan's character. Overholser describes how, in an unprovoked attack, Morgan and his cohorts shot a starving Indian and hanged three others at Sun River. The Indians had only come to ask the whites for food. In retaliation, a war party killed one of the attendants and burned the Sun River government farm in April 1865, whose purpose was to teach agriculture to the Blackfeet. The same war party also killed a sheepherder and forced the abandonment of St. Peter's Mission.

Morgan built an adobe livery stable and corral on the corner of Block 25 at Main and Benton streets. He dug a well behind it. Legend has it that he also built a house on the premises. Around the time of Hynson's hanging, locals say that Morgan's wife died and his house on Block 25 burned down (although there is no record of either event). The Virginia City *Montana Post* recorded Morgan's death on November 14, 1868, a few months after Hynson's hanging. The 1870 census confirms that Morgan and his wife had died, recording the couple's orphaned six-year-old son, Henry, in residence in Fort Benton with Jeff Perkins and his wife and daughter. Perkins' life also later proved unlucky. In 1875, the judge handed Perkins a five-year term at Deer Lodge for shooting a saloon proprietor in self-defense. The sentence was unusually harsh for those times although Perkins served only one year of his term.

In the mid-1860s, relationships between whites and Blackfeet steadily deteriorated. The gold rush brought an influx of miners, settlers, and whiskey traders that encroached upon Blackfeet territory. W. S. Stocking described an incident with the Blackfeet in the town's streets that helped shape Block 25's grim reputation. There were approximately twenty-five white men in Fort Benton when a Blackfeet war party clattered into town on high-spirited horses. According to Stocking, the men fought Indians all over town and killed several, throwing their bodies in the well John Morgan had dug before his death. The well where the bodies lay, and still lie today, afterwards became known as the Place of Skulls. During this same skirmish, one wounded Indian hid overnight in his carpenter son-in-law's workbench. Teamsters came into town the next morning, adding considerably to the number of white males, and they thoroughly searched the town. They found the Indian and dragged him to Block 25 where he was promptly hanged.

After John Morgan's death, his livery passed to other owners, and a small log house fronting Main Street, built on the block in 1868, served as the county jail; the gallows stood next to it. Even though Fort Benton had its share of bad characters, the jail actually saw few prisoners. On November 28, 1872, a soldier and two teamsters in the employ of the Diamond R Company were on a drunken binge that turned potentially violent. They were arrested and locked safely in the jail before they could do bodily harm to Fort Bentonites or destroy personal property. At three the next morning, nearby residents awoke to the smell of heavy smoke and discovered the log jail enveloped in flames. By the time neighbors detected the fire, the cabin was a total loss. Authorities assumed that the three prisoners had been burned alive in the conflagration. When the smoldering ruins cooled enough to allow investigation, the charred remains of only two men were found among the ashes.

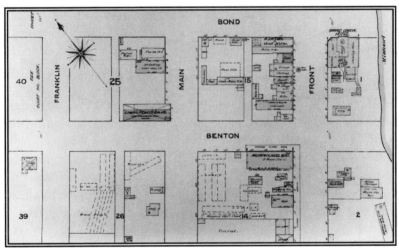

1884 Sanborn Map of Fort Benton and Block 25 with the livery and Roosevelt's Store
COURTESY MONTANA HISTORICAL SOCIETY RESEARCH CENTER

Buttons belonging to the soldier and one of the teamsters confirmed their identities, while officials found a belt belonging to the third man, Frank Thompson, a distance away from the fire. This provided some clues, hinting that Thompson likely killed the other two, made it out of the burning jail alive, and escaped.

After these dark events on Block 25, local citizens began calling it the Hoo Doo Block, believing the site accursed. Nearly all of the town's violent acts and tragedies seemed to take place there. Nevertheless, Morgan's adobe livery under a string of different owners did a brisk business. By the early 1880s, William Rowe and Ed Lewis operated the Benton Stables. On the site of the old jail, Ferdinand C. Roosevelt decided to build a furniture store. The frame building was nearly finished when a freak wind, described as a tornado, tore the boards apart and blew the entire structure into the river. The sudden whirlwind touched not a board of any other building. Roosevelt was undaunted, however, and began again, this time completing his store in 1884. He filled both first and second floors and a warehouse at the back with furniture. The rooms were so full that customers could scarcely turn around. The Oddfellows' Hall, a two-story brick building next door, was constructed at the same time and housed the offices and print shop of the *River Press*.

On a calm July evening in 1885, mosquitoes hummed and the river lapped at the sides of the government steamers *Josephine* and *Missouri* down at the levee. A slight west wind carried piano music from some saloon along Front Street, voices faintly mixed with laughter, and someone singing a bawdy ballad drifted along with the welcome breeze on this warm and humid summer night. At 11:15, a cry went up. By the time a crowd gathered, a fire had engulfed Roosevelt's Main Street store on Block 25, making it impossible to save even those articles of furniture nearest the front door. Roosevelt appeared on the scene, frantic that his wife might be inside. She, however, had been visiting friends and was not in the building.

Crews from the *Missouri* and the *Josephine* pitched in, some forming a water brigade and others helping to douse the flames while Fort Benton's inexperienced fire department, having never fought such a conflagration, tried desperately to get the pump engine working. Within ten minutes it became obvious that the building was a total loss, and the men directed their efforts at saving the adjacent brick structure. They hauled the printing equipment and contents of the office of the *River Press* into the street, but the building was a near total loss, too. None of those afflicted had sufficient insurance. The property owners did not rebuild on Block 25.

The old livery stable on the opposite corner of the block at Main and Benton, its adobe walls covered with boards, went unharmed. Now the sole occupant of the block, the Benton Stables continued to support Ed Lewis who had bought out his partner, William Rowe. In 1890, Lewis' brother George joined the business. From time to time, neighbors whispered about the ghost of the soldier who had burned in the jail years before; they said he haunted the neighborhood, spooking the horses in the livery stable, and wandering aimlessly along Main Street over the empty, overgrown lots of Block 25.

On March 30, 1894, the *Kalispell Inter Lake* carried a curious front-page news item about the haunting of a house on Fort Benton's Main Street. This incident, according to the reporter, was the talk of the town. The ghost inhabited an abandoned house and its white form could be seen in the windows, moving from room to room. A group of young men had vowed to discover if it was a hoax. There was no follow up report, nor did the *River Press* ever make mention of the incident that supposedly "took the town by storm." Perhaps it was kept quiet so as not to rekindle fears about Block 25 and thus discourage residents from walking along Main Street after dark.

The Lewis brothers rebuilt the old wood-covered adobe stable in 1895. Ed Lewis fell ill in the spring of 1897 and died the following November. His brother George remained in the livery business on Block 25. An alley separated the east and west halves of the block, and by 1902 the west half along Franklin Street had been built up with several homes and businesses. Only the Lewis livery, the forgotten body-filled well Morgan dug so many years before, and the ghosts of those who perished remained on the east half of Block 25 at the turn of the twentieth century. In a final burst of evil energy, fire consumed the new Lewis livery stable. George Lewis promptly relocated his business.

A brave citizen who put no stock in *hoo doo* built a home on the corner of Bond and Main, the site of the old jail. According to locals, the house never saw events out of the ordinary, and in the minds of many, its construction signaled the end of the supposed curse. Renumbering of the original townsite lots, twice, helped to erase the stigma of the Hoo Doo Block. Block 25 became Block 129 by 1910 and then Block 164, as it is today. It remains a curious fact that most of the tragedies that occurred in Fort Benton's early history occurred on the Main Street half of this block. W.S. Stocking summed up the history of the Hoo Doo Block in 1906: "At the end of forty years there is one building on one corner … —a dwelling house, and good luck seems to attend the occupant—from which it may be argued that the 'hoodoo' has exhausted its power for evil."

Sources
The murder of China Mary is recorded in the *Helena Weekly Herald*, September 12 and 19, 1867; Nathaniel Langford, *Vigilante Days and Ways,* relates the hanging of Bill Hynson. The Sanborn-Perris Fire Insurance Maps of Fort Benton (1884, 1888, 1902, 1910 and 1920), Overholser's *Fort Benton: The World's Innermost Port* and the Winfield Scott Stocking Papers, SC 797, at the MHS Research Center provided much of the background for this story. Newspaper clippings include River Press, July 15, 1885; November 17, 1897; *Helena Herald,* December 4, 1872; and the *Montana Post,* November 27, 1868. John G. Lepley's *Birthplace of Montana: A History of Fort Benton* as well as a conversation with the author provided excellent clues. Lepley's book includes a photograph of the log jail and gallows (p. 53) before it burned.

DIGGING UP THE DEAD

She walks the grounds in broad daylight, a sad woman with two small children clinging to her long skirts, picking her way among the tombstones. Across the uneven soil she wanders, among the remembrances of the dead near the tall, marble obelisk that marks her final resting place. Mary Dunphy is a statistic, an example of one of the worst terrors of life in remote Montana Territory during the 1880s. And her presence, lingering in the old graveyard, makes her more than a faceless name on a stone monument.

Mrs. Dunphy was a victim of her own selfless good heart. In the late fall of 1885 a diphtheria epidemic threatened the residents of Lewis and Clark County. By January of 1886 when the disease had taken its deadly toll, a number of children had died. Among the dead were five-year-old Blanche and eight-year-old Jennie, daughters of prominent Helena physician Ben C. Brooke who was powerless to intervene when the disease attacked his own children. Five of Calvin and Margaret Beach's ten children, ages ranging from four to fifteen, died between August and December. The Beaches lived on a farm in the Prickly Pear Valley. Neighbors were too afraid of the disease to assist the family, so Calvin Beach had to attend to the burials with his own teams and wagon, five different times. Noah and Rosella Harris, ages eleven and fifteen, who also lived out in the Prickly Pear Valley, died in November. Felix Kuehn, almost two, and his older sister Norma Alada, who was almost five, died in December.

Diphtheria was fatal in one out of two cases. The disease tortured both the afflicted and the parents, forced to watch helplessly as their child struggled for breath and suffocated. A tough, grayish membrane characterizes the disease. It spreads across the little one's tonsils and throat. Although diphtheria usually struck children between the ages of two and fourteen, adults sometimes fell victim too. Mary Dunphy died of the disease on Christmas Eve, the day after Norma Kuehn. Mrs. Dunphy had nursed both the Kuehn

Mrs. Dunphy's Tombstone in the Benton Avenue Cemetery
COURTESY KATIE BAUMLER

children and sat beside little Felix as he died. She was too ill to attend Norma at the end.

The mid-nineteenth century witnessed remarkable strides in medicine, including the diphtheria antitoxin, first available to the public in 1895. It was, however, a decade too late to help the victims of that 1885 epidemic.

The number of Helena cemeteries and burial records speak to the random cruelty of epidemics. Diphtheria, whooping cough, scarlet fever, measles, and tuberculosis were among the common afflictions, constant threats and worries that loomed over early communities. Human life then was very fragile, and the victims of these diseases and other causes of death serve as classic examples of Helena's complicated interment history. The graves of the Brooke, Beach, and Harris children illustrate a bizarre historical fact: there was frequent movement of the community's early dead. The Kuehn children, Mary Dunphy, and Mary's husband Elijah, who died three years after his wife, further demonstrate what happened to the graves of pioneers whose parents moved on or who left no heirs: they were usually forgotten, their graves left to crumble and deteriorate with neglect.

With Helena's first recorded death, that of Dr. L. Rodney Pococke of tuberculosis in spring 1865, the mining camp had need of a burial ground. Masons conducted the funeral with great formality and fanfare, and it was the first formal gathering of the order in Helena. Fellow Masons buried Pococke where, within several months of his demise, a city cemetery would be well established on high ground overlooking the gulch. By 1868, at least two more cemeteries served Helena, the Catholic Cemetery on Oakes and the Jewish Home of Peace adjacent to present-day Capital High School. The old Catholic Cemetery is now the site of Robinson Park, but the Home of Peace remains active. Both these cemeteries were well outside the original townsite; the "in town" City Cemetery generally served the Protestant, non-sectarian and substantial Masonic population. There were certainly other, smaller early cemeteries in use briefly. "Boot Hill," for example (see "The Fruit of the Hangman's Tree") was the location of at least one burial, recorded unofficially by an eyewitness, because of its proximity to the "hangman's tree."

When Helena became the territorial capital in 1875, the capital city wanted its buildings and community resources to showcase its importance. In addition to a federal assay office—one of only five in the nation—under construction on Broadway, a grand new school worthy of the territorial capital was in the planning stages. Old Central School, the first graded school in the territory, opened in January 1876. (The present Central School, built on the same site, had replaced the original building by 1921.) The rise overlooking the gulch was the best, most visible location to build the school, but that entailed moving part of the City Cemetery, active now for a decade. It was neither an easy nor a pleasant task, moving a cemetery.

Not all the graves had markers, for one thing, and so in many cases it was a game of move-them-when-you-find-them. The method of burial, too, in roughly and hastily made pine boxes or worse, left corpses in various stages of decomposition. This made removal difficult and grisly. Another problem was where to put the newly unburied dead.

Lewis and Clark County created Benton Avenue Cemetery in 1870, and so it provided the solution to the latter problem. Benton Avenue became the receptacle for burials clearly marked with tombstones or wooden markers as well as unmarked graves encountered during the digging of the school's foundation. Among the graves transferred to Benton Avenue was that of Langford Peel, killed in a saloon affray in 1867. Wilbur Sanders took a fancy to the wooden headboard that marked Langford's grave, likely thinking it should be saved for posterity. Sanders took the man's wooden grave marker home to his house at nearby 7th and Ewing. There in his attic it stayed until the 1930s when the Sanders family gave it to the Montana Historical Society. It remains in the collection today, a rare, well-preserved relic of Helena's earliest history. The epitaph reads:

> In Life Beloved by his Friends
> And Respected by His Enemies
> Vengence [sic] is Mine
> Sayeth the Lord
> I know that My Redeemer Liveth

Peel himself lost out; his new grave at Benton Avenue was, and is today, unmarked.

On May 30, 1883, Helena celebrated the first observance of Memorial Day—or "Decoration Day" as it was originally known—with a mile-long procession that made its way from Harmonia Hall on Broadway out of the city to Benton Avenue Cemetery. Nearly 1500 people marched in the procession, including some fifty veterans of the Civil War and a few veterans of the war with Mexico. The Silver Coronet Band provided music. Ladies and gentlemen in carriages joined the crowd at the cemetery, bringing flowers to place on the graves of their loved ones. The Reverend T. V. Moore officiated as chaplain. This observance, the *Helena Daily Herald* pointed out a few days later on June 2, brought to light the deplorable condition of the city's Protestant and Catholic cemeteries whose wooden head and foot boards had deteriorated and could not be deciphered:

> Some of the noblest men and women ... lie buried there; yet their resting places cannot be identified. After considerable inquiry, we do not find that plot of the lots ... is kept. The county gravedigger keeps no record of interments. He digs a hole and covers a corpse and the name of the dead is buried in the same oblivion as is his body ...

An informal tally taken at this time revealed that only one-fourth of the graves in the city's several cemeteries had markers. The assessment included the forgotten graves that remained in the old City Cemetery near the grounds of Central School, Benton Avenue, and the Catholic Cemetery on Oakes.

When Forestvale opened in 1890, it immediately became the favored burial place for Protestant and non-sectarian families. Many prominent pioneer families, who had parents and children buried at Benton Avenue, moved their relatives to the more desirable new cemetery. Argyle Parkinson and Anna Davenport were children of prominent early Helena pioneers who were among the first, after Rodney Pococke, to die in the new settlement. Argyle, an infant, died of brain fever in the spring of 1865 and ten-year-old Anna succumbed to the effects of measles contracted en route to Montana on the steamboat *St. John*. She died after several months' confinement in the fall of 1865. Another Davenport child died of scarlet fever in early February of 1875. Incomplete records indicate these children were all buried in the old cemetery on the site of Central School. The two families moved their children first from the City Cemetery to Benton Avenue, and again from Benton Avenue to Forestvale, where their headstones today are included in their respective family plots. Interment records indicate that sometimes, as in the case of these children, a disinterment and re-interment actually occurred, but in other cases headstones at Forestvale may be commemorative only and remains were not actually transferred.

The opening of Forestvale Cemetery, with its architect-designed entryway and beautifully landscaped grounds, coincided with improvements to the city upon statehood in 1889 that disturbed the sleep of the dead. Helena High School, for example, built next door to Central School at the corner of Warren and Lawrence streets, relieved overcrowding and allowed high school students their own facility but encroached on the old cemetery. The high school was long in completion, from 1890 to 1893. During this three-year period, additional graves that still dotted the former grounds of the old City Cemetery were moved, some to Forestvale and some to Benton Avenue.

Forestvale records specifically indicate some of these re-interments by name and date spanning from the late 1880s to the early 1890s. There is no record of re-interments at Benton Avenue from this time period. However, the dozens of unmarked graves, very close together, especially in the northwest quadrant, clearly indicate this activity. Unidentified bodies from the old city cemetery were a problem during this period in Helena. The *Helena Herald* reported on April 14, 1893, that a coffin washed out of the Lawrence Street cut after a heavy rain had burst open in the street. The well-preserved, unidentified red-haired miner was re-interred at the "new cemetery," likely Forestvale. Mrs. Lucille Topping admits to spending her recesses watching these ghoulish activities:

> Of course, many were found later, nameless. When my uncle graduated from high school in 1885—he was attending H.S. in what is now Central—remains were still being found. When I was in 7th grade in the stone building [i.e. the new Helena High School]—Lawrence Street was being cut though and bodies found. We spent our recess periods sitting on the bank.

Some of the unknown persons most certainly ended up at the older, less frequently used Benton Avenue Cemetery, and all those unearthed before Forestvale's opening in 1890 would have necessarily been re-interred there.

The death of loved ones prompted Helena families to bury their dead at Forestvale, but it was not enough to bury the newly dead in the grand new cemetery. Family ties and companionship run deep, even in death, and family loss provided impetus for the removal of loved ones interred at Benton Avenue. The entire Brooke family, for example, including the children's father and mother, were removed from Benton Avenue and re-interred at Forestvale upon the death of their daughter-in-law, Bertha Brooke, in 1920.

By 1966, neglect had taken a toll on the Benton Avenue Cemetery. Lucy Baker, a secretary in the office of Governor Tim Babcock, passed by it each morning on her way to work. Distressed at this lack of respect for Helena's early settlers, Mrs. Baker determined to do something about it and challenged the community to help her. Recruiting friends and neighbors with rakes, shovels, and hoes, she organized a cleanup. One hundred volunteers carted out trash, weeded, and raked. The one-time call for help stretched into months, and then years. Mrs. Baker arranged for students at Carroll College to take care of the grounds and organized a campaign to finance it called

"Pennies from Heaven." Media took up the cry for help and offered support. On Memorial Day, May 30, 1968, state and local officials rededicated the Benton Avenue Cemetery. Lucy Baker received a citation from Keep America Beautiful for her unique reclamation project and a representative from Washington, D.C., came to officiate at the ceremony.

During the next seven years, Lucy Baker recorded markers, names, and dates compiling a list of interments at Benton Avenue. The Governor's Commission on Historic Preservation designated the cemetery a historical site in 1974. Mrs. Baker moved out of state, but continued her crusade through voluminous correspondence. Yet the pioneer cemetery again began to deteriorate. In 1998 the Benton Avenue Cemetery Association reorganized and now is an active group taking the lead in bringing recognition to it and keeping the cemetery clean and well maintained. Lucy Baker's dream of listing the Benton Avenue Cemetery on the National Register of Historic Places came to fruition in 2003.

Although a simple pioneer cemetery, its most distinctive feature is the wrought iron fencing that surrounds individual family plots. A pineapple, the southern symbol for welcome, marks the corners of one; a graceful lyre forms a centerpiece in the gate of the enclosure around another. Wood, marble, metal, and granite chronicle the change in fashion and progression from imported marble or catalogue-order markers to locally crafted monuments. The only landscaping is ancient lilacs, small shrubs, and an occasional bloom that family members who once tended their loved ones' graves planted there.

Nancy Cormier and Karen Fred are cemetery board members who always lend a hand on the yearly cleanup crew. On one of these cleanup days, they and other board members were going about their tasks when a car drove up the alley along the cemetery's south side. The driver honked the horn, jumped out of the car and began gesturing frantically. Nancy recalls that one of workers ambled over, curious to see what was behind this woman's wild gesturing. "Just thought you'd like to know," she said, "that there are people walking in this cemetery."

"Well, of course there are," said the worker. What was she trying to say? "No, no," the driver explained. "I mean that there are, you know, *people,* like *dead* people, gathered over there, watching you work. There's a woman in a long dress with two little children, and others gathered over there," she said, pointing to the area at the back of the grounds near the Kuehn and Dunphy graves. The incredulous crewmember returned to the group reporting what he had just heard.

Shortly thereafter, Nancy came across a reference to the diphtheria epidemic and the connection between the Kuehn children and Mrs. Dunphy. Their graves are in the same general area where the woman claimed to have seen the crowd of ghostly observers. Mrs. Dunphy's obelisk is plainly visible from the road, representative of the old style marble obelisks that mark the cemetery's most historic graves. The Kuehn children's tombstone is one of three, exactly alike, likely ordered from a catalogue and inscribed locally, the most charming and the most poignant of all the tombstones at Benton Avenue. It is a child-sized chair with a hat tossed upon it, little shoes tucked underneath, clothing draped across the back, tossed there as if some other diversion captured the attention of its little owner who then quickly cast it aside. The epitaph reads simply, "How we miss them."

The caretakers at Benton Avenue like to think that Mrs. Dunphy and Felix and Norma Kuehn know how much they care about the place, and what they, and others have tried to do. Some see proof of Mrs. Dunphy's continued presence in an odd photograph taken in October 2003 during an evening tour of the cemetery. The group paused at Mrs. Dunphy's grave and one member took some digital photographs. Low to the ground, on Mrs. Dunphy's obelisk, was a very large, bright, circle of light, or orb—a sure sign, according to some, that supernatural forces are at work.

Sources

Charleen Spalding has done much of Helena's cemetery research available at the Montana Historical Society's Research Center. The National Register nomination form for the Benton Avenue Cemetery, compiled by the author at the request of the Benton Avenue Cemetery Association and with the help of Charleen Spalding, is housed at the State Historic Preservation Office. It includes a thorough bibliography, detailed history of the cemetery, and the history of interments in Helena from the town's beginnings to the present day. The Benton Avenue Cemetery Association continues to care for the cemetery grounds.

SPEAKING WITH ARTIFACTS: CONVERSATIONS WITH GEORGE

By means of the intuitive and parapsychological a whole new vista of man and his past stands ready to be grasped. As an anthropologist and as an archaeologist trained in these fields, it makes sense to me to seize the opportunity to pursue and study the data thus provided. This should take first priority.

J. Norman Emerson, "Father of Canadian Archaeology," 1973

George McMullen is a man of rare intuitive ability who has developed his skills for the benefit of science and man's understanding of his past. He sums up his philosophy this way: "Honesty, humility, respect for the dignity of all living creatures. That is about what I am, or try to be. And I think that accounts for an awful lot of my ability … ."

A native of Ontario, Canada, George was born in 1920 to parents of Canadian and English heritage. He had a rough beginning. His father died soon after he was born, leaving his mother to raise four children. When George was five, his thirteen-year-old sister died. His mother remarried and then his eleven-year-old brother died. As the youngster tried to cope with family changes and hardships, he began to realize that he was not like his siblings.

George *knew* things. Playmates accused him of cheating at games like hide-and-seek because he could see their hiding places in his mind's eye. Card games, too, were problematic because he always knew what cards the other players held. It was hard to find friends, difficult to weather the teasing of his peers, and so George chose to keep to himself. With the encouragement of an elderly neighbor who understood the youngster's difficulties, George learned to meditate. He spent long hours in the swampy forest near his home in Weston, Ontario, learning every tree and creature. He practiced meditating and experienced renewal from it.

A solitary explorer, George roamed the countryside and in so doing discovered the tools of ancient peoples scattered across the landscape. He had an intense curiosity about these artifacts and the people who made them. Through many hours of practice and meditation, George believed he had gained awareness and visions that allowed him to see the people who made the tools and how they used them.

Graduation from high school, marriage in 1942, and three children brought George a relatively normal family life. He worked hard at various occupations to provide for his family and kept his abilities mostly to himself, giving his wife and children all the material possessions they needed. But he says, " … it wasn't what I wanted. I had all the things that make a person happy, but I wasn't happy. Material things just didn't interest me." In 1969 George began a working relationship with Dr. J. Norman Emerson, director of Archaeological Studies at the University of Toronto. Dr. Emerson, an expert on the Ontario Iroquois, was the founder of the Canadian Archaeological Association and revered by many as the "Father of Canadian Archaeology." The two formed a dynamic partnership that lasted until Dr. Emerson's death in 1978.

During their collaboration, Dr. Emerson and George visited sites in southern Ontario, Upper New York State, and abroad. Dr. Emerson kept track of George's successes. With eighty percent or better accuracy, his ability to confirm information and suggest direction proved invaluable. For example, once he visited a site where archaeologists had been working without success. George first ascertained what they had been seeking and then suggested where they might find it. Six weeks later he returned to the site and sure enough, they had excavated where George had indicated and found what they had been in search of for the past two years. Because of revelations like this, Dr. Emerson came to realize that George's intuitive ability " … wasn't a parlor game, but that it was a tool, a tool that they could use in the work that they were doing that could save them years of time."

George further explained, "I couldn't begin to tell you the things I felt, the pain I suffered … . I was determined not to subject my wife and children to that ridicule. So that's why I always kept a low profile. It hasn't been until the last twenty-five years that people have begun to look at metaphysical things and that it's become popular. I believe that I have brought some morals to what I do … . You don't have to pay for it to listen to what I have to say. I won't do that."

The abilities George developed with the help of his elderly neighbor are not unique, he suggests, but rather exist in each of us. George, however, believes that because of his circumstances, his isolation, and his retreat into himself, he was able to develop his intuitive skills to a very high degree of sophistication. Learning how to meditate was the key. It takes most people a long time to reach the total state of relaxation that allows the mind to take over. George, though, can reach this state in about five seconds. When he holds an object, he feels "the energy of the person who made it … . The residue of their energy stays there." George maintains that all things, whether living or not, have energy. Since the sum of energy can neither be created nor destroyed, energy from people, places, and things—no matter how old—remains timeless. This, in very simple terms, is what allows George to "read" or "psychometrize" a site or an object.

Initially in their collaboration, Dr. Emerson liked to test George's ability. On one occasion Dr. Emerson gave George some coins a woman had sent to him. Emerson did not know what they were. He wanted to prove that if he knew nothing about them, George could not have knowledge about them either, nor could he be reading Emerson's mind as some believed. George said, "I described the coins, and where they came from, and the woman who had them, and the place where she lived, and where she had found them. That really blew his mind, and after that there were no more games; it was serious business … ."

As Dr. Emerson discovered, George's intuitive skills could be used in combination with more conventional methods of collecting scientific data. George's "intuitive archaeology," according to Dr. Emerson, is "the ability to know without reason or study." George is not of Native American descent, but because of his intuitive experiences, he strives to write from the their point of view. His books include *Red Snake* (1993), *One White Crow* (1994), and *Running Bear* (1996).

Over the years, George has made many trips to Native American sites in Montana. Whitney S. Hibbard is among the friends and acquaintances he has made over the years. George allowed Hibbard to study how and why he gathers descriptive information. With an interest in archaeology and broad professional experience in criminal justice and psychic criminology, Hibbard has been a criminal justice planner and a licensed private investigator. He has also practiced forensic hypnosis, taught martial arts, and with the late psychologist Ray Worring, George's longtime friend and associate, authored a manual on the use of psychics in criminal investigation. Hibbard's interests and skills put him in a good position to work with George. Hibbard's investigative training and interest in psychic research gave him the special analytical expertise and interviewing skills needed for the project. The meticulous study, published in 2000, includes a transcript of the interviews he conducted with George.

A part of one interview took place in Hellgate Canyon in Broadwater County, a rock art site important to the early people of the region. As George received information about events in the canyon while in a meditative state, he answered Hibbard's questions. When George visits a site, he first must find a point of reference, some object—a tree, a rock formation, a stream— that exists today as it existed then. Once he has a contextual link to orient himself to the site, George can locate other related objects such as buildings or artifacts. While the mechanics of George's intuitive methods are detailed in the study, his impressions of the past are of most interest here. His interviews offer fascinating glimpses into another time.

Hellgate Canyon has a series of spectacular pictographs that have been known by whites since the Montana gold rush in the 1860s. Archaeologists say that they are of great age, about five thousand years old. Unlike some pictographs, the Hellgate panels contain no animals or hunters. Rather, dots, lines, arrows, and headless and armless figures that seem to be levitating sprawl across the great limestone cliff in a dramatic demonstration of a style less dramatically classified as "Central Montana Abstract." Forty handprints in red-smeared paint, some the size of a child's and others obviously strong like a warrior's, are poignant traces of a long ago presence. The paintings are so ancient that any interpretation is pure conjecture. Even so, there are many theories. One, according to Baptiste Mathias, a Kutenai Indian, is that spirits with supernatural powers dwelled in the canyon around the pictographs. Youths would come to the site to vision quest, add their names in pictograph form, and note in dots or lines how many days they remained in the place. Some archaeologists, however, suggest that the dots, lines, and limbless figures reflect shamans' ritualistic trances and that the distorted pictographic images are evidence of an altered state, believed to be the portal to the supernatural. Shamans may have induced trances through various means such as dancing, rapid breathing, or use of hallucinogenic plants and used the resulting altered state to invoke any number of outcomes such as supernatural journeys, rain, good luck in hunting, or success in battle.

Hibbard conducted a portion of his interviews in the vicinity of one of these pictograph panels painted on the steep face of the limestone. George spoke in one interview, describing his experience as it was occurring. He began by describing the awe-inspiring, narrow canyon, explaining that he had to find out why the Indians came through the place. "It was a short cut,"

George explained. "But it has more meaning than that." He then told Hibbard that a larger rival group controlled the land to the south. The narrow canyon was a secret, known only to those traveling through it. It was a refuge and thus a spiritual place. George said that he was receiving this information from a shaman who had lived six hundred years ago. The shaman told him that the people "believe this canyon has sacred meaning because they were shown this in mythology as an escape route by some animal. It's a deer. A deer went in here and went through and they followed, that way they dodged the enemy … . Since then it's been considered sacred … . He [the shaman] says this is where the animals talk." A crow cawed overhead as if to demonstrate, and George went on to say that the shaman could talk with the animals and hear what the stream rushing past had to say.

The shaman had been forewarned of George's coming, and George could feel the charge in the air. Spirits of the rocks, the stream, everything around him was full of energy. George explained:

> I call him the guardian shaman because no one could come through this territory without him seeing them or knowing about it. And nothing happened here that he didn't know about. He lived his life here, his whole life. His body is up in a crevice in one of these rocks, up the top there [above the pictograph at the top of the limestone cliff]. They placed his body in a crevice and piled rocks over the top of him because this is his canyon.

George attributes his experiences to others who show him the way. He was four when his spirit guides first began to help him gather information. These spirit guides lead him into the past by painting a picture in thoughts and images, building upon details, so that George can "see" and actually experience the past as it happens.

Hibbard continued the interviews at other sites archaeologists have identified as key to ancient peoples. At one site George explained his sensory and auditory experiences in this way:

> Right now I can hear children laughing. I can feel it. And when I go out on site, because of that energy, I'll be able to talk with those people. I can smell what they're cooking. I can see what the world was like then. What I see is the people themselves. When I get back to that time and how I feel is evident in my

own physical being, whether it's hot, cold, rainy, snowy, if there's a battle going on, or a celebration, and I can feel the sadness and a compassion for the people. I always feel a little sadness at the conditions they had to live in.

At another site, the experience was intensely emotional. Sometimes, he admits, he is afraid of what he might find because the experience is real:

I looked closely at the skeletal remains and could see they were unusual because the bones were not laid out as they should be but were scattered around in broken sections. I then focused on the time they died and the first thing I felt was a crushing sound of buffalo hooves approaching. I saw a man and a woman running holding the hands of a child between them … . I stood there with such compassion for these poor people who had lived so long ago.

For the historian, George offers an interesting, if unconventional, method of gathering information. When facts are uncertain or questionable, his information provides possible alternative answers. In 1995 George and the his friend, Ray Worring, who was a counseling psychologist and pioneer in the application of psychics in criminal investigation, came together with staff and other interested persons at the Montana Historical Society. George is not a Montanan, and he has little or no knowledge of Montana's history, but on a visit to the state he agreed to apply his intuition to several artifacts in the collections with incomplete histories. He was not privy to any prior information about them. Among the items were Henry Plummer's shotgun, two swords that belonged to Thomas Francis Meagher, John X. Beidler's rifle, and a pile of leather reins attached to a crude kind of belt or harness. The latter item reputedly also belonged to Beidler. The entire session was documented on videotape; a copy of the tape is in the possession of Patrick Marsolek of Helena.

The first item the museum registrar brought to the table was Henry Plummer's shotgun. Unbeknownst to George, historians have long discussed, debated, argued, and written about the guilt or innocence of Plummer, the sheriff at Bannack who was hanged by vigilantes in January of 1864. They believed Plummer secretly led a gang of road agents who terrorized the region during the height of the first Montana gold rushes. Nathaniel Langford's *Vigilante Days and Ways* and Thomas Dimsdale's *Vigilantes of Montana* lay out the case for Plummer's guilt, and both authors witnessed some of the events they recorded. More recently, however, a few vocal historians have suggested that Plummer's hanging was politically motivated during a period of intense Civil War conflict and that he was an innocent man framed by his accusers. In their book *Hanging the Sheriff*, Ruth Mather and Fred Boswell make the case for Henry Plummer's innocence. Modern support-ers of the two different sides are passionate in their beliefs and the contro-versy continues. Needless to say, the spectators were especially interested in George's impressions of Henry Plummer's shotgun.

George put on white cotton gloves as the museum required for handling artifacts. The gloves did not seem to impede the "reading." Ray opened the dialogue saying," We have a weapon here and it looks like a flintlock, double-barreled shotgun. Looks like it's been used quite a bit."

"Yes," George agreed, "It's a sawed off shotgun." He picked up the gun, hefted it, sighted it, and caressed the barrel.

"It's maybe had many owners, but can you describe some?" Ray gently prodded.

"Yeah," said George, "People have died in front of this gun."

George put the gun down, sat back from the table and thought about it. Then picked up the gun a second time. Ray asked, "Is the person using it a law enforcement person?"

George answered, "If he was, he was a crook." Then he hefted the gun again and said, " It's not something you aim. Just point it." After several moments lost in thought George said, "He was somewhat of a hero locally. Uh huh. I think what keeps the man alive is the fact that he took a lot of money and buried it somewhere."

"Well George, tell me *where*. All these rocks and bones are nice, but … " said Ray, referring to some stone tools that George had discussed previously. The spectators laughed.

"The only thing that makes this rifle important is the man who owned it. The gun is nothing special. Still, the man who had it … " George's voice trailed off.

Ray asked, "Any idea what his name was, what he looked like? Describe where he lived."

"Someplace in Montana," George offered, "not too far from here." Bannack is about 188 miles from Helena. George seemed unable, however, to come up with a name.

"Mmmhmm," said George, caressing the barrel, "See this twist? … The way they wrapped the barrel. Uh, yes."

Ray asked, "Negative or positive feel?"

"Negative. I think he was a bad actor myself. He had a reputation in the neighborhood. A folk hero ... ." Again, George's voice trailed off.

Ray volunteered, "They think this was Henry Plummer's gun. Plummer was the sheriff of Bannack, Montana, thought to be head of a gang."

George continued, "He didn't have any ethics. He was not a very moral person. You are right. His name was Plummer. I was going to say Carpenter." Everyone laughed.

"Any sense how he died?" the registrar asked.

"Violent, " George answered.

George's final comment seemed to underscore the dangerous weapon that it was. He said, "Not very many people have handled that gun. You keep it under lock and key?" The registrar assured him that it was kept in a safe place.

She next brought the two swords to the table. Thomas Francis Meagher is also something of an enigma, the subject of fierce debate even today between his supporters and detractors. Meagher was born in Ireland and became a leader in the Irish independence movement. Captured by the British and banished to Tasmania, he escaped and fled to New York. He organized and led the hard-driving Irish Brigade during the Civil War before coming to Montana as territorial secretary. He soon took on the role of acting governor as well. Meagher's death has sparked much speculation. Did the general who reputedly drowned in the Missouri River on July 1, 1867, trip and fall from the deck of a steamship because he was ill or in a drunken stupor? Was he shot before he fell overboard? Was he pushed? His body was never found, and his disappearance is perhaps Montana's most enduring unsolved mystery.

"Well," said Ray, "tell us about the man who owned these."

"He liked swords," said George matter-of-factly, running gloved hands over the hilt of the first sword. The spectators laughed.

"What kind of person was he, what happened to him?" asked George.

George put the sword down, and sat back from the table. "He got killed," he said. "Not with anything like this," indicting the swords. "He drowned." There was a pause, and George went further, "He was pushed off a boat," he said, his voice hushed. "In a lake, in fresh water. River? Lake? It was wide, though, a river."

Indicating the two swords, Ray asked, "Did he ever use these? Are they ceremonial?"

Indicating the first sword, George noted, "This was ceremonial."

After some moments of silence, as George stroked the swords, lifted them, and caressed them through his gloves, Ray asked, "Was his enemy related to him? Was he in any organization, political?"

"I would say it's politically motivated. This guy got to be a pain in the butt. This guy was great on ceremony." George seemed sure of himself.

"What's the significance for him of the ceremonial sword?" asked Ray.

"I think it was presented to him," said George. "He was arrogant. He made a lot of enemies. He suffered for it."

"Why was he killed?"

"I don't know. I think it was politically motivated. He had to go. Once you get into politics … ." Then, again picking up the first sword, he said, "This was made in a special place. I would say England or someplace. Came from some special place."

"Was he part of a special order?"

"Yeah, he belonged to some special order like Masonic or something. This is like a Masonic sword." (If, according to one theory, the vigilantes murdered Meagher, the reference to Masons is significant. Not all vigilantes were Masons, but Masons did figure prominently among them.)

"Was the guy related who pushed him?" asked Ray.

"I can't get that. It wasn't a close relationship. This fellow just made himself disliked. Very stubborn in his views, very arrogant, very ceremonial. He was one hundred percent military, very much American, very patriotic," George concluded his remarks. He had in fact described Meagher very well. The man was particularly renowned for his gift of oratory and for his patriotic speeches. George was then informed that the swords belonged to Meagher, and that it is his statue that is on the front lawn of the State Capitol, just across the street from the Historical Society. "Oh," said George, impressed, "Is that right?"

The final items the registrar laid on the table were the Beidler rifle and the pile of leather. The staff had no idea what the jumbled leather, cracked with age, had been used for, just that it had come to the society together with the rifle. They hoped that perhaps George could offer some clues or explanation. Beidler, unlike Plummer, was known to be an enthusiastic vigilante, and enjoyed the license his status as Deputy U.S. Marshall allowed. The registrar opened this final segment of the session asking George, "What kind of a guy was he?"

"A Springfield, no less," said George. "Good taste. Beautiful weapon. He liked to shoot." Picking up the pile of leather, George asked the staff,

John X. Beidler
COURTESY MONTANA HISTORICAL SOCIETY PHOTOGRAPH ARCHIVES 940-844

"How did they use this on a horse? It is a rawhide rope. Should be oiled to preserve it. Do you think you know what this is?"

A spectator answered, "George, we hope that you will tell us what it was used for."

Again addressing the museum staff, George asked, "Did this go around his leg?" indicating the rawhide. No one answered his question, and George picked up the gun, held it, hefted it, felt its weight. Then he again picked up the leather. "Whatever it was, it wasn't nice."

"Didn't do nice things?" Ray added.

George shook his head, licked his lips, and swallowed. "It wasn't very good. I don't know what ... ," he pushed the leather away and sat back from the table. "I don't like it. Don't like it." George looked very uncomfortable.

"Tell us what you think it might be," Ray prodded.

"Seems to me like it was to put around a prisoner, or slave. Put around his neck and drag him. That's the feeling I get, anyway. I don't like it. Reminds me of something unlawful. This person was taking the law into his or her own hands. At least that's the feeling I get. This here is a beautiful gun. More than the person. But uh, that," George indicated the gun, "has killed people. That," now indicating the leather pile, "didn't do any good. That bothers me."

"Did the same person own the two items?" asked one of the spectators. This was a question the staff hoped to resolve. George didn't answer.

Ray then volunteered some information, "X. Beidler was a vigilante. You are right. He liked guns and had a sadistic streak."

George nodded, indicating the gun and the ropes, and showing his distaste, remarked, "There's death in both of those things."

Thus ended the unusual session. George had not answered some of the questions, or provided all the answers. He had, however, added a new and unique dimension to some controversial topics, and provided sufficient corroboration for historians to consider. While many mainstream professionals may be skeptical of the work that George does, some archaeologists and historians are beginning to understand and appreciate the doors that George can open. His has been a long road and not a chosen path. Nonetheless, George feels under some obligation to share his intuitive talents, and does so generously. Perhaps one day many will embrace and fully appreciate his significant contributions.

Sources

The Montana Historical Society's museum registrar Janet Sperry, now retired, provided initial information about the session at the Montana Historical Society and Patrick Marsolek graciously loaned the videotape from which the partial transcripts were extracted. Biographical and methodological information about George McMullen is from Whitney S. Hibbard's "A Case Study of an Intuitive Archaeologist," in *Exceptional Human Experience: Studies of the Unitive / Spontaneous / Imaginal*, Volume 16, no. 1, 2000. Reporter Martin Kidston described the Hellgate Canyon pictographs in the *Helena Independent Record*, April 17, 2000. Both *Discover* (June, 1998) and *Science News* (October 5, 1996) include informative articles on the correlation between pictographs and altered states.

THE HANGING
OF PETER PELKEY

Tales of spook lights, ghost lights, or earthlights richly embroider folklore and legends. They have been known to different ages and cultures by many descriptive epithets. Ancient Romans called them *ignis fatuus* (literally "foolish fire") and in seventeenth-century England they were known as "friar's lantern" or "will o'the wisp." Scientists have various explanations for these phenomena such as electrical discharges (St. Elmo's Fire), organic luminescences (foxfire), temperature inversions, the moon's reflection on mineral veins, and modern-day headlights. Most who claim to have seen them remain unconvinced by these attempts to demystify personal experience.

Across the United States tales of such sightings can be found in nearly every state and county. In October 1894, for example, President Grover Cleveland saw a mysterious glow from a Pullman window as his train sped through the mountains of North Carolina. He immediately summoned the conductor who informed the president that he had seen the Maco Station light. Reported in the press, it became the South's most famous ghost light. The light has been seen since the 1860s when a freak accident took the life of conductor Joe Baldwin. The last car of his train somehow separated from the others. As another train sped toward the stranded car, Baldwin swung his lantern in warning, but the oncoming train did not stop and Baldwin was decapitated. Observers say the light moves in an arc, like the swinging lantern. Until the tracks were taken up in 1977, the light was mistaken for a real signal so many times that the signalmen used red and green lanterns to distinguish theirs from the ghost light. Other famous ghost light locations in the United States include Marfa, Texas, where the Texas Historical Commission erected a marker describing the history of the unexplained phenomenon; Silver Cliff's cemetery west of Pueblo, Colorado; and Hornet, Missouri.

Montana has its own tales of ghost lights. Ethel Castner and Eva Stober mention one incident in their book, *Belt Valley History*. In 1917 several people reported powerful search-type lights circling over the hill and sweeping the city. The observers could not determine the source of the mysterious lights. Gene Maier in the *Lewistown News Argus,* December 13, 1987, wrote of a strange light on his grandparents' homestead ten miles south of Grass Range. Similar to the Maco light, "It was like someone walking along, swinging a lantern." From 1907 until his grandparents left the homestead in the 1930s, the light was active. When Maier happened upon the current owner in the 1980s and mentioned the mystery, the owner said that he had seen it too, but had told no one.

Ghost lights also appeared following one of the most gruesome murders ever recorded in Lewis and Clark County. In September of 1880 authorities went to check on Charles Tacke whose ranch was in the Prickly Pear Valley about four miles east of town, just off the Bozeman road. Tacke's brother had reported him missing. After checking Tacke's cabin, an awful stench led authorities to discover the rancher's bloody corpse buried under several hundred pounds of lime. Body moisture caused the lime to slack and heat, rapidly decomposing the remains. The murder weapon, an ax clotted with blood, lay buried with the victim and tufts of hair and pools of blood revealed the path along which the killer had dragged the body. Pelkey's subsequent arrest, trial, and hanging led to a series of ghostly visitations witnessed by hundreds of local residents. Not only did the Helena newspapers report the supernatural events, but Father Lawrence Palladino, a well-known early-day priest and chronicler of the early church in Montana, also attended Pelkey before his execution and corroborated the events. Besides detailed newspaper accounts of the facts, Father Palladino wrote his personal version included in his history, *Indian and White in the Northwest.* The phenomenon was no simple haunting, and the events remain unexplained to this day.

The period during which these events occurred, between 1880 and 1881, was an unusual time for several reasons. For one thing, the weather was extreme. There was so much snowfall during the winter of 1880-81 that on April 18, 1881, a *Helena Daily Herald* reporter commented that the number of bodies beginning to come to light during the spring thaw was remarkable: "Never in our recollection have [there been] so many cases of men found dead as this spring in Montana." And there were other events, too, that made this particular time period one of uneasiness. Thomas Edison had just introduced the incandescent electric light bulb to the public and a new railway system stretched from ocean to ocean. By 1883, it would reach across Montana. Citizens correctly speculated that before long, new technologies would radically alter their lives.

On the brink of these changes the world seemed poised, teetering between a bright future and the abyss, much like that in the paintings that depict sailors in a ship about to fall over the edge of the world. A dire prediction that the end of the world would come in 1881 fueled the pessimism of some. Local papers from time to time discussed the sixteenth-century prophesy made by a cave-dwelling recluse in Norfolk, England, known as Mother Shipton. The prophetess foresaw the invention of cars, submarines, airplanes, and even spoke of the western gold rushes. Like Nostradamus, she foretold calamities such as the Great Fire of London. Local newspapers speculated that the series of strange events related to the heinous murder of Charles Tacke might have been connected to Mother Shipton's end-of-the-world prophesy.

The crime itself came about in a bizarre manner. Peter Pelkey was a twenty-four-year-old French Canadian who drifted from the lumber camps of Maine to New Hampshire and Minnesota before ending up in Tacke's employ. Pelkey's physician described him as a "wild man" who grew up on his own in the woods. Father Lawrence Palladino agreed that Pelkey never learned to restrain his passions. Tacke himself was something of a recluse, a thrifty bachelor living in a very old log cabin despite the prosperity of his ranching enterprise. Pelkey and Tacke made a strange combination, although the two seemed to get along well.

According to Pelkey's account of the crime, he and his employer were in the log stable together. A number of hogs had died of cholera and the two men were preparing to catch the remaining hogs to pull out their blackened teeth, then commonly believed to be a precaution against spread of this highly contagious disease. Tacke bent down to catch a hog, and Pelkey picked up the ax to toss it out of the way. He accidentally hit Tacke on the head causing a wound that bled profusely. Pelkey claimed that the sight of blood made him so crazy and excited that he struck Tacke twice more over the head, killing him. Then Pelkey feared the hogs would eat the body, and so he dragged the dead man into the manger and poured two barrels of lime over the lifeless body for good measure. When Pelkey noticed one of Tacke's feet sticking out of the lime, he took up the ax and chopped the foot off, then jumped on it to bury it in the lime as well.

Pelkey had the presence of mind to rifle Tacke's pockets, take what money he could find from the cabin, and make his getaway. But as Pelkey later told his confessor, Father Palladino, there was a witness to the ghoulish business. Tacke's fine stallion was stabled in the stall next to the bloody, lime-covered corpse. Pelkey saddled the valuable animal intending to ride hell-bent for Fort Benton, but the horse—perhaps in loyalty to his dead master—refused to cooperate. He constantly turned his massive head to snap at his rider's legs until Pelkey finally had to kneel in the saddle to protect himself from the vicious jaws. The spirited horse would only move in fits and starts while Pelkey beat him mercilessly. It took the horse and rider all night long to go about eighteen miles. Pelkey finally reached the Dearborn Crossing later in the afternoon the following day, trading the horse for a swifter mount and $80 in cash. Authorities soon identified the horse as Tacke's. Thus they followed Pelkey's trail and arrested him.

Once incarcerated in the Lewis and Clark County Jail in Helena, Father Palladino visited Pelkey and found him to be indeed a hard-looking case, "seemingly stolid, stupid, and devoid of human feelings," uncommunicative and incoherent. Father Palladino wrote that Pelkey's demeanor suddenly changed, however. On a later visit, Pelkey told the priest about a strange experience. It was night, and as he lay on his cot wide awake, he saw a blinding light in the corner of his cell. The light struck terror into his heart. When it dissipated, Pelkey was transformed. The guards noticed immediately that his appearance had somehow changed and he no longer spoke in grunts but with articulated intelligence. Father Palladino gave him Catholic instruction and a few days before his execution, the priest enrolled Pelkey in the Brown Scapular of Our Lady. The Catholic Church teaches that those who die wearing this scapular shall not suffer eternal fire. Pelkey wore the two small pieces of cloth, attached with a cord over his shoulders, to his execution.

A reporter interviewed Pelkey the night before the hanging. The reporter asked the condemned man if it annoyed him to hear the men outside constructing the scaffold. Pelkey replied, "Not at all. I told the boys to fix her up in good shape ... I am afraid of nothing. I am chuck full of sand and vinegar ... . I shall die game ... . It is no harder for me to face the rope than to eat a piece of pie."

Early on February 4, 1881, crowds of men and boys and a few women (whose presence shocked the reporter) thronged about the jail yard adjacent to Courthouse Square. In a congenial mood, they packed so densely onto the rooftops of the nearby sheds to get a good view that several roofs collapsed. People plummeted to the ground but no one suffered serious injuries. At half-past eleven a blanket-wrapped coffin was placed under the scaffold.

Jailers escorted Pelkey out of the jail at 11:45; the crowd fell silent as the death warrant was read. Pelkey bowed and nodded to several in the crowd. Father Palladino, Sheriff Jeffries and other officials escorted the prisoner to the gallows, applied the restraints, adjusted the noose, and gave the signal. The sheriff cut the cord, springing the iron trap and Pelkey fell through the opening. His heart continued to beat for 14 minutes, and at 16 minutes doctors pronounced him dead, his neck broken by the fall. Burial records of the Cathedral of the Sacred Hearts show that Pelkey was interred under the name Peter Pelletier in the Catholic Cemetery on Oakes, now the site of Robinson Park. His grave lies unmarked and undisturbed, as do hundreds of others, somewhere in that residential neighborhood.

Wild rumors soon began to spread throughout town that in the dead of night strange lights appeared on Tacke's deserted ranch. They hovered over the house and floated around the property, sometimes gliding along the fence rail, over the fields, moving inside the house and stable. The papers reported the incidents in detail, and according to Father Palladino, the "entire community became absorbed in the apparition." Theories to explain the strange lights included the connection to Mother Shipton and the end of the world. Some proposed that the lights were electric and had escaped from Mr. Edison's laboratory. Others believed that the lights were the ghost of Peter Pelkey, looking for the rest of Tacke's reported wealth; others argued that it was Tacke himself, come to check on his property.

Numerous witnesses to the Helena sightings described what they saw; all agreed that the lights visited the various corrals and pens, the house, and the fields. The lights were erratic, and periodically rose in the air as high as forty feet. A neighbor of Tacke's said that "the lights looked like what might be thrown from a red glass lantern at first," but grew paler and lighter in color as time passed. He claimed to have seen from one to four lights of an evening, and that he first saw them when the snow began to fall. They moved independently in different directions, sometimes settling on the fence corners. Another neighbor said that he first saw the lights in the fall as he was returning from town where he had sold some produce. They appeared to him as clear, bright lights moving around the Tacke property, rising in the air, and eventually moving slowly out over the valley until lost to sight.

The ghost lights persisted for several months. Hundreds drove out each evening to observe them to the consternation of Tacke's brother who feared some tourist would accidentally set fire to the place. Father Palladino admitted that when he and his colleagues were asked their opinion about the lights, they would imply that someone who wanted to buy the ranch had simply made the story up to scare other buyers off. But Father Palladino concluded in his narrative: "[W]e must candidly confess that the strange occurrence has ever been, and still is to this very day, an unsolved riddle in our mind."

Sources

According to Government Land Office maps, Tacke's homestead was located just west of the present townsite of East Helena. The Helena newspapers carried the story of the murder and all the gory details as well as detailed accounts of the hanging. Father Palladino told of Pelkey's transformation and the subsequent ghost lights in *Indian and White in the Northwest*.

CELESTIA ALICE EARP

"It is the most brutal, cruel assassination we have ever been called upon to chronicle in the whole course of our reportorial career, and one that has no circumstances to palliate its atrocity," wrote the *Madisonian* reporter on March 29, 1881. The crime resulted in the brutal death of thirty-two-year-old widow Celestia Alice Earp. She was a lovely, charming, and industrious woman who had come to Bozeman from Wharton, Ohio, some eighteen months previous. She had a sister in Bozeman and two brothers farming in Gallatin County. Celestia's husband, Private Richard J. Earp, had served in the 15th Ohio Volunteer Infantry, Company G. He was reportedly a casualty of the Civil War.

Mrs. Earp supported herself working for prominent Bozeman families, including that of Charles Rich, and as a chambermaid at the Laclede Hotel. She carefully saved her money. When she received her husband's $900 government pension, she used her astute business sense to file a homestead claim on 160 acres in the Flathead Pass area twenty miles north of Bozeman. But she was unable to improve the property alone. Upon the recommendation of friends, Mrs. Earp hired John Douglass, a local bachelor, to do the heaviest chores.

John Douglass was soon infatuated with Mrs. Earp. Whether he loved her for her looks or for her money he never said, but his advances were persistent and disagreeable. Mrs. Earp finally moved from her homestead back to Bozeman. When he heard that she was receiving the attentions of another man, Douglass became enraged and began threatening her with bodily harm if she did not consent to marry him. At the Pacific Hotel in Bozeman, Douglass confronted Mrs. Earp. He aimed his pistol at her and threatened to kill her. Mrs. Earp grabbed the gun and threw in it an open trunk, slammed the lid down, and locked it. Friends kept her hidden from Douglass until she decided that there was no way out of the situation. So she made plans to flee the Territory and go back to her family in Ohio.

Mrs. Earp bought a ticket to Virginia City, and George Ash took her by private conveyance to meet the stage along the road. At the stage stop at Red Bluff, two miles east of Norris, she and her fellow passengers spent the night. When Douglass came looking for Mrs. Earp, she refused to speak with him. She voiced her fear to the other passengers that Douglass would kill her. The next morning as the stage left Red Bluff, Mrs. Earp in a frightened state foolishly rode in the open, alongside the driver. It was a fatal mistake.

Douglass had been following her every movement. He overtook the stage and fired two shots. Both bullets hit their marks; one hit her in the back and went through both lungs, another hit her in the shoulder and arm. Douglass brandished his weapon and demanded that the stage driver stop. Mrs. Earp lost consciousness only for a moment, then quickly came to. When Douglass saw this, he remarked, "What! You ain't dead yet!" and fired three times more; only one bullet found its mark, hitting her in the head. Douglass stopped to reload his Smith & Wesson. The stage driver, a man by the name of Delaney, took the opportunity to put his whip to the horses, driving the short distance to Sterling with Douglass chasing him all the way.

Dave O'Brien of Pony arrested Douglass at Sterling without incident and took him to the Madison County jail at Virginia City. News of the shooting preceded their arrival, and the entire town milled around the courthouse waiting to catch a glimpse of the monster that had committed such a heinous crime. Mortally wounded, Mrs. Earp was taken from Sterling to the nearest house, that of R. M. Goin, where she lay fully conscious and in possession of her faculties until she died thirty-six hours later. During this time of intense suffering, Mrs. Earp chose an administrator, left messages for her relatives, and made her will. She left her possessions to her parents in Ohio and her clothing to her sister.

Officials conveyed Mrs. Earp's body to Bozeman where the ladies of the Presbyterian Society prepared her for burial. Although her wishes were to be buried next to her husband in Ohio, there is no indication relatives sent her body east. According to the newspapers, many attended the funeral service that took place in Bozeman. The article noted, "Although the work of the day has been sad, the weather has been delightful." The location of Mrs. Earp's burial, if it was in Bozeman, went unrecorded. That was not unusual, however; Bozeman cemetery records of this early era are sadly incomplete.

Douglass meanwhile was in residence at the Madison County jail in the courthouse basement and public sentiment ran against him. The *Madisonian* reported on May 7, 1881, that if what he said was true, this crime was not his only misdeed. He admitted to having committed robberies and murders aplenty in a constant battle against society. In fact said the paper, " ... it would have been an excellent thing for society had he been strangled in infancy." His escapades were so numerous that " ... their recital would make the hair of a Bowery boy stand on end ... ."

Douglass went to trial, was convicted of murder and sentenced to die. He reportedly asked to be hanged as soon as possible. A few days before the execution, Mrs. Earp's sister visited Douglass in his cell. The *Helena Weekly Herald* reported on May 30, 1881, that the brief interview was "not very touching, reproaches on one side and callousness on the other being the principal features of it." Officials erected a temporary courtyard and gallows in the jail yard adjacent to the present Madison County Courthouse. The *Madisonian* reported the details of the execution on May 28, 1881, with a headline that read, "The Demon Douglass Done to Death and Ends his Earthly Existence by Elevating Execution." The new method utilized a 250-pound weight, poised on a trap door at the opposite end of the hangman's rope, which rested on a heavy beam some twelve feet overhead. The executioner stood hidden from view within a boxlike enclosure. When the trap was sprung, an unrepentant Douglass met his maker with little more than a final twitch. Officials removed his body an hour later and buried him in a corner of the Virginia City cemetery. "Just retribution," said the *Madisonian,* "for the particular crime it was intended to atone, [the execution] has removed from society a man who was a constant menace to its peace." Memories of the brutal death of Celestia Alice Earp faded into obscurity.

Many decades later in 1965, as workmen installed new plumbing at the AMC Sullivan Photo Shop at 107 East Main Street in Bozeman, they made a bizarre discovery. The building, constructed in 1888, rose from the ashes of a community disaster. Businessman William M. Nevitt owned a frame hardware store that stood on Main Street between Bozeman and Rouse Avenues. A fire started in his building causing $40,000 in damages and left a two-hundred-foot hole on Main Street. Nevitt rebuilt his business at 107-113 East Main Street. The elegant Nevitt Block had room for four stores, upstairs lodgings, and originally a peaked tower that no longer exists. The arched windows, fancy cut stone, and decorative brickwork of the Nevitt Block made it an impressive addition to Main Street. It remains one of Bozeman's oldest Main Street buildings. Sherman G. Phillips bought the Nevitt Block in 1897 and one storefront became the Phillips Book Store as it remains today.

The AMC Sullivan Photo Company occupied one of the storefronts. The

Sullivans had known since improvements were made in 1949 that there was an oddly protruding rock slab, "a bump in the floor," in their basement. They had thought it was just part of the structure and a nuisance, something that was easy to trip over. When the workmen removed the slab they discovered it was marble. After a closer inspection, they discovered that the slab was a tombstone, in perfect condition. The inscription read:

CELESTIA,
Wife of
RICHARD J. EARP
Died
March 26, 1881
Aged
32 Y.   12 D.
Dearest Celestia thou hast left us
Here thy loss we deeply feel
But tis God that hath bereft us
He can all our sorrows heal.

Montana State University historian Merrill Burlingame investigated the inscription and unearthed the tragic story of Celestia Alice Earp in 1965. The tombstone eventually ended up on display at the McGill Museum, founded by Dr. Burlingame and Butte physician Dr. Caroline McGill to hold her extensive collection of antiques. That museum was the forerunner of the present-day Museum of the Rockies. Some of the McGill collection is today housed at the Museum of the Rockies, but what became of Celestia's tombstone is thus far not known, nor has anyone solved the mystery of how the tombstone ended up in the Main Street basement of the photo shop.

Before his execution, Douglas was asked if he had a last request. He replied that he had all the people in Bozeman half scared of him. All he wanted in the next world was to come back for an hour or two to finish the job. Said the *Helena Herald*, "If departed spirits can return to earth, Bozeman may look out … "

Sources

The Helena, Bozeman, and Virginia City newspapers all carried extensive stories about the murder and subsequent hanging of Douglass. Dr. Merrill Burlingame recounts the story of the discovery of the tombstone and recounts the murder of Celestia Alice Earp in the *Bozeman Daily Chronicle*, January 17, 1965.

LEGACY OF THE GRANT-KOHRS RANCH

President Richard Nixon put his signature to a Congressional bill in 1970 that helped preserve an important slice of the American West in Montana. The Department of the Interior had designated the Grant-Kohrs Ranch a National Historic Landmark in 1960. The 1970 bill allowed the National Park Foundation to purchase a portion of the ranch property that included the historic main house and outbuildings. Although in dire need of rehabilitation, the property offered a unique opportunity to interpret nineteenth-century cattle ranching. Ranch owner Conrad Kohrs Warren, grandson of cattle baron Conrad Kohrs, generously donated the family furnishings of the main house and contents of the outbuildings. Warren continued to work the remaining ranch land and live in the home he built across the railroad tracks in 1934. The Park Service began restoration of the landmark buildings in 1974.

Employees tackled the work head on. They brought in Belgian draft horses and Shorthorn cattle, the kind of purebred stock Grant-Kohrs ranchers had prized. The idea was to preserve a working nineteenth-century cattle ranch "for the benefit and inspiration of present and future generations." Workers catalogued everything from rusted tools and projectile points to the fine china that once graced Augusta Kohrs' table. Like an army of sleuths, they went over every inch of the grounds, identifying, cleaning, and fixing. The buildings yielded up some of their secrets. Cats, for example, played an important role in the long traditions of the working ranch and still go in and out the little cat holes in the ancient barns and granary. The modern-day detectives uncovered crumbling skeletons of the little mousers in nooks and crannies where they had crept, as cats will do, in sickness or old age. Little cats' bones, however, are not the only secrets hidden at Grant-Kohrs Ranch, as Park Service employees have discovered over the years.

Repairs brought new life to the buildings but preserved their intended functions, their historic fabric, and their individual character. Augusta Kohrs' furniture from the main house came out of storage, and the ranch opened to the public in 1977. To wander among the buildings is to step back to the time the ranch founders knew. These stockmen built a far-reaching empire in the valley that once served as a travel corridor to generations of native peoples and supported abundant wildlife.

Long before telephone poles, roads, railroad tracks, and houses sprang up to mar the view, a curious sedimentary cone nearly forty feet high dominated the valley in what is today southwestern Montana. Within the cone a thermal spring bubbled. On cold clear days, the steam that issued forth from this mound could be seen for miles. Native peoples, explorers, trappers, and traders took notice of the oddity. The mound with steam issuing mysteriously from its peak looked like a huge Indian lodge with smoke from a campfire curling out the top. The Shoshone knew the cone as *It Soo Kee En Carne,* "the lodge of the white-tailed deer." It held spiritual significance and power to the native peoples who trekked through the valley. Grasses grew thickly at the base of the mound bringing the white-tailed deer to graze there while saline deposits from the hot spring created a saltlick, offering further enticement. Known today as the Warm Springs Mound, it is some fifteen miles south of the Grant-Kohrs Ranch on the property of the Montana State Hospital. The historical significance of the mound and its impact on the valley have been acknowledged by listing in the National Register of Historic Places, but buildings now hide it from public view.

The Clark Fork of the Columbia River runs through the valley while the headwaters of the Missouri River at Three Forks is not too distant to the east. The valley is thus strategically located along a well-worn travel corridor. The peaceful valley was a place of summer encampment where Blackfeet, Pend d'Oreille, Nez Perce, Salish, Kootenai, and Shoshone families and hunting parties gathered. French trappers and traders also found it a place to rendezvous. The French translated *It Soo Kee En Carne* as *La Loge Du Chevreuil.* Father Pierre-Jean DeSmet, who later founded St. Mary's Mission at present-day Stevensville, met the Salish at *La Loge Du Chevreuil* in 1840. At the base of the mound he held the first Christian service in what would later become Montana.

The French name grew to include not just the mound, but the valley as well. White settlers who later discovered its bounty shortened the French translation to Deer Lodge. Long before the first Montana gold rush brought miners to southwestern Montana, former trader Richard Grant and his two sons, John and James, drove cattle into the nearby Beaverhead Basin to graze for the winter. In the spring, they drove the fattened herd west to the Oregon Trail to trade with westward immigrants. The Grants offered one fresh animal for two that were footsore and trail weary. They exchanged horses, cattle, or oxen, depending upon the travelers' needs, then wintered the animals and conditioned them. In this way, trading along the Emigrant Road, the enterprising Grants built up a sizable herd.

By 1857 Johnny Grant, whose mother had been of French and Indian descent, had at least five children and several Indian wives. The Grants, along with a company of other men and their Indian wives and children, returned to the rich grazing land of southwestern Montana. Johnny and his wife Quarra, a Bannock woman, split off from the group and brought their cattle into the valley of the "lodge of the white tailed deer" where they wintered. The cottonwood and willow trees along the river bottom sheltered their grazing cattle from the winter wind. All that season the herd mingled with deer and migrating buffalo, sharing the bunchgrass that stretched in places nearly as far as the eye could see, rippling in the wind like fields of grain. The valley proved an irresistible home to Johnny and Quarra Grant. They returned again in 1859 with two hundred and fifty head of horses and eight hundred cattle, this time to settle in the Deer Lodge Valley. They built a log cabin and a small trading post at the valley's north end, trading with the many Indians who traveled through.

In spring 1860 Johnny Grant left the valley to seek out others who might want to settle nearby. Indians, Mexicans, Canadian Métis like Johnny himself, and whites soon joined the Grants in the Deer Lodge Valley. It was a lively, ethnically diverse settlement called Grantsville, as early pioneers Granville and James Stuart recorded. The Grants hosted frequent all-night balls and social affairs with the locals dressed in a colorful mix of beaded buckskins and trade calico. But in the spring of 1861, floodwaters took the Grants' cabin, and the family moved to the new settlement of Cottonwood. They chose a suitable location to build a log cabin overlooking the line of cottonwoods that followed the Clark Fork, or Deer Lodge, River.

Johnny Grant built two cabins and joined them together for his large extended family. Edwin Ruthven Purple, who visited the Grants in the summer of 1862, wrote that Johnny offered him gracious hospitality. Grant, according to Purple, had at that time three Indian wives: "[S]urrounded by his half breeds, Indian servants, and their families, with a half dozen old French mountaineers and Trappers who have married Indian women for his neighbors, Grant lives in as happy and free a manner as did the ancient Patriarchs." Pioneer Francis M. Thompson claimed in a news article published in 1922 that Grant had a wife from every tribe that frequented the Deer Lodge Valley. When trouble with Indians was brewing, he carefully determined which tribe was involved, then brought out his wife and children from that group, hiding other family members. While this may be an exaggeration, by 1863 Grant had had eleven children with at least four different women.

First Sketch of the Johnny Grant House, circa 1862
COURTESY MONTANA HISTORICAL SOCIETY PHOTOGRAPH ARCHIVES 943-361

In fall 1862 Johnny Grant built one of the first clapboard homes in the territory. Its twenty-eight glass windowpanes packed in sawdust and shipped at great expense by steamboat to Fort Benton, then freighted overland to the valley, were an expression of the Grants' wealth and importance. It was a fine house, and Quarra took charge. However, change was in the wind. Gold discovered at Grasshopper Creek in 1862 and at Alder Gulch in 1863 brought miners and white settlers to the area. Racial tension among the Métis, Indians, and whites ended the days when neighbors were tolerant of other cultures and inter-racial marriages. Grant's worth stood at half a million dollars, a symbol of Métis prosperity, but he was soon to suffer losses.

Grant must have realized the valley was becoming unsafe for his family. vigilantes organized late in 1863 to combat lawlessness in the region. In 1865

Indians ran off most of Grant's cattle, and the following year an arson fire set by persons unknown destroyed his best barn. Soon after, the United States revenue officer paid Grant a visit and seized seven hundred gallons of liquor with which Grant had stocked his saloon. Grant told the *Montana Post* that if he could find a safer place, he would leave and "take my children away from such a rough country as Montana." A friend provided a solution. Conrad Kohrs, whom in the past Grant had assisted financially, arranged to purchase the ranch for $19,200 in August 1866. Grant sold the buildings and their contents, including the house and many of the furnishings he and Quarra had purchased from the east and shipped at great expense. In the end Grant did take his children away from the settlement now known as Deer Lodge, but Quarra did not live to accompany them.

In September following the sale of his ranch, Grant took his oldest daughter to St. Louis to enroll her in school and then traveled to Manitoba, Canada, to arrange a place for his family to live. He returned to the Deer Lodge Valley in spring 1867, only to find that on February 24, Quarra had died of tuberculosis. She left behind six children, four boys and two girls. William at ten was the oldest and Charles Henri, who had been born during Grant's absence, was five months old. In between were David, eight; Julienne, seven; John, five; and Ellen, four. Grant wrote of Quarra in his memoirs:

> She was a thorough Indian woman and not handsome, but a better and more clever woman could not be found, without education. She was a good mother, industrious and gay in her moods and friendly with everyone regardless of nationality or color. She could speak several Indian languages as well as English and French. She was expert with her needle too and could ride horses that many could not. My little Quarra, when I heard of her death my first thought was the great loss our children sustained. She had been such a good mother.

Despite Grant's wayward eye for other women, and that he already had another wife in mind to take care of his children once he reached Manitoba, he confessed that he would truly miss Quarra. From members of his household Grant learned that Quarra had expressed sorrow that her husband was not there at the time of her death. Her last request, however, was to see her children. She took little Charles Henri in her arms and held him so tightly he cried. The children sorely missed her presence in their lives.

Grant thus left the Deer Lodge Valley and the settlement of Deer Lodge, formerly called Cottonwood, which he had helped to found. He took his bereaved family and his many horses with him to Manitoba. Conrad Kohrs took possession of the ranch property, its buildings, and their contents. The large, two-story, white house with the green shutters, twenty-eight windows, and tall chimneys—very grand indeed for this remote valley in the 1860s—stood in stark contrast to the barns, earthen-floored corrals, and surrounding grasslands.

Conrad Kohrs returned east to marry in 1868. He brought his nineteen-year-old bride, Augusta, to Montana. The Kohrses raised their children on the ranch and the couple enlarged the house in the 1890s. The furnishings reflect the elegance with which Augusta ran her household, although a few pieces—rosewood parlor chairs and a pie safe in particular—date to Quarra Grant's years. The ranch was the largest in the valley, and Kohrs and his half-brother and partner John Bielenberg, a life-long bachelor, prospered. Theirs was among the best stock in Montana. Bielenberg introduced the first thoroughbred stallions into the territory in the early 1870s while Kohrs, who had mining interests and also served in the state legislature, focused on cattle raising. He pioneered cattle ranching techniques, business management and investments, feed production, and cattle breeding. The operation shipped eight to ten thousand head to market every year. Ownership of the working ranch remained in the Kohrs family through grandson Conrad Warren until the 1970s when the Park Service began its restoration. Over the years, a few employees have become acquainted with at least some of the deeper secrets of the ranch.

Chief Ranger Matt Connor signed on with the National Park Service as a ranger at Grant Kohrs Ranch in January 2001. He enjoyed his first months, settling in, getting used to the routine. By October, Matt was comfortable around the historic buildings. As Halloween approached, Matt and his wife were excited because, for the first time, they lived in a family-oriented safe neighborhood in Deer Lodge where kids still enjoyed trick-or-treating door-to-door.

So on this special Halloween, Matt was in a hurry to lock up the buildings and head home. He wanted to be sure that he would be there when the doorbell began to ring. The weather was not cooperating. In fact, it was a downright nasty afternoon, unusually dark with thunderclouds overhead. He checked the house, noting that everything was okay there. Matt hurried along, walking briskly to the edge of the ranch buildings, checking to make sure everything was locked up. He made his way along the bunkhouses that had been built around the two joined cabins—originally the Grants' first home on the ranch. He moved toward the granary. As he passed the 1870s draft horse barn on his left, he saw that the door had its customary padlock. At certain times of the year there were horses stabled in the great old barn, but the horses were out to pasture just now and the door was padlocked, as it should have been.

Matt made a second check, set the alarm in the house, and following his usual routine, came back for a third and final check of the outbuildings. Again, he cut through the yard, made his way along the bunkhouses, and headed toward the granary and the barn. As he glanced to his left toward the barn, he saw the door standing wide open. "How could that be?" Matt said to himself. "Maybe the padlock wasn't really fastened and the wind blew the door open." He knew this was unlikely but could think of no other logical explanation unless someone else was on the property. This was an unforeseen annoyance, something that would make him late getting home. He quickened his step and approached the barn. As he came up to the door, he saw that the wind had not just blown it open; no, it was chained open, and the chain was hooked to the old bent nail the staff used to keep the door from slamming shut.

"Hello," Matt called out, "Is anybody here?" It was starting to rain; large spatters began to hit the gravel as the wind picked up.

Matt stepped into the old barn, which was naturally so dark that, standing inside even with the door open, it was impossible to see more than a few feet, a situation the Park Service had tried to remedy by installing electric lights. Matt saw that the overhead lights were not on, but something was very peculiar. A strange, glowing, bright light bathed the barn's normally dark interior. It was bright, almost blinding, like the light a photographer uses in his studio during a portrait sitting. This brilliant light spilled over the windowless stalls. It cast an odd luminescence over the ancient wood worn smooth by generations of equine inhabitants. Matt looked for the source of the light as he thought to himself, "Maybe the windows are open in the other part of the building." They were not, and even if they had been, the weather was so gloomy that the windows would not have been the source of such radiance. "Maybe the lights are on in the loft," reasoned Matt, unwilling to accept this strange phenomenon. But the lights were not on in the loft, and the barn was empty of human visitors.

Matt was now even more anxious to get home. He was going to be late, and he was rushing around the barn trying frantically to figure out this mystery. Finally, he could find no explanation for the open door or light, so he shrugged and moved to the door, took the chain from the bent nail, pulled the door shut, and began to put the padlock through its chain. As he fiddled with the lock, he heard a familiar sound inside: the distinctive sound of cowboy boots crossing the floor.

"This is just crazy! Who are these jokers, playing around when I need to get home? I haven't time for this nonsense, not tonight!" thought Matt. He distinctly heard two sets of cowboy boots and two men in the barn. He could hear them moving about inside, as if they were just doing their chores. He listened intently to the boots as they moved about; then he also began to hear conversation. They were talking in low tones, so low that he could not make out the words. It sounded like a normal, everyday conversation between a couple of cowboys.

As Matt stood with his ear to the entry, he heard the top of the grain bin, just on the other side of the door, flip open and bang in his ear. Thunk! He heard the scoop hit the grain. Then he heard the cowboy dip deeply into it, get a hefty scoopful, and dump it into a waiting bucket. He could hear the *plunk* as the first grain hit the metal, then *swoosh* as the rest poured into the bottom. Matt again heard the scoop hit the grain in the bin followed by the *plunk, swoosh* rhythm of grain shoveling. "Wait a minute," said Matt aloud. It still did not strike him as abnormal, only that these pranks were making him late. Matt undid the padlock, pushed open the heavy door, and again entered the barn. No one was there. He looked into the bin and saw that it was empty. There was not even one stray kernel of grain left over from its last use. "Hmmm," Matt thought, irritated. In retrospect, he remembers that neither the open barn door, nor the weird bright light, nor the sounds of the mumbling cowboys spooked him. The situation still didn't strike him as out of the ordinary exactly, just that it was darn irritating when he was in such a rush to get home.

As Matt again pulled the door shut and began to work the padlock, he again heard the cowboys. Their mumbling conversation droned on, and their boots dragged. They were just a couple of hands, lazy and slow, doing their chores halfheartedly when the boss was not around to goad them into efficiency. Matt listened again intently, and as he did so, he heard the pair come out of the barn. He distinctly heard their slow footsteps hit the gravel. Clu-CLUNK. Clu-CLUNK. Clu-CLUNK.

"Well," thought Matt, now beginning to realize that he had just been privy to an extraordinary event, "these boys must really want to be here, and I am not going to be the one to chase them out. They belong here."

Matt never again heard the cowboys in the barn, nor did he experience anything similar on subsequent Halloweens during his time at the ranch. Even so, at least during his several Halloweens at the Grant-Kohrs Ranch, Matt never liked to lock the barn. He preferred to keep it open for those lazy and slow, yet very persistent, cowboys.

Other events have occurred at the ranch, though, fueling the notion that forces springing from a deep sense of history and residents long since departed are at work. Staff sometimes find harness moved from one place to another in the draft horse barn, and tack left unbraided in the evening will mysteriously be braided the next morning. Matt and other employees have reported footsteps, two distinct sets of them, upstairs in the Warren house when no one is there, and cigar smoke sometimes wafts through the rooms where no one smokes.

On one occasion Grant-Kohrs veteran ranger Lyndel Meikle was working in her office in the Warren House during a storm when some inner voice told her to go check the main house. Lyndel has always made a practice of talking to the spirits of the place. "Call fast if you need me," has become her sign off, repeated every evening when she locks up to head home. That little inner voice was strong and so odd, coming at that particular moment. It was only three in the afternoon. There was no reason to go over to the main house across the railroad tracks, but that little voice was so insistent she could not ignore it. Lyndel rushed over and once inside, she found the inner storm windows open and blowing in, falling dangerously close to fragile artifacts. A few seconds' delay would have been disastrous.

Lyndel has several other tales to tell about the property. One incident compares to that of Matt's encounter with the cowboys in the barn. In 1950 Con Warren converted three rooms on the second floor of the main house into an apartment for a resident caretaker. The rooms at the top of the stairs were designed to house an employee with a family. These rooms were original to the Grants' home, and likely served as bedrooms for Quarra Grant and her children and, later, for Conrad and Augusta Kohrs and their children, too.

The foreman who lived in the apartment with his wife in 1954 had a young son, Jack, who was about nine years old. The living–working arrangement was quite convenient, and the family enjoyed looking after the old house that had such a long history. One night the foreman and his wife had settled in for a comfortable sleep. As her husband slept, the wife awakened to the sound of crying. She distinctly heard the plaintive little voice of a child calling "Mama! Mama!" Thinking it belonged to her own little boy, she threw back the covers, got out of bed and raced to her son's room. The little boy was sound asleep. Thinking, that perhaps he had cried out in his sleep, she made sure he was okay, as any parent would do, adjusted the covers around him, and returned to bed. Lying in the dark, she distinctly heard the little voice again, "Mama? Mama?" It was a sound so poignant in the deep dark quiet that it brought tears to her eyes. Again she went to check on her child, but as before, nothing was amiss.

Throughout the night "Mama! Mama? Mama?" punctuated her dreams, and she slept poorly for hearing the sad little voice, calling out in the dark, for the mother who never answered. With the morning light, she thought she had dreamed the whole incident. As she was getting dressed, however, she glanced at the mirror over her dresser. There in a corner, as clear as could be, she saw a small, smudgy handprint.

"How could Jack have gotten up there?" she marveled, thinking that her son would have had to go to some creative means to figure out a way to leave his handprint in such a place. Then she began to wonder about the logistics. She called Jack into the room, boosted him up and had him place his hand over the print. It did not match. Her blood ran cold. Some other child, not her own, had been in her room that night.

Lyndel has been a ranger at the ranch for more years than she cares to count and knows its secrets better than most. Although she recently moved off the property, Lyndel lived there for much of her career as a ranger. She had grown accustomed to the quirky alarm in the main house that inexplicably goes off on its own. One night, not long after the September 11 terrorist attack that brought increased security measures across the nation, Lyndel returned late from a homeland security detail assigned to guard the dam and power plant at Bighorn Canyon. She was exhausted after twenty-one shifts of twelve hours each. About three AM, the alarm in the main house went off. Lyndel knew it was nothing, but she had to go over to check the house and turn it off. She unlocked the door, checked the parlor, the dining room, and the rest of the first floor, climbed the stairs, and found all in order. Headed back downstairs, Lyndel suddenly became overwhelmed, and out of utter weariness sank down on a stair. With her head in her hands, terribly depressed, she felt the stress of the last three weeks take over. Then sitting there in the quiet house, in the darkness, she noticed, or thought she noticed, something pleasant in the air. She raised her head and breathed deeply. "What is that?" she thought to herself. It was not her imagination. It became stronger and began to surround her. It was lovely, calming, nostalgic, and old-fashioned. It smelled like the drawers in Augusta Kohrs' dresser where the same faint scent of lavender still lingers, infused into the old wood.

Lyndel's heavy mood began to lift. Lavender enveloped her for a moment, wrapping her in its sweetness like an elusive memory. Then, quite suddenly, it was gone. Who was responsible for the healing spell the lavender cast about her? Quarra Grant? Augusta Kohrs? Some other benevolent spirit? Lyndel will never know for certain, but she is grateful to whomever, or whatever, it was. The peace that came in the brief encounter meant a great deal to her that night.

Sources

The National Register nomination for *It Soo Kee En Carne* at the State Historic Preservation Office in Helena furnished the information for the historical context of the Deer Lodge Valley. Grant–Kohrs Ranch history is easily accessible on the Internet through Park Service websites. Lyndel Meikle has ably edited the Grant memoir under the title *Very Close to Trouble* (1996). The memoir contains Grant's description of Quarra as well as information about his personal life and his children. Edwin Ruthven Purple's gold rush narrative, *Perilous Passage,* edited by Kenneth N. Owens (1995) includes a description of the Grants' hospitality. Patricia Nell Warren, the daughter of Conrad Kohrs Warren, has written beautifully about the history of her family's ranch, notably in *Persimmon Hill*, a publication of the National Cowboy Hall of Fame and the Western Heritage Center (May, 1985). These materials reside in the Montana Historical Society Research Center's vertical files on the Kohrs family.

A GHOST WITHIN A GHOST

You can see most of what is left of the fort from the highway, huge buildings with hollow windows, the sunlight piercing their emptiness. They dot the great expanse of flat grassland that sweeps across the windy landscape. But down the road, at the end of a gravel driveway, the surviving buildings lie hidden from the highway. These buildings are still in use, lived in, and allow the visitor a glimpse of another time. Fort Assinniboine was the largest military fort in Montana, its troops charged with patrolling the northern plains. Officials placed the fort in one of the most strategic points in the Northwest along what we call today the Old Forts Trail. The trail included Forts Benton and Assinniboine in Montana Territory and Forts Walsh and Battleford in Saskatchewan, Canada. Construction of Fort Assinniboine began in 1879. Some eight hundred soldiers were stationed there at its peak; the soldiers commanded such a presence in the desolate area that only a low board fence enclosed the fort. It needed no battlements. Unfortunately, internal threats posed greater risks than external foes. In the first years deadly pneumonia took a handful of soldiers; other diseases, accidents, bad water, extreme weather, fire ants, and swarms of mosquitoes compounded the difficulties of the men garrisoned there.

Although on alert many times, Fort Assinniboine troops saw no direct action. Famed General "Black Jack" Pershing came to this remote post in 1895 as a First Lieutenant in the 10th Cavalry, a unit of African-American soldiers. Pershing's nickname derives from this period in his career when he was the officer in charge of the unit. The fort's importance was on the wane but luck was on Pershing's side when he met General Nelson Miles at Fort Assinniboine and accompanied the general on a two-day prairie chicken hunt. It was fortuitous for Pershing's career since, partly because of this friendship, Pershing got himself appointed instructor at West Point. The unmarried officers' quarters where Pershing once lived still stands, a grand red-brick structure with an imposing turret.

During Fort Assinniboine's first two years, trade in buffalo robes and furs was said to be enormous. Col. C. A. Broadwater, who later built Helena's famed Broadwater Hotel and Natatorium, operated the trading post and stage line. R. L. McCullough soon joined Broadwater and the partners did business as Broadwater and McCullough. Mrs. McCullough's reminiscences of life at the fort offer a colorful picture. For the women and children whose husbands and fathers were stationed there, the fort was a small city surrounded by wilderness. Fort Assinniboine was the center of an elite group where officers, their families, and a select group of civilian personnel made their own society. The first soldiers carried fish in canvas buckets from Birch Creek to plant in Beaver Creek where none had been before. Then they not only had fresh fish for their tables, but sport in catching them. Wives and children soon arrived. There were dinner tables set with silver, crystal, and china; dances to the accompaniment of the regiment band; and plays, riding parties, and ice sailing. In winter, blizzards caused little concern as everything needed was snug within the confines of the fort. The children attended school, the reverend conducted services, the women baked cakes and pies, and everyone participated in the community in one way or another. But by 1895 when Pershing entered the scene, the region was changing and the area was no longer so remote.

In 1911 the last soldiers departed, abandoning the fort to the elements. The barracks, dance hall, stables, chapel, library, hospital, and other facilities sat empty, and the cement sidewalk slowly crumbled. In 1915 the State of Montana purchased the buildings still standing on the site along with some 2,000 acres for agricultural purposes. The federal government sold the rest of the military reserve's land at auction. In 1916 the state turned the property over to the Northern Montana College of Havre and the facility became an Agricultural Experiment Station. The first project was testing dry land tillage methods.

With the collapse of the homesteading era, the dry land farming experiments ceased and the fort went on to host a variety of public functions. Public meetings, 4-H camp, women's camp, farmers' gathering place, and the site of the annual Presbyterian youth conference were some of its functions during the 1920s and early 1930s. By 1934 the southern portion of the fort housed homeless victims of the depression and drifters, many of whom came into Havre riding the rails. In exchange for food and a warm place to sleep, relief workers put the transients to work repairing the fort's buildings and keeping the camp clean for those who needed housing during the lean 1930s.

An elderly local man, recently deceased, told former legislator and long-time Havre resident Toni Hagener about an unforgettable experience he had at the fort. As a youngster of twelve or so, he attended summer camp at the fort. The boys were housed on the first floor of one of the barracks built for enlisted men. The young campers slept side by side in rows like the soldiers had before them. The kids enjoyed the usual camp activities—crafts, sports, campfires, and camaraderie—and as kids will be kids, they also did some things they were not supposed to do. Every chance they got, the boys would sneak up to the second floor of the barracks, which was strictly forbidden.

Ruins of the barracks at Fort Assinniboine, 1954
COURTESY MONTANA HISTORICAL SOCIETY PHOTOGRAPH ARCHIVES 946-953

On the second floor was one long room with a path down the center. On either side, piled to the ceiling, were the fort's administrative records, which included bookkeeping logs, fitness reports, and documentation on all the prisoners who saw the inside of the fort's jail. Also among the records were stacks of books that held the quartermaster's logs. These oversized books provided unusual sport for the mischievous boys. One boy would serve as lookout at the bottom of the stairs. Upstairs, the boys would each take a book, get a running start down the long corridor, and flop down on the open volumes. The slide down that corridor was marvelous! The wind rushed past and for that split second, time stopped. Again and again the boys would take turns. It was almost as good as sledding down a steep hill. If they got caught, punishment was nothing more serious than peeling potatoes for the camp cook or taking an extra turn at dishes after dinner. It was always worth the risk.

By the time the boys rolled into their bunks at the end of the day, they were usually too tired to cause much mischief, and they slept soundly until the morning wake up call. But one early morning incident left the old man with frightening memories that lingered vividly fifty years later. He opened his eyes to the semi-darkness, wondering what had disturbed his sound sleep. It wasn't his usual habit to awaken before he had to. He seemed to recall in his hazy, sleepy mind that there was some out-of-the-ordinary sound like ... like ... hmmm ... . He drifted off to sleep again. Then he started awake, and listened intently, wondering if anyone else had heard it. He took inventory of the sleeping forms nearest him trying to determine if anyone had moved. All the boys were sound asleep. "Must have been a dream," he thought. No one else seemed to be stirring, so he settled back again into his pillow. Suddenly he heard what he thought he had dreamed. There was a rustling kind of sound and then footsteps overhead. "There couldn't be anyone upstairs at this hour," he thought. But the dim light also prevented him from determining if any of his fellow campers were out of their bunks and wandering around above him.

Compelled by curiosity, he folded his blanket back, quietly let his feet hit the floor, one at a time, and tiptoed to the end of the long room full of sleeping campers. He reached the end of the barracks and heard the sounds again, coming from upstairs. He paused at the bottom step and looked up into the darkness that enveloped the upper story. There! He heard the sound again. Faint-like. It sounded like, well, like ... he didn't know what it sounded like. So the youngster screwed up his courage and quietly took the steps one at a time. He reached the top and stepped into the long room. The windows let in a faint light between the stacks of old books and papers. Moonlight filtered into the room, pooling in intervals beneath the windows. At the far end of the room, at the end of the paper-lined corridor where the boys had so enjoyed their forbidden sport, an elderly man sat crossed-legged on the floor. He had a stack of books at his side, the old quartermaster's logs. The boy recognized them right away. The man's grizzled, unkempt hair and scraggly gray beard hid his features, but the boy could see what he was doing. In his lap he held a book, and he sat hunched over it, turning pages as if searching for something. The boy stood frozen, hidden in the shadows. At least, he hoped the shadows were dark enough to keep him hidden. As he watched the man, he could see the pages in the book turn. Nothing else moved, just the pages in the book. The boy did not know what to do. Slowly he backed up to the stairs, turned and took them two at a time, trying all the while to be as quiet as he could. But he was frightened! He quickly made his way back to the bunk, climbed in and thought about what he had just seen. Who could that man be? And what was he looking for up there in the dark?

The boy waited, shaking in his bed, until the faint streaks of dawn began to color the sky, turning it from dark blue to shades of rose. Then he couldn't bear the silence and the fear anymore. He reached over and punched his friend. "Hey! Shh!" he hissed in his friend's ear, "Wake up! You won't believe what I saw upstairs." Motioning to his friend to follow, the boy again crept out of bed and led the way to the stairs. Up the two went, taking each step like thieves in the night. At the top of the stairs, in the pale half-light, they could see him. The old man was still at his task, turning pages in the quartermaster's reports. The boys' eyes met, and each saw that the other was as gray as ashes in a cold fireplace. Both boys mutually turned and fled noisily down the stairs to their bunks. It was strange that none of the other boys so much as shifted position in bed. The two friends stared at the door waiting for whomever it was to sneak down and quietly let himself out the door. But they never saw anyone come down.

Soon reveille sounded and the other boys tumbled out of their bunks. The two who had seen the old man turning pages waited for the right moment, then scampered up the stairs to check. Of course the old man was gone, and whatever books had been at his elbow were neatly replaced. Neither boy doubted what he had seen early that morning, but neither could explain it.

In 1954 the barracks burned down but not before the papers, records, and quartermaster's logs had been gathered and stored elsewhere. When the boy was himself an elderly man, he still wondered who it was that he and his friend had seen. He had long ago come to the conclusion that it was the ghost of some old soldier returned to search for he knew not what. During his long life, the man often wondered if the grizzled old timer he had seen on the early morning so long ago still walked the grounds of the old fort, and sifted through the ashes of the building that no longer stood, a ghost within a ghost.

Sources

Toni Hagener supplied much of the information for this story. Other sources include the National Register of Historic Places nomination housed at the State Historic Preservation Office in Helena, the Fort Assinniboine vertical file at the MHS Research Center, and the Old Forts Trail interpretive signage for Fort Assinniboine.

School Spirit

Most college campuses have their eerie tales, passed down from student to student. Such tales are part of college life, told in the wee hours when fatigue takes over and the pages of the textbooks begin to blur. At such times, when too much coffee prevents sleep, students swap tales and relate their personal experiences. Older students share the lore they have learned with younger classmates. Within this social framework, the special camaraderie among young scholars effectively perpetuates tales of haunted places and ethereal visitors.

Take the University of Montana-Western in Dillon, for example, where students report the ghostly notes of a piano filtering down from a room on the top floor of Old Main Hall. The simple tune flows through the hallways and catches in the stairwells. They say the player is a ten-year-old, practicing in a music room where long ago she took lessons. As the story goes, the little girl lived across the street from campus. One day after her lesson, she left her books in the classroom. Racing back to get them, she forgot to look both ways and a car mowed her down. Now the ghostly notes of her piano piece keep the memory of the tragedy alive among the students.

Then there is the haunted theater at Montana State University in Bozeman where a theater director fell down a metal stairway and sustained a severe concussion. Depression set in and a few weeks later during a production, he shot and killed himself. The incident occurred in his office. Students who never knew this director report seeing him in the building, and describe him perfectly. Various kinds of phenomena frequently occur in the theater. And among the popular stories at the University of Montana at Missoula is the one about the coed who stabbed herself with a metal comb (so they claim) because her father lost his shirt in the stock market crash of 1929. Students say that she and her German shepherd walk the lofty corridors of Brantly Hall. Custodians report slamming doors, footsteps, and the image of a dark-haired woman in the mirrors of the women's restroom at University Hall.

Carroll College in Helena has its stories, too, and more than its share of places haunted by the past. Tales about the Carroll campus are so numerous and the same stories span so many decades, told among students who have no associations with each other, that even skeptics say there might be something to them. The aftermath of a tragic accident, haunted buildings, ghostly nuns, and a beloved and saintly priest make the college one of Montana's most haunted places.

Carroll College traces its roots to the vision of Bishop John Brondel who came to Helena in 1883. He found the fledgling territorial capital teeming with energy, but there were only a dozen Jesuit priests scattered throughout the territory. Their far-flung congregations required long journeys to conduct periodic services, a time-consuming effort that took them away from missionary work. In addition, there were five diocesan priests serving a fast-growing population. These priests were not native-born Montanans, but even if they had been, there was no educational facility to train them at home. Bishop Brondel immediately saw that Montana needed to train its own clergy to minister to the territory's 15,000 Catholics. The bishop dreamed of founding a school to facilitate his idea and received permission to raise funds for it. He died in 1903, however, before his dream could come to fruition.

John P. Carroll, president of St. Joseph's College in Iowa, became Bishop of the Diocese of Helena in 1904 following Bishop Brondel's death. Bishop Carroll brought expertise in academia and immediately took up the cause to build the college. To raise funds he sold mining properties willed to the Diocese and chose the prominent hilltop as a perfect location for the campus.

It was not until September 27, 1909, that the cornerstone of the first college building was laid. The event coincided by happenstance with a presidential visit. President Howard Taft came through Helena on an ambitious railway tour around the country. At the instigation of Senator Tom Carter, the President's motorcade diverted to Benton Avenue and up the hill to the formal ceremony in progress. Thus with the impromptu aid of President Taft, Bishop Brondel's dream began to take physical shape. Beautiful, regal St. Charles Hall, designed by St. Helena Cathedral's architect A. O. Von Herbulis, was, and still is, the centerpiece of the present college campus. Its solid walls of native red porphyry, peaked gables, and bright red roof are a focal point of the Helena community.

The location of the campus on the hill east of Benton Avenue affords a sweeping view of the Prickly Pear Valley. It was a much-coveted location. Upon statehood in 1889, officials had set their sights on the hilltop, optimistically platting it as Capitol Hill. It would have been ideal for a statehouse, but in the end Montana looked elsewhere, building its capitol on donated land east of town. Samuel Hauser simply wanted too much money for his Capitol Hill.

Samuel Hauser's daughter had acquired Capitol Hill. She and others generously donated fifty acres for the building of the school, named Mount St. Charles College in honor of St. Charles Borromeo, patron of learning and the arts. The school at first accepted boys ten years and older offering four years preparatory education and four years of college. By 1924 two additions to St. Charles Hall completed the original campus plans. Other new buildings gradually increased the size of the campus, including the addition of Borromeo Hall in 1957. Named for the College's patron saint, Borromeo Hall was intended as a residence hall for young men studying for the priesthood and for elderly priests who had retired.

The school's social structure began to change with the gradual addition of women to the campus in different capacities. Two Catholic women's orders helped shape the transition. St. Albert's Hall was built in 1924 to accommodate twelve Dominican sisters who arrived from Germany in 1925. The homesick sisters used to joke that they were far from home without so much as stamp money to send a letter to their families. Until 1934, the sisters were responsible for all janitorial duties, and they prepared all the meals for students and faculty on campus until 1961. The Sisters of Charity, already in residence at St. John's Hospital in Helena, began teaching nursing classes affiliated with Carroll College in the mid-1940s. The students were housed off campus at Immaculata Hall on Catholic Hill. This paved the way for Carroll to admit women students.

Today the College numbers fourteen hundred students and has a fine reputation as a nationally ranked liberal arts college with a long history of excellence. Its beautiful campus is not only rich in colorful traditions; it is also rich in legend. Many of the tales that wind their way through several generations of Carroll students are not verifiable. Others are not so difficult to trace or explain. A priest who committed suicide, for example, or another who fell down a flight of stairs—these are apocryphal rumors. Certainly, retired faculty members have died on campus, but almost always of the infirmities of old age. A few were in the prime of life. Father Patrick

McVeigh, for example, at thirty-eight was head of the Science Department when he died very suddenly at seven in the morning, February 20, 1933, of a heart condition. The *Helena Independent Record* of February 24, 1933, noted that an honor guard of students stood over his casket as he lay in state on campus before removal to the Cathedral for public funeral. These incidents add to the more mysterious aspects of Carroll's history.

St. Charles Hall on the Carroll College Campus, ca. 1930s
COURTESY MONTANA HISTORICAL SOCIETY PHOTOGRAPH ARCHIVES PAC 97-41.2

There are places on campus where the past seems to resonate. St. Charles Hall is one such place that is tied to a story, unfortunately rooted in truth, stemming from a tragic incident that continues to spin its threads among Carroll students. In January 1964 a promising twenty-one-year-old football letterman and junior class president suffered a devastating fall. The *Helena Independent Record* of January 13, 1964, reported that according to the young man's mother, he " ... had gone to the dormitory bathroom to brush his teeth and blacked out, striking his head against the wash basin." He was taken to St. John's Hospital and remained awake, seeming to respond to treatment until doctors performed the first of two operations the following evening. He never regained consciousness following the first surgery. Suffering a subdural hematoma with intra-cerebral hemorrhage, the young man died after pneumonia set in three weeks later, on February 7. The popular young resident of St. Charles Hall, according to his obituary, was a linebacker studying biology with plans to go into medicine. Faculty and students struggled with his loss and remembered him in their prayers.

After the incident, residents of St. Charles Hall began to report something disturbing about the dormitory bathroom where the tragedy occurred. Perhaps these students knew about the young football player's accident and had over-active imaginations. As the story goes, however, a student would stand at the washbasin, brushing his teeth or washing his face. A random glance into the mirror over the sink sometimes produced a horrifying image. Reflected in the mirror was a young man standing behind and slightly to the side, so as to reveal his head and upper torso. Blood was flowing profusely from a gaping wound to his forehead. The first reaction was to whirl around to see who was in the mirror. But there was never anyone to match the reflection. These glimpses frightened not only students who claimed firsthand sighting, but also others who lived on that floor and elsewhere in St. Charles Hall.

The stories about the bathroom began to include other elements. Students claimed that blood would flow from the faucet, and bloodstains in the sink and on the floor reappeared every time maintenance staff cleaned them. The explanation was that pranksters had splattered red paint in the basin and on the floor. The stories were so enduring, however, that eventually this fourth-floor bathroom was closed, locked, and used only for storage. Maybe, as some maintain, it was simply too expensive to renovate; maybe there were other reasons. A St. Charles Hall dorm director in the late 1980s claims partial responsibility for fabricating a few of the stories about the fourth floor. While he does not deny that the building has an unusual energy, he insists that the young man who fell in the bathroom never even lived at St. Charles Hall. This is very odd indeed, since the obituary in the *Helena Independent Record* on February 7, 1964, clearly states otherwise. Whatever the reason for the closure of the bathroom, it has been locked for years and remains off limits to this day. Its closure is a further curiosity since it is one of the dorm's largest bathrooms and its plumbing, according to maintenance workers, is fine. A few years ago, Helena's KTVH Channel 12 did a Halloween story on the bathroom and took the camera inside. That footage remains the public's only glimpse inside the locked room.

Char Helmick Pentecost spent a memorable year on the fourth floor of St. Charles Hall in the early 1990s. It was her first semester living in St. Charles. After a long day moving into her new room, Char turned out the light and settled in, looking forward to a good night's rest. She was on the brink of sleep when she became aware of heavy, rhythmic breathing, as if someone in a deep sleep was in the room with her. The breathing seemed to come from the floor next to her bed. Char flipped on the light, but of course no one else was in the room. Again she nearly drifted off only to be startled again by the heavy breathing. After going through this scenario several times, Char finally turned on her radio to muffle the sound. The next day the new residents of the fourth floor gathered for their first meeting. The floor monitor sat at the head of the group. The first thing she said was, "So, has anyone heard the breathing yet?" Everyone looked at each other feeling uncomfortable, but no one wanted to speak up. It was evident that Char was not the only girl who heard the ghostly sleeper.

Later in the year, Char and some of the other girls on the fourth floor gathered in the lounge to study for finals. It was late, almost midnight, and they decided to call it a night. Before heading to their rooms, they stood visiting near the locked bathroom, used at this time to store extra dorm furniture. Suddenly they heard loud scraping sounds coming from inside the locked bathroom. It sounded like metal dorm furniture being scooted on the floor. The girls stood quietly looking around the group, each silently imploring the others to acknowledge that they heard it too. All eyes looked to the padlock, still secure on the door. That was the only time Char heard sounds coming from the bathroom, but throughout the school year, she and the other girls on the floor regularly heard the ghostly breathing. Most just slept with their radios on as a matter of course.

There are many other stories about St. Charles Hall that have been consistent throughout the last half century. The priest who committed suicide is one persistent legend. A row of discolored stones at the back of the building is supposedly where the death occurred. The stones are of a slightly lighter color than the masonry on the rest of the building. There is also the legend of the student who jumped or fell out a top story window; his body is supposedly sometimes seen plummeting past the windows of the lower floors. There is the tale that has to do with a priest or a student who fell down a stairwell, and yet another tells of an old priest with a cane, tapping in the halls. Likely most of these legends are just that. Students, however, consistently report that on certain walls nothing can be hung. Pictures, nails, thumbtacks, tape, sticky wax—nothing will stay on them. Many, many students who have lived in St. Charles Hall swear that there are noises in the night like tapping sounds that come from the walls. Others report a phantom visitor, knocking on their doors, tapping down the halls. So many have experienced these noisy visitations over the decades that he even has a name. They call him "The Tapper."

Helena High School English teacher Don Pogreba spent nearly seven years at Carroll, from 1992 to 1998, as a student and then as a debate coach. Don lived in Borromeo Hall, the 1957 facility originally intended as a residence hall for student priests and retired faculty. By the 1990s, however, Borromeo Hall housed students, but Don also had an office there. One afternoon he had gone to his room to take a nap. It had been a very bad day and he was stressed out. As he began to drift off, he felt a hand on his shoulder. Don describes it as an old, dry hand, like his grandmother's. His grandmother, to whom he had been very close, had recently passed away. It was a very comforting experience, one that he looks back on as pleasant and reassuring. He felt that his grandmother had been there, telling him not to worry, that it would all work out.

There may be several other explanations, however, for Don's experience. Borromeo's use as housing for elderly priests offers one possibility. Another is that through different generations of students in the various residence halls at Carroll there are reports of someone who comes to sit by the bedside of those who are sick or unhappy, quietly keeping vigil until the crisis has passed. It is interesting to note that this same experience is common among Virginia City residents and visitors who live near, or stay in, the Bonanza Inn. The building was formerly St. Mary's Catholic Hospital operated by the Sisters of Charity (see "Mother Irene" in *Spirit Tailings*). It doesn't seem far-fetched at Carroll that the Dominican sisters, far from home themselves and in domestic service, might also take on the role of temporary mothering, and the Dominican sisters would have frequented the rooms of Borromeo Hall, keeping them clean and tidy. Don, at the time of his experience, was unaware of the stories of the visiting nun. He agrees that this might explain the bony hand on his shoulder, but he finds these other possibilities more disconcerting than his familial explanation.

St. Albert's Hall, however, is where most students have been introduced to the Dominican sisters. The former convent was once a student dormitory and serves now as the Student Union. Students who lived in this hall have their own stories about the visiting nuns. For a time St. Albert's Hall housed the campus radio station. Students who gave radio broadcasts from St. Albert's were familiar with the nuns, too. The radio show would begin at 6:30 on Sunday mornings and run until 10 o'clock. Promptly at 6:30, footsteps would begin at the head of the hallway, set a deliberate pace, the same every time. There was a pause at each door down the hall as the footsteps came closer. When they arrived to pause at the studio door, students say that they could always feel someone on the other side of the door looking in. There was a general consensus among the students that this was the sisters' morning wakeup routine, enacted so many times over the decades without varying that it continued long after the nuns left the campus.

Stories about Carroll faculty extend beyond the campus into the community. An urban legend well known in Helena involves Father Paul B. Kirchen who was among Carroll's best-loved and most revered professors. Father Kirchen taught languages at the college from 1929 until his retirement in 1973. Throughout his years at Carroll and after his retirement, Father Kirchen was a familiar figure who championed the community's downtrodden and outcast. He fed the transients who camped behind the college in the 1950s, collecting student leftovers and distributing them among the men who eventually became known as "backdoor alumni." Everything he had he gave away, including a coat off his back that once belonged to a bishop. He distributed his Social Security checks to the needy saying, "It's God's money." He was a friend and counselor to students after his retirement, and walked all over town in shoes that didn't fit him, visiting the needy. People did not refuse Father Kirchen. He had a way of enlisting aid, always asking for rides to various places so he could do his work. "He was irresistible," said former Helena mayor Russ Ritter. "People never refused him anything."

Father Kirchen refused to take it easy. "I don't need to slow down," he said. "There are just lots of things to do." When the beloved father died of a heart attack at eighty-four in 1989, everyone regardless of religious affiliation mourned his loss. Flags at Carroll and over city offices flew at half-mast in remembrance of the saintly priest who, just a week before his death, had been visiting Helena's needy. Father Kirchen's passing left a great hole in the community.

After Father Kirchen's death, stories about him began to emerge. Among these were reports of the sighting of an elderly priest walking the streets of Helena. He wore shoes that were too big for him. Throughout the decade following his death, there were occasional reports of an elderly priest begging for rides from passing motorists. The motorist would stop, the priest would climb into the backseat, and the driver would take him to whatever destination he requested. Upon stopping to discharge the passenger, however, the driver would discover that the backseat was empty.

Carroll College is rightly proud of its long traditions, of its many dedicated educators, and its reputation for academic excellence. But for alumni like Char Helmick Pentecost and Don Pogreba, the years spent in academic pursuits taught them something they could not learn in the classroom, that Carroll College is a place of exceptional school spirit.

Sources

Excellent historical context for Carroll College can be found in an unpublished speech delivered by Father William Greytak and alumnus David McGoldrick on November 4, 1991 at http://www.carroll.edu/community/images/jackscastle.pdf (February 15, 2004). In addition, Lewis and Clark County Death Certificates and newspaper articles related to the individuals mentioned are all housed on microfilm at the MHS Library Research Center in Helena. The obituary for Father Paul Kirchen can be found in the *Helena Independent Record,* April 21, 1989. Debra Munn in *Big Sky Ghosts,* Volume One, includes a version of the haunting of Carroll College. In a striking coincidence, on February 7, 2004, I came across the young football player's obituary. I had no prior knowledge of the date of his death, and happened to stumble upon it on the fortieth anniversary.

The Centerville Ghost

Centerville huddles precariously against the slope of the richest hill on earth, astride a hillside so steep that each house sits nearly on top of its neighbor. Back yards tumble into each other, challenging the housewife who hangs her wash on the clothesline. At the turn of the twentieth century, the collective Centerville community was overwhelmingly foreign born, of European ancestry. These folk who came to the Land of Opportunity kept the traditions of their forebears. The cultural heritage these adventurous immigrants brought to the great American melting pot, and especially the industrial giant that was Butte, enriched the colorful fabric that even today, several generations later, makes Butte a unique and special place.

A century ago Dublin Gulch in Centerville, a suburb of Butte, was home to many young men not long from Cork and Limerick. They came to America with young wives or married nice girls of similar Irish Catholic backgrounds, and together they had broods of children—the first generation born outside the Emerald Isle. These hardy Irish transplants found Butte a place where there was always work. But they also found the miner's life tough. Centerville's population crowded into small company-owned cottages, filling the stuffy rooms with crying babies, extended families of aunts, uncles, and cousins, and boarders who helped pay the exorbitant rent that always seemed to eat up most of their wages.

Looming headframes dotted the hillside, a constant reminder of men by the hundreds tunneling like so many ants inside the treacherous labyrinth of the mines, a hell inside the hill. In the winter, the clammy underground was bad enough, but above the mines, a pall of sulfuric smoke hung thickly over the hill. Lamps had to be lit at noon in the crowded kitchens where the womenfolk labored over endless chores. Danger haunted every miner, every hour of every day. And it haunted his family, too.

In this ripe setting for horror stories, tales of banshees and ghosts carried across the Atlantic and told around Centerville's kitchen tables found a place in the collective memory of the mining community. Belief in the supernatural was the norm, and while the creatures that figured in the folk tales always seemed to hover barely out of reach in one's imagination, they made the shadows in dark alleys come alive after dark. It didn't take much to fuel active imaginations in a place where mining accidents were so common-place, and if a man escaped death in the bowels of the hillside or in the jaws of the heavy machinery, the miner's con—consumption—was like as not to get him in the end. In such a place, the Grim Reaper could come with his random knock on any door at any moment. Superstition colored birth, death, and life in between. The Irish of Dublin Gulch feared the banshee's wail, warning that a death was close at hand. The thought was enough to give even the brawniest miner the cold, hard creeps.

On September 6, 1897, a horrendous crime gave the population of Centerville something to talk about beyond the usual worries of mining. Shift boss James Shea was making his way home from work at the Mountain Consolidated No. 2 during the noon hour. There had been some trouble the day before at the mine. Thomas Lane's heavy drinking of late had caused Shea no small concern. Lane had been drinking again the day before despite warnings, and so Shea had fired him—a drunk miner put all the other men at risk.

On this September day, Shea was not thinking about the incident with Lane or about anything else in particular as he neared the Mullin Hotel. But Lane lay in wait upon the porch with murder on his mind. As Shea approached the hotel, Lane raised his firearm, shut one eye, took aim and opened fire, pumping five bullets into his former boss. The victim dragged himself to a nearby doorstep as his blood drained into the dusty street. Deputy Sheriff McGlynn quickly arrived on the scene and momentarily held the murderer at bay, but there was one bullet left in the chamber. Lane turned it on himself and blew his brains out, thus saving officials the trouble of a trial and a hanging. The folk of Centerville were used to death and dying, but the deliberate and public manner in which the two men met their fates left the community reeling. And it also made Centerville and Dublin Gulch fertile ground for haunting stories.

A few years after the murder-suicide of Shea and Lane, the people of Centerville began to report frightening encounters. The first occurred late one Saturday night when several concertgoers were on the way home from a John Philip Sousa performance at the local opera house. The *Anaconda Standard* of March 6, 1901, carried the tale of a young man who had missed the last streetcar after the concert. He and his companion had been forced to walk home to Centerville. As they came to West Center Street, the pair saw a black-clad figure emerge from an alley and move toward the car track. The two paid little heed at first, mistaking the solitary wanderer for some lone woman on her way home from a nearby neighbor's, but at the top of the hill, the shadowy form stopped, obviously waiting for them. When the two got to the top of the hill, they became apprehensive, thinking it might be a robber:

> But the figure threw up a black veil, disclosing its face. For a moment we were transfixed in amazement, for the features, whether male or female, being or spirit, were most horribly distorted, marked, and were illuminated by blue streaks of sulfur ... . Before we could recover from the fright, the being uttered a piercing scream, turned and fled down the track, moaning and screaming as it went.

A few days later the *Standard* ran a letter to the editor from a miner who described his encounter with the black-robed figure. He had just come off his shift at eleven PM and was on his way home to Centerville. Following his usual route up Dublin Gulch to the railroad tracks and then west toward Main Street, he had just reached the Mountain Con. No. 2 when he saw a figure in black. It materialized out of nowhere, and stepped directly in his path as he approached. He stepped to one side to pass it, but the thing stepped in front of him. The miner took a step right and so did the ghost, or banshee, or whatever it was. Each time the miner stepped to one side or the other to pass the figure, it stepped in front of him to block his way:

> My first impulse was to run, but on second thought I found I could not move. For a moment we stood there. I could not take my eyes from it, and I know it was glaring at me from beneath the folds of the long black veil that covered its face. Raising one arm above its head, I followed the movement. In the hand was a grinning skull. With the other hand it threw back the veil, revealing the most horrible looking countenance that I have ever looked upon. The face of a Chinese joss would be an angel in comparison. Around the face hovered an unearthly blue light quite different from that produced by phosphorus.

Then uttering a soul-piercing shriek, it turned and fled up the trail leading in the direction of Summit Street and disappeared in the cluster of houses in the rear of Murphy's Saloon. I had no desire to follow it, nor do I wish to see it again.

The "Dark Ghost of Centerville" became the topic of discussion over every back fence. Neighborhoods all over Butte were abuzz with accounts of the dark intruder. Stories circulated wildly. It was like the opening phrase whispered in a game of "Gossip" that gains momentum with each retelling. Accounts varied widely, but most noted that the ghost was clad in a black robe and had some sort of eerie blue phosphorescence about it. One man, however, who claimed to have encountered the ghost said its face was that of a woman he had known. She had died in Centerville the year before.

The *Butte Miner* and the *Standard* printed accounts of the sightings almost daily for two weeks, scaring and disrupting the community. The doors of Centerville's neighborhood markets closed at dusk, leaving the main street deserted. Youngsters accustomed to roaming the streets went to bed early with their parents' bedtime admonition to be good or the "ghost'll git ya" ringing in their ears. Articles reported that a young woman had been kidnapped by the specter in the dark of night, tied to a fence post, and left shivering. A blacksmith on his way to work at four AM found the victim nearly frozen and frightened to death. Although miners coming off shift and late night revelers had passed very near her, the gag placed in her mouth left her unable to call for help. In a second incident, two boys were found unconscious in an abandoned cabin. Coming to their senses, they both told how the talons of a monster had buffeted them about. Although they bore no marks, they would not change their story. In yet another encounter, a woman with a baby fell while running from the grisly apparition. The dark-clad banshee snatched up the baby, delivered it to the mother, and sped off shrieking. Miners Will Smeleer and Will Osborne went looking for the dark ghost, too. When it suddenly popped out at them from behind a rock, the two stood frozen, watching helplessly as it threw up its arms and "a phosphorescent light appeared at the point where its head and face ought to be." They began running when the ghost let out a blood-curdling shriek. Smeleer tripped, cutting his face severely.

These incidents and injuries to the citizens of Butte prompted local law enforcement to investigate. A posse of local lawmen gathered, their firearms loaded with rock salt to keep the spirit at bay, to ghost hunt along the slope.

IN WEIRD PURSUIT
OF A REAL GHOST

Or It May Be a Case of a Job
Put Up by Solid Flesh
and Blood.

MANY WILD TALES TOLD

Newspaper Sketch of the Centerville Ghost
ANACONDA STANDARD, MARCH 17, 1901

They had no encounters. However, acting police sergeant Tom Walsh, Jack Murphy, Michael Colhane, and two newsmen resolved to see if they, too, could encounter Centerville's now famous phantom. It was just past midnight when the five ventured out. They decided to concentrate their efforts on the dark, shadowy cut of the B. A. & P. Railroad that led to the mines on the hill. There in a hollow was the deserted cabin rumored to be associated with the black-robed being and where the two young boys had fallen prey. They found nothing there. Colhane and Murphy separated from the other three to inspect some ore cars. As they headed under the Main Street footbridge, the moon pooled along the tracks and cast shadows on the hillside. A tall stately figure suddenly appeared out of nowhere, gliding down the steep embankment to stand directly in front of them. It paused and then moved in the direction of the ramshackle cabin. The sight sent a chill down the spines of Murphy and Colhane. Both men were so frightened they stood there trembling.

"Halt! Are you man or ghost?" shouted Murphy.

The black-robed spirit, or whatever it was, slowly raised both hands toward the sky and noiselessly seemed to glide over the rough ground, still moving in the direction of the cabin. The men could see it, outlined in the faint light of the moon. They gathered their wits, aimed their rifles, and each fired a shot at the specter from a distance of about ten feet. When the deputy and newsmen reached the badly shaken Murphy and Colhane, they had quite a tale to tell about their close encounter. They claimed that the uplifted hands seemed to be transparent, appearing blood red like a hand held over an electric light. Just before they fired their rifles, a dull red glow appeared in the breast of the creature providing a well-marked target. Its head also seemed to glow the same dull red. The men were very frightened. As the group made its way back, they met two Finns who also claimed to have seen the ghost gliding toward the lonely cabin.

The *Standard* put the spirit to rest on St. Patrick's Day, 1901, hinting that the whole thing was a prank. There were several theories. Perhaps the culprit was a spurned lover trying to scare his rival, or a buyer trying to clinch a real estate deal by "hoo-dooing" the property of a superstitious owner. Or, perhaps it really was the ghost of Thomas Lane, come back in search of another shift boss who did him wrong. Whatever the explanation, the ghost succeeded in "whitening the hairs of the few to whom he appeared" and sent children to bed, for once, at a decent hour. The ghost likely made no more appearances because, the newspapers speculated, the shots had scared him off. Further, said the *Standard*, "It is a safe guess that the ghost will boast of his pranks when the fever has blown over."

No one claimed responsibility however. Two decades later the memory of the Centerville ghost was still alive. In 1922 those who had been young-sters back in 1901 now had children of their own, and they still shivered as they walked past the old streetcar tracks in Centerville. Given the true panic the ghost created, perhaps reporters were seeking to put the minds of Centerville's good citizens at ease by making light of what might have been a true haunting. Regardless of the motivation, no one came forward, at least not for decades.

In 1922 a story in the Montana News Association Insert of February 13 claimed that old-time newsman "Silver Dick" Butler made the whole story up on a slow news day. And maybe he really did. But in 1930, laundryman Joe Duffy claimed that he planted the story and newsmen took it up. By the power of suggestion, many people soon claimed sightings of the dark ghost. Duffy claimed that Murphy and Colhane were just coming off a drinking binge, and what they saw, or thought they saw, was brought on by alcohol-induced hallucinations. The guns that they had been given were loaded with blanks.

In the final newspaper account of the Centerville ghost, the paper reported that two men confronted it. They asked why it made its appearance late at night, and what it wanted. The dark ghost answered willingly, saying that it had a heavy weight to carry, and was burdened with trouble. It said that the late hours of the night suited it because that was the quietest time and helped it to contemplate its difficulties. It then promised the men that it would appear no more, and the citizens of Centerville and Butte could resume their nightly activities without fear. This contrived interview differs from other accounts of the ghost and was likely intended to put the minds of citizens at ease in an effort to ward off a more serious panic.

Most people believe that the Centerville ghost was nothing more than a hoax. But who can say what really lies at the murky bottom of the Berkley Pit, Butte's infamous lake of liquid as poisonous as battery acid? If the dark ghost had earthly remains, it could be that they now lie in that toxic graveyard, along with remnants of neighborhoods where children once played. It would be a fitting grave for a specter that brought terror to the community. If that is where the dark ghost ended up, the good citizens of Centerville can only hope that is where he stays.

Sources

The local papers carried many stories of the Centerville ghost, including the *Anaconda Standard,* March 6, 9, 12, 13, and 17; and *The Butte Miner,* March 3, 12, and 14. A follow-up article appeared in the Montana News Association Inserts on February 13, 1922. Lorie Hutson wrote an article in *The Montana Standard,* October 30, 1999, recounting some of the Centerville Ghost story; the *Butte Centennial Recollections* by Neil Lynch (1979) also retells the story.

REMNANTS OF A COPPER KING

The day began with a depressing, steady rain; it was a fitting omen for what residents feared would be the end of an era in Hamilton, Montana. "It was as if the heavens were crying," said museum curator Erma Owings. Cars that filled the parking lot on that wet Saturday in August of 1986 revealed a diverse crowd: out-of-state license plates from across the country were interspersed with those from Montana. On the grounds of Riverside, once the largest and grandest summer home in the Northwest, the serious collector and the curious tourist mingled with Hamiltonians young and old. More than a thousand people had gathered at the rambling estate of Copper King Marcus Daly in anticipation of the sale that many in the community had long feared.

Although Marcus Daly himself had been dead more than eighty years, his presence lingered in the small community in Montana's beautiful Bitterroot Valley. After his death, Margaret Daly's bequest built the town's hospital in her husband's memory, and it was she who donated the land upon which the library was built. The extensive fields of Daly's Bitter Root Stock Farm and the palatial grounds of his estate comprise much of the local scenery.

Marcus Daly came to America in the mid-nineteenth century as a fifteen-year-old penniless Irish immigrant. He had an uncanny eye for spotting rich copper ores. He also had the foresight to see that copper prices would skyrocket, a boom market driven in the 1880s by the new luxuries of electricity and telephones. Daly's economic intuition won over his investors and with their backing, Daly purchased seemingly worthless Butte silver mines from owners who lacked his understanding of the technological revolution underway. These mines made Daly a millionaire. He built the largest smelter in the world and founded the town of Anaconda to serve it. To shore up his copper mines and fuel his Anaconda smelter—an industrial monster that swallowed 40,000 board feet of timber every day—Daly needed an endless supply of wood. He looked to the rich timberlands in the Bitterroot Valley.

The emerald valley reminded Daly of his native Ireland, and he bought and acquired 22,000 acres. He built a sawmill along the Bitterroot River and platted the town of Hamilton in 1890. It was a company town. Daly built a bank, endowed churches, brought in handpicked professionals to run his business concerns, and enticed builders and carpenters to the area to erect fine homes and business blocks for his employees.

But it was Daly's love of horses that kept him personally close to the Bitterroot Valley. He believed it was the ideal place to breed and train the thoroughbred racehorses he so prized. Daly's theory was that horses trained at higher altitudes were stronger and developed better stamina. He built an indoor racetrack, hired the best veterinarians in the world, and imported young jockeys to ride his horses.

Daly's Bitter Root Stock Farm produced champions of whom he was especially proud. One of these was Montana, a horse with a personality as dark as his sleek coat. He was a mean, formidable giant. It is said that the horse would wait for a mouse to enter his feed bin and when it did, his massive jaws would crush the little creature. At these times in particular, when Montana had blood in his teeth, it was not safe to be anywhere near him. But Daly's beloved Tammany was Montana's opposite. A horse with a sweeter disposition could not be found, and despite the work the horse was expected to do, he was Daly's special pet. Tammany was the winner of both the Lawrence Realization and Withers Stake races at New York's Belmont Park in 1892. The next year, a crowd of 15,000 witnessed Tammany defeat Lamplighter by four lengths in a legendary match race at New Jersey's Guttenberg track. The win established Tammany as the East's best thorough-bred racer from 1892 to 1894. Tammany Castle, the poignantly beautiful stable Daly built for his great and gentle champion, presides at the top of a long, graceful drive. Cork floors half-a-foot thick imported from Spain protected the stallions from slipping, and the heated stalls were lined with velvet. Although still pungent with the smell of horses and hay, Tammany Castle has long been empty.

Marcus Daly and his wife, Margaret, settled permanently in the early 1890s on the vast estate comprised of some five ranches. The Daly's four children—Margaret, Mary, Marcus II, and Harriot—spent much of their youth at Riverside, the family home along the Bitterroot River. By 1900 Daly had amassed his fortune but was still embroiled in bitter feuding with his archrival, Copper King William A. Clark of Butte. In a strange twist, Margaret Daly's sister was married to a brother of Clark's, drawing these two mortal enemies together in a familial bond. The wily, unscrupulous Clark had just succeeded in buying his way into the U.S. Senate, defeating Daly's attempts to block his election. Daly was on a business trip, homesick for Montana. He checked into The Netherlands Hotel in New York City on November 11, 1900, for a needed night's rest. The following morning, surrounded by his immediate family, Daly succumbed to diabetes and a bad heart. He was only 58. His will, probated in Powell County, Montana, valued his assets—not including real estate, stocks, or bonds—at ten million dollars.

Some months later, Hamilton's citizens gathered at the depot with heavy hearts to bid adieu to Daly's string of prized racehorses. Nearly two hundred thoroughbreds were bound for Madison Square Garden in New York City where they were auctioned at a dispersal sale. The New York auction netted $403,000. This and two other sales of Bitter Root stock in San Francisco made the total price of Daly's horses the most impressive dispersal of racing stock in American history. Daly had had the right idea, and would have been proud to know that his Bitter Root stock bloodlines went on to produce many notable animals including Kentucky Derby winners Regret, Paul Jones, Zev, and Flying Ebony.

Unlike Montana's other Copper Kings who took their wealth elsewhere, the Daly family remained tied to Montana and their beloved Bitterroot Valley. Margaret Daly, a very capable woman, assumed control of her husband's holdings, and each year spent May through October at her home in the valley. Marcus and Margaret Daly together had planned a new Riverside that would replace the older Queen Anne style home where the family had known such good times. That was not to be. Mrs. Daly delayed these plans upon her husband's death. She carried on as before, spending the warmer months of every year in Montana.

Six years passed and then in 1906 Margaret Daly announced plans to proceed with building plans for a new home. When the Georgian Revival style mansion was finished in 1910, it was without question the largest, most lavish summer home in the West. Designed by Missoula architect A. J. Gibson, its 24,000 square feet included twenty-four bedrooms, fifteen bathrooms, and three dining rooms. The exclusive firm of Hurlburt and Hurlburt of Baltimore spent months furnishing the interior. Imported Italian marble adorned the seven fireplaces, cut glass or brass knobs opened every door, call bells summoned the thirteen servants, and the bathtubs were edged in gold.

Riverside was Mrs. Daly's retreat and she loved it. It was a place where she could relax and entertain her international guests who came for extended periods of time. She loved her gardens too, especially the roses that grew in lavish profusion, in rich shades of red, yellow, white, and pink. Their scent perfumed the summer evenings, and the fragrant buds and flowers in crystal vases and silver bowls decorated Riverside's every room.

Mrs. Daly had just gotten back into a normal rhythm in 1911 after the carpenters, decorators, and artisans had completed their work. But tragedy tempered Mrs. Daly's elation. Margaret Daly-Brown, the Dalys' eldest married daughter, had abruptly left Montana for New York feeling unwell. Doctors had advised an immediate change to a lower altitude, and what amounted to an entire hospital staff accompanied her on the train from Montana back to New York. The day after her homecoming, Margaret died of a heart ailment leaving two small daughters. Her death at such a young age was the unfortunate part of her father's vast legacy.

The other two Daly daughters married well. Harriot, the youngest daughter, wed wealthy Count Anton Sigray of Hungary and spent much of her time abroad. Her husband—later imprisoned at the Nazi concentration camp of Mauthausen during World War II—was a member of the Hungarian Upper House. The middle daughter, Mary, known affectionately as "Molly," was the wife of New York attorney James W. Gerard. Molly spent the long, languid summers with her mother, entertaining guests that sometimes filled the spacious Riverside to capacity.

Margaret Daly, the grand matriarch, was a good person who always looked for opportunities to help others. She also had a strong sense of likes and dislikes. Pearls and roses were her favorite luxuries. Mrs. Daly insisted upon every detail being planned and perfect for her guests: horseback riding in the mornings, formal dinners each evening at seven sharp, and coffee on the sun porch. At bedtime she gathered all the children around her while she read to them. Mrs. Daly had some good friends in the community, and they were sometimes invited to afternoon teas and games of bridge or whist, but most of Hamilton could only wonder and imagine what life was like inside the grand Daly stronghold. Those who delivered groceries or supplies to the mansion's back door rolled their eyes in awe of the place.

The Daly's only son, Marcus II, was not like his father. He was conservative and quiet where his father had been lively and spirited. Young Marcus was skilled at financial matters and Margaret came to rely on him in helping manage the vast family holdings. Marcus II was an avid hunter whose trophy room at the mansion was a marvel that never ceased to amaze Riverside's visitors. The room, added in 1913, doubled as an occasional dining room and card room. It was full of heads, skins, and other souvenirs of extensive hunting trips in North America, Africa, and many other foreign countries. One local visitor who attended a card party in the trophy room at the Daly mansion remarked that it was very strange to "look up to see all those animals looking down at you."

The only son of the copper king was the last Daly child to marry. In 1919 he wed Evelon Herrenreich Young. The marriage was unhappy, and the couple separated; Marcus gained custody of their son, Marcus III. The boy was twelve when the Daly legacy struck again. Marcus II was on a hunting trip in Virginia when he died suddenly of a heart attack on November 7, 1930, within a few days of the thirtieth anniversary of his father's death. Marcus II was only 48. The boy became the ward of his grandmother and spent his summers, as he had always done, with her at Riverside.

As she had for several decades, matriarch Margaret Daly continued to preside over her mansion. She directed the tending of her rose and flower gardens and entertained both guests from town and far-flung places in lavish style. She bestowed charitable gifts upon the city of Hamilton, including the Marcus Daly Memorial Hospital, founded in 1931, in memory of her husband. During the summers she spent at Riverside, every room had a bouquet of fresh flowers, especially roses. Those privy to the mansion's inner hospitality remember that roses of every conceivable color and shade perfumed the grand home.

In July 1941 in her bedroom at Riverside, Margaret Daly quietly passed away at the age of 88 with Molly at her side. She was interred with her husband in the family mausoleum at Greenwood Cemetery in Brooklyn, New York. The grand rooms at Riverside, accustomed to hosting parties and guests during the busy summer months, fell silent. The draperies and many of the furnishings were put in storage. The family boarded up their beloved home and in so doing, boarded up a lifestyle that died with Margaret Daly. The house remained thus for the next forty years. Local youths, dared by their peers, stole in through the coal chute to steal up the stairs to the billiard room and pocket a ball or two. Residents of the valley who passed by imagined the vast empty spaces, now home to mice and squirrels and little creatures of the night. The wind swept through the hollow hallways, leaves swooshed down the chimneys into the seven hearths, and the snow blew in under the doorsills.

A world away in war-torn Europe, Harriot Daly Sigray's daughter Margit had inherited her grandfather's love of horses. Now a woman of middle age, Margit had spent her youth riding trails in the Hungarian countryside with her father, the count. Margit never knew her grandfather Daly, but she loved her grandmother's Riverside, having visited there throughout her childhood.

Riverside's living room, circa 1941-1942. "Musicale" hangs at left
COURTESY MONTANA HISTORICAL SOCIETY PHOTOGRAPH ARCHIVES 955-297

During the German occupation of Austria, both Margit and her mother Harriot aided the resistance. Margit risked her own safety to give sanctuary to some of the famous Lipizzaner stallions caught up in the cruelty of the war. In 1946 Margit fled with her mother to the United States where they were soon reunited with the count, whose concentration camp had been liberated by the American forces. Margit, an attractive spinster, married fellow Hungarian refugee Baron George B. Bessenyey in 1958, but he died scarcely a year after their wedding. The Countess Margit, deeply involved in equestrian pursuits, acquired ownership of the Bitter Root Stock Farm, buying out her cousins, and returned to her mother's idyllic childhood home. But the cold, empty mansion was not to her taste. Margit remodeled a small house nearby and trained the Hungarian horses she loved. Her Bitterroot Hungarian Horse Farm carried on the bloodlines of the horses General Patton had rescued in war-torn Europe. He brought the horses to the States for use by the American cavalry, but the cavalry disbanded in 1949. The horses were put out for stud and the countess eventually acquired several. Their offspring would have made her grandfather Daly, a great judge of horseflesh, extremely proud.

Marcus Daly III died in November 1970 carrying on two grim family traditions. First, he died relatively young. At 50, like his grandfather and father, he was in the prime of life when he, as did they, died suddenly. Second, his death occurred, like those of the other two Daly men, in November in a year ending in zero.

The final end of the Montana fairy tale came, however, when the countess died in New York City in 1984; she had just returned from a visit to her native Hungary. Margit's remains were returned to her beloved valley and buried in Hamilton overlooking the land that bound her as it had her grandparents. Margit is the only direct descendant of Marcus Daly buried at Hamilton's Riverview Cemetery. A few days after her funeral, many of Margit's favorite horses, big beauties that she had so prized, were put down. This was not at the countess' request, but because they were in their twenties and caretakers felt it would be for the best. The several heirs—cousins and Margit's stepchildren—worried about what to do with the vast estate. Taxes, estimated in the millions, were sucking the Daly assets dry. The empty mansion continued to deteriorate.

Francis Bessenyey, Margit's stepson, sought out local support and began negotiations with local banker Tom Brader and the Montana Historical Society to develop a plan for eventual state ownership of the Daly Mansion. In 1986 local Hamiltonians joined together to form the Daly Mansion Preservation Trust. Their unlikely dream was to buy the mansion from the Daly heirs, furnish it, and open it to the public. The entire community dreaded the upcoming day when Riverside's contents were to go on the auction block, but there was some hope that local purchase of some of the estate items might help mitigate the loss of family heirlooms, antiques, art, and furnishings that made Riverside such a symbol of the community's roots. Skeptics feared that buyers would purchase the Daly family's possessions and take them away from Montana to furnish homes or museums out of state. The Trust had raised a meager $10,000 to purchase items that once furnished Riverside. They wondered if such a small amount was even worth the effort.

Despite the dreary weather, as the auction got underway, the crowd of wealthy buyers caught the spirit, and nostalgia mixed with sadness gave way to something quite extraordinary. Morris Gardner of Gardner Auction Service chose a stuffed dog on wheels, manufactured by F.A.O. Schwarz in 1932, to open the bidding. According to the *Ravalli Republic* the following Monday morning, Gardner carefully chose the dog as the first item, knowing that it would set the tone for the day. The paper declined to print what price the buyer paid for the dog, but noted that she remarked, "I knew I was spending several hundred dollars too much for it, but I was buying history so I was willing … ." Records show the dog actually sold for $1,000. And that was how the sale went, with people willing to pay top dollar for treasures of the past.

As the sale progressed, the Trust began to bid. Each time it purchased an item, its cheering section clapped and whistled. At the top of the Trust's wish list was a mahogany dining suite. But the Trust had bid all its money and was about to lose when strangers chipped in the difference; the Trust got the set for $27,000. The crowd went wild. Soon strangers were bidding and buying and donating items back to the Trust while the crowd cheered them on. At the end of the sale, the Trust had acquired $67,825 worth of furniture, rugs, and art, and other buyers were inspired to donate or loan items back to the mansion for eventual display. Benevolent Mrs. Daly, who so loved her Riverside home, surely watched over the proceedings, smiling at the crowd as the miracle unfolded.

A beautiful print of a famous painting entitled "Musicale" was among the art the Trust purchased back for the mansion. The painting depicts a high church official, a cardinal, dressed in his red robes, seated next to a piano. He is sipping a cup of tea, enjoying a duet played by an elegant young woman at the piano and a gentleman violinist. Lesley Pappier of Hamilton, presently a docent at the Daly Mansion, relates a well-known incident with the picture.

As Mrs. Pappier tells it, after the auction, workers brought all the purchased items into the mansion. Among them was the crated painting. Workers uncrated and hung "Musicale" on the south wall in the living room where it was originally hung. Later, a decorator moved the painting to the music room. When workers returned the next morning to finish their unpacking, the picture lay on the floor. Assuming that it had fallen off the wall, they were astounded to discover that the picture was undamaged; neither the fragile gilt frame nor the glass had so much as a scratch. The picture was again hung in the music room. Next morning, once again, the picture lay on the floor. How very strange, they thought. Either someone is playing tricks, or there is a message in all this. The staff went through some old Daly family photographs of the mansion and found "Musicale" in one of them. But the picture was hanging in the living room. So they hung the picture in the living room in its original place, and there it has remained.

The Trust's dream became reality when ownership of Riverside was transferred from the Daly heirs to the State of Montana in 1987 in exchange for forgiveness of a portion of the estate taxes. The Daly Mansion Preservation Trust then leased the property that same year. Although the future was promising, the mansion went through a tumultuous period under numerous directors. If the Dalys were watching over their estate, it must have been with some pain because these were difficult times.

Doug Johnson became director of the Daly Mansion Trust in August of 1990. His permanent appointment relieved his wife who had served as the last of more than half a dozen interim directors within the last few years. Doug would serve as director for the next twelve years. At the beginning of his tenure, the alarm system at the mansion was hardly state-of-the-art. It required staff, usually Doug, to turn the system off and on manually. The alarm system was housed in the back hall where there was a pastry room and two walk-in coolers. To enable the system, Doug had to walk into a cooler, set the alarm, and then exit out the mansion's back door.

During the first few months after he became director, Doug was conscientious about his care of the alarms. After numerous trips to set the system, he realized that there seemed to be a faint odor lingering in the back hallway. It was a very pleasant scent, like roses, and Doug dismissed it, thinking that a tourist or a docent had likely worn too much perfume and left a trail of it wafting though the back hall. Then one day as he opened the heavy door to take care of the alarm, the scent of roses *inside* the archaic fortress-like cooler was overpowering, "It was so strong," said Doug, "that it nearly knocked me over."

Although Doug had been noticing the scent of roses for some time, he had not mentioned it to his wife. She, of course, had become quite familiar with the building and its quirks during her stint as director. After the overpowering encounter in the cooler, he finally asked her if she had ever noticed the scent of roses around the back hall. She replied, "Oh yes. It's just Mrs. Daly." Doug's wife had drawn her own conclusions some time ago. Doug continued to notice the smell of roses throughout August and September. The lights also plagued him. If he left them off, they would be on in the morning; if he left them on, they would be off.

With November, the essence of roses seemed to dissipate. Perhaps Mrs. Daly retreated to the shadows, or moved on with the seasons as she had in life. But one night, in the middle of the night, the alarm inside the mansion went off. Doug crawled out of bed, dressed hurriedly, and met the police there. They could find nothing amiss. He had no sooner gotten home and crawled back into bed when the alarm went off again. He went back to Riverside, but again the police could find nothing wrong. Doug returned home only to return to the mansion a third time when the alarm sounded. There was simply no explanation, and the timing was very odd. It was November 7, 1990, the 20th anniversary of the death of Marcus Daly III.

A few nights later the alarm again went off, tripped by some unseen intruder. Again, there was no explanation. And it happened a second time that night, November 10, the anniversary of Marcus Daly II's death. A few days later, on November 12, the anniversary of the death of patriarch Marcus Daly himself, Doug was called to the mansion in the middle of the night when someone, or something, again tripped the alarm. There was never any explanation for these malfunctions, if that is what they were. Nor has it happened since.

During this same period, just after Doug assumed his role as Trust director, there was another odd incident. Professional decorators had been hired to decorate the mansion for a special public event during the Christmas season. The decorator chose red as the color scheme for the dining room. "Musicale," hanging in its place in the living room, caught the eye of the decorator because the rich red of the cardinal's robes were a perfect complement to the color scheme. So "Musicale" was temporarily hung over the mantel in the dining room. Although the painting remained on the wall this time, a series of disasters befell the unfortunate decorator's painstaking efforts to decorate the room. A mouse ate some of the crucial decorative elements; the tree fell over; and the lights, on an automatic timer, malfunctioned. Mrs. Daly thus expressed her disapproval of "Musicale" in its temporary place.

Many believe Mrs. Daly frequently makes the rounds of her home, and the scent of roses is today common among those who have spent time at the mansion. Even one-time tourists who know nothing of the Daly family have experienced this phenomenon. Brianna Chaffin, however, had an experience at the mansion that was even more dramatic and personal than the incidents with the picture and the unexplained tripping of the alarms. It was an oddly appropriate encounter, one that she will not forget.

Brianna is a direct descendant of Anthony Chaffin, the original owner

Margaret Daly
COURTESY DALY MANSION

of the land upon which Riverside was built. Her 6th grade class planned a field trip to the mansion. The students made their way through the many rooms, listening to the tour guide. Brianna was fascinated with the mansion, partly because of her own family's connection to it. As they went through the various rooms on the second floor, Brianna became aware of the faint scent of roses. It played around her subconscious, and she was enjoying herself. As the group moved into Mrs. Daly's bedroom, the scent became stronger as Brianna stood in the room. The other students moved on leaving Brianna alone. Something caught her eye. As she looked toward the elegant dressing table, she distinctly saw someone standing there. There was no mistake; there stood Mrs. Daly herself, wearing an elegant evening gown with a train. The dress was the color of her red roses. "She was just there," says Brianna, "and she was smiling at me."

Brianna was transfixed at what she saw, and the two looked at each other, the girl and the ghost. All the while Mrs. Daly smiled benevolently. When Brianna broke the gaze, the moment was over and she rushed out of the room into the hall. Her classmates were immediately aware that something extraordinary had happened. Brianna was deathly pale and obviously shaken. When she thought about it later, Brianna decided that it was as if Mrs. Daly revealed herself that day to say to her, "You see what your family made possible for my family?" Mrs. Daly's sweet smile was her way of saying thank you. After her fright lost its edge, Brianna realized that this was a gift, one that she will always cherish.

Oversight of the mansion, still under state ownership and maintained by the Trust, transferred in 2003 from the Montana Historical Society to The University of Montana. Francis Bessenyey, so instrumental in the preservation of the landmark home and the idea of local involvement in its operation, continues to own some 600 acres surrounding the property. He has always been, and still is, a good friend to the Trust. Since no disruptive, unexplained events have occurred in recent years, these arrangements seem to suit the Daly family. And Mrs. Daly, on rare occasions, still delights the staff and special visitors with a gentle whiff of her beloved roses.

Sources

Sources are plentiful about the Daly family, the preservation of the Mansion, and its history. The Montana Historical Society's Research Center vertical files include resources on the Daly family and the property. In addition, *Historic Preservation* (September/October 1988) includes a good article on the preservation of the Mansion. Obituaries on the Daly family include, Marcus Daly III, *Ravalli Republican*, November 9, 1970; Marcus Daly II, *Anaconda Standard*, November 11, 1930; and Margaret Daly, *Ravalli Republican*, July 17, 1941. Ada Powell's *The Dalys of the Bitter Root* is the best source for anecdotal information about the Daly family. The National Register nomination for the Daly Mansion is housed at the State Historic Preservation Office, Helena. Jeanette McKee, Doug Johnson, Lesley Pappier, and staff at the Daly Mansion graciously assisted in the compilation of factual information.

GHOSTLY TRANSPORT

The train came gliding up the tracks between Hamilton and Grantsdale. It appeared at the same place each night, opposite a tiny graveyard that lay in a field near the residence of C. B. Hart. The cars came chugging along, smoke pouring from the engine. But this train did not announce itself with the clacking of the rails as steel met steel, and there was no melancholy whistle echoing through the valley to announce its arrival. Silent as the mist, the ghost train slid on its route through the Bitterroot Valley, night after night, as punctual as the setting sun.

For Louis Pennoyer it was a frightening burden to be the only witness to the phantom train. Pennoyer and his wife, Julia, settled in the beautiful Bitterroot Valley to farm the property that he owned. Pennoyer was a family man, a hard worker, and his home lay perched upon a mountain slope north of Roaring Lion Canyon across the Bitterroot River. It was a lovely place to settle with a clear view of the broad expanse of the sprawling valley between Sleeping Child to the south and Corvallis to the north. Marcus Daly's Hamilton was just a few years old, a bustling little burg full of industry, and Pennoyer could see that too in his bird's eye view of the valley. Sometimes smoke curled from chimneys and cook fires in the clear winter air, a sign that Daly's timber mill was operating and crews were being fed. The Pennoyers, who came from Minnesota, found the valley a good place to work and raise their little daughter.

The apparition was troubling to Pennoyer and to his neighbors as well. No one called him crazy when Pennoyer reported it to his community. He felt an obligation and indeed, his fellow farmers respected the young family man who had no reason to fabricate such a strange tale. Pennoyer said that the scene was always the same. As the train sped along, at a certain place he saw a man appear in the west doorway of the express car. Something seemed wrong, and the man took up a lantern, frantically waving it in the air. The man kept up his frenzied movements for two, maybe three, minutes. It was this element that was so disturbing to the neighbors. The ghostly crewman and his frantic gestures directed at an unseen danger down the tracks surely signaled something dreadful. If the train was the harbinger of a disaster as many believed, what could it be and when would it happen? The folk of the Bitterroot Valley could only wonder.

Trains are inanimate objects, true, but they take on a personality, a character, that is compelling and mesmerizing. This identity helps to explain credible reports of phantom trains rumbling through the countryside, puffing and chugging. To the witness, it is just as real as the train that stops traffic at a crossing. "Phantom transport" this is called, a term that applies to trains as well as cars, planes, ships, wagons, and other forms of spectral conveyance.

Reports of phantom trains most often mark the place of a disaster, as in the case of Joe Baldwin and the Maco Station Light (see "The Hanging of Peter Pelkey"). Another famous example marks the catastrophe that occurred on a bridge near Dundee, Scotland, in 1879. Civil engineer Thomas Bouch designed the bridge of eighty-five spans across the Firth of Tay. Completed in 1878, it was two miles long, the longest bridge in the world at that time.

On December 28, 1879, a train crowded with holiday travelers made its way across the bridge. There was a violent storm at the time of the crossing. Rain pelted the cars and unusually high winds tore at the eighty-five spans. Midway across the bridge as cars of the train swayed dangerously, caught by the wind, the bridge collapsed sending the all cars and their passengers into the churning waters below. More than seventy people, counted only by the number of ticket stubs sold at the station in Fife, lost their lives; rescuers could not recover all the bodies, so no one knows exactly how many died. One thing was certain: there were no survivors.

To this day, the piers of Bouch's bridge stand just above the water line running alongside the entire length of the present-day bridge. It is an unnerving sight for those who know their history. Eerie, too, are the reports that began to surface sometime after the collapse, which continue to the present day. Witnesses say they have seen a phantom train rumbling across the bridge. When the train reaches the halfway point, the six-car train disappears as if the bridge has collapsed.

Not all phantom train reports, though, are the aftermath of a railroad disaster. President Abraham Lincoln's funeral train is the subject of a famous case of ghostly transport that memorializes Lincoln's final solemn journey to his birthplace for interment. In April of 1865, the assassinated president first lay in state in the East Room of the White House. After his funeral, the train bearing the coffin with his remains left Washington, D.C., for Springfield, Illinois, where Lincoln was to be interred. A second coffin bore the remains of the Lincoln's 11-year-old son, Willie, who died of a fever in 1862. The historic facts surrounding this funeral cortege are macabre.

President Lincoln may have had an interest in the supernatural, and some believe that he dabbled in spiritualism in the hope of contacting his beloved little boy. Willie's temporary resting place was in Washington rather than the family home in Springfield because the president did not want his son buried so far away. The embalmer did such a good job in preserving the child's natural appearance that Lincoln supposedly had him disinterred twice in order to look upon him again. Willie's final resting place was to be Springfield, and upon Lincoln's death, his coffin was once more disinterred and sent along with the President's remains.

The funeral train left Washington on April 21 and followed the route Lincoln had taken as he journeyed to the nation's capital to take the oath of office in 1861. The train moved slowly with nine stops along the way including Baltimore, Philadelphia, New York, and Chicago. Nine million people, one-fifth of the nation's population at that time, viewed the train. At each stop, officials took the body from its Pullman and placed it upon a catafalque for public display in city halls and auditoriums. In Philadelphia, 300,000 mourners waited five hours in a line three miles long to file through Independence Hall and view the corpse. The somber, tedious journey took two weeks.

The public could not forget such an episode. Over the years in the anniversary month of Lincoln's assassination, there have been many sightings of a train festooned in black. It mournfully wends its way, slowly chugging along the same route that the President's funeral train traveled in April of 1865. The cars travel the eight states from Washington, D.C., to Springfield, making a regular appearance at Urbana, Illinois, on the same tracks the funeral train traveled. Blue-coated military men surround the Pullman car where the president's body lies next to his son. The guards are no ordinary soldiers. These are skeletons, their white, fleshless skulls grinning insanely. The train's crew and engineer are also skeletons with bones that flash bright white. As the train passes in eerie silence along the tracks, clocks reportedly stop. Willie and the president disembark hand in hand just before the apparition disappears. Clocks then resume ticking, running five to ten minutes behind.

Disasters and momentous events such as these are one thing, but the third kind—like Louis Pennoyer saw in the Bitterroot Valley—are more unusual. If the sightings that seem to predict a future event have credence, these trains do warrant cause for alarm. The appearance, for example, of ghost trains on two separate occasions foretold the well-documented head-on collision of two Canadian Pacific Railway trains traveling through the cutbanks on the way from Medicine Hat to Dunmore Junction in Alberta, Canada, on July 8, 1908. Fireman Gus Day was on the train on two separate occasions a few weeks before the crash with different engineers at the throttle. In the same spot, two miles out of Medicine Hat, a phantom train came around a bend; its headlight was so eerily, uncharacteristically bright that it lit the night sky. The shrill whistle struck terror into Day and the engineers. The engineer at the first sighting was Bob Towhey and at the second sighting, J. Nicholson. On each occasion they watched as the lighted passenger cars sped by much too close. Crew and passengers on the ghostly train waved at the horrified observers before the vision dissolved into thin air. A few weeks later, the collision of two trains occurred at that exact spot. A fireman, a conductor, seven passengers, and J. Nicholson and Bob Towhey, the two engineers who witnessed the phantom train with Gus Day, died in the wreck. Years later after his retirement, Day recounted the incident for the *Vancouver Sun*.

Louis Pennoyer, however, in the Bitterroot Valley in 1893 knew nothing of the Tay Bridge, Lincoln's funeral train, or ghostly transport. Because of the wildly gesturing crewman who obviously saw something ahead, he and many others believed this sighting predicted the future. But how should the folk of the Bitterroot Valley interpret the omen? At this time in America, there was plenty to predict. The silver mining industry was about to topple with the repeal of the Sherman Silver Purchase Act. Worse, an economic panic hit in mid-year, causing a financial collapse and economic depression.

On the upside, though, the World's Columbian Exposition opened in Chicago on May 1, 1893. Commemorating the 400th anniversary of Columbus' discovery of the New World, it had a tremendous, enduring effect on myriad facets of American life. The Montana newspapers ran frequent coverage of the world-renowned exposition that established Columbus Day as a national holiday. It was the venue for modern products such as Aunt Jemima syrup, Cream of Wheat, and Juicy Fruit gum; it popularized hamburgers and carbonated soda; it introduced ragtime; and it prompted the City Beautiful movement that dominated American architecture across the nation for the next two decades.

These events still lay ahead as 1892 ended and the New Year of 1893 dawned. During this time of transition, Louis Pennoyer repeatedly witnessed the strange phenomenon in the Bitterroot Valley. Every evening just after dusk, when evening cast its shadows over the winter fields lying fallow, over the farmhouses dotting the valley, and over horses and cows in their pastures, the train sped past. The lantern winked in the dark, illuminating the man and his frantic movements. Then the man moved away from the door and disappeared inside the car as if the car had swallowed him without a trace. The train continued its slow, silent glide along the tracks until it was lost in the darkness somewhere between Hamilton and Grantsdale.

The valley buzzed with speculation over the meaning of the ghostly portent. There had to be a message somewhere in such an odd occurrence. Some believed it signaled the coming of a new railroad line over Skalkaho Pass. Others thought that the train meant Darby would become the valley's main settlement. But some who disapproved of worldly attractions like the Columbian Exposition and their influence were convinced that these frivolous, expensive undertakings brought dire consequences. The *Bitterroot Times* reported that pessimistic hypochondriacs believed that the train foreshadowed the introduction of cholera into the United States during the Exposition. None of these things, however, came to pass.

Oddly enough, a deadly disease did lurk in the Bitterroot Valley. Since 1873 spotted fever, or "black measles," had affected residents. While this strange disease was known in somewhat milder form in many other places, in the Bitterroot Valley it was particularly virulent and almost always fatal. Some thought this strange fever came from the sawdust piles of Marcus Daly's timber mills. Others thought it was from the wind blowing over decaying vegetation. Others believed drinking melted snow in the spring was the cause. Governor Edwin Norris in 1912 advised that any publicity about spotted fever would adversely affect settlement in the Bitterroot Valley. Not until 1919, with the deaths of State Senator and Mrs. Tyler Warden of Lolo from spotted fever, would the disease receive national attention.

In the 1920s Hamilton became the site of the Rocky Mountain Laboratory, where large-scale rearing of infected ticks and research into the tick-borne disease known as Rocky Mountain spotted fever led to effective treatment. Those "pessimistic hypochondriacs" forecast the wrong disease but were on the right track.

For Louis Pennoyer on his mountainside in 1893, the misty apparition never came clear. Speculators were left to wonder what it meant as Pennoyer's vision faded into obscurity. It is only in retrospect that Bitterroot residents might look back and reflect on the winter of 1893, the meaning of the ghost train, and what it symbolized as it glided through the valley.

Sources

The story foretelling the crash of the Canadian Pacific Railway is available on the West Coast Railway's website at http://www.wcra.org/features/ghost-train.htm (October 3, 2004). The Tay Bridge disaster is well covered in Internet sources including http://www.tts1.demon.co.uk/tay.html (August 19, 2004) by Tom Martin. A brief description of Lincoln's funeral and the phantom of it at Urbana, Illinois can be found at http://dcpages.com/Events/Holidays/Halloween/Abraham_Lincoln.shtml (September 12, 2004). The *Bitterroot Times*, January 7, 1893, reported Pennoyer's vision.

THE BISHOP OF ALL OUTDOORS

I t was late July of 1900 in Auburn, New York. Reverend John Brainard, Civil War veteran and beloved rector of St. Peter's Episcopal Church, fainted during Friday morning chapel services. Dr. Brainard, who was getting on in years, was indisposed for a wedding ceremony. As luck would have it, the young chaplain of a visiting fire department, Triumph Hose Company No. 1 of Homer, was in town to offer the welcome address for the annual Central New York Firemen's Convention. Dr. Brainard's associates recruited the young chaplain to perform the wedding. The young minister soon ingratiated himself to Dr. Brainard and just a month later, announcement came that the youthful chaplain had been named assistant rector at St. Peter's. The young man, Reverend Leonard Christler, began his new assignment under Dr. Brainard August 12, 1900.

Before long the new reverend had assumed most of the elder Dr. Brainard's responsibilities, performing weddings, baptisms, and burial services. According to a contemporary minister in a neighboring town, he usurped the elder minister's duties. Gradually, the young ambitious reverend became the primary officiate at St. Peter's. When Dr. Brainard's wife, Cornelia, died in 1905, it was Christler who officiated at the funeral. By 1906, Christler was performing nearly all the services that once were Dr. Brainard's domain. Finally the ailing old gentleman's health was so poor that he announced his retirement. But to the surprise of many in the community, he did not name Christler his successor.

In fact, Dr. Brainard went to great lengths to have the young reverend reassigned elsewhere. He manufactured a better offer to effect Christler's resignation. According to Reverend Robert C. Ayers, Rector Emeritus at St. Peter's, Dr. Brainard persuaded Montana's Bishop Brewer, former rector of Trinity Church in Watertown, New York, to offer the ambitious Christler the title "Archdeacon." Dr. Brainard predicted that Christler would be so impressed by the title that "he would knuckle down and hustle the work." In this way Dr. Brainard succeeded in getting Christler disengaged from St. Peter's with no ill feelings and reassigned to missionary work along the remote, windswept hi-line in northern Montana.

There are, of course, two sides to this story. Christler, the son of a mill worker, endeared himself to the laborers and workingmen of Auburn, much to the dismay of the prominent, upper crust members of St. Peter's congregation. To the social elite Christler may have seemed an upstart and ambitious boor, but to the working class he was a brother who visited the needy, kept vigil with the sick confined in the hospital, and played Santa Claus to the children of Auburn's hard working labor force. While the Reverend Arthur Byron-Curtiss, a contemporary of Christler's, described him as "awfully pompous, conceited and aggressive," the parish societies petitioned the Vestry on Christler's behalf. Many others protested his transfer to Montana, begging him not to go. The *Auburn Daily* headlines on April 20, 1906, read, "Rev. Christler Must Stay!" Two hundred laborers signed a petition and a delegation delivered it offering "generous financial support if he would make up his mind to stay among the citizens of Auburn." But the Vestry would not change its mind, and Christler offered his sincere gratitude but declined their offers.

And so the Reverend Leonard Christler came west to Montana in 1907, reassigned to what was called the Milk River Field. He worked along the hi-line across the vast northern expanse among railroaders and homesteaders, eventually helping to build churches in communities such as Malta and Glasgow. Havre served as the reverend's home headquarters. Mindful of the social differences among the parishioners in his last post, he closed his first sermon in Havre with this prayer:

> Good Lord, keep me in all my ministry from becoming a frump or a pious non entity, and grant me sufficient good sense to fall not into the ways of the shabby snobbish or ignorant of the world in order to be good and manly.

There in Havre in 1908, Reverend Christler laid the cornerstone of St. Mark's Episcopal Church, and oversaw its progress year by year with a copy of the plans always in his back pocket. The church was long in the building, but Reverend Christler accomplished the nearly impossible. He secured donation of the stone from the Kain brothers' quarry in Helena and persuaded James J. Hill of the Great Northern Railroad to ship it to Havre at no expense. Finally the beautiful church was finished in 1918. The stone building is still in use today, a credit to the man who had the fortitude to see it to completion.

In his travels among the far-flung hi-line communities from Glacier National Park to the North Dakota border, Christler styled himself the "Bishop of All Outdoors," and by that title he was widely known, universally accepted, and well liked. He had a great gift for oratory, and he was a familiar figure wearing a long black coat that reached below the knees of his six-foot frame. A wide-brimmed western style hat covered an ample head of brown curly hair. Enigmatic and magnetic, Christler cut a handsome figure.

In 1914 Christler returned to Auburn to marry Anna Wadsworth, the daughter of the prominent owner of a scythe factory whose funeral Christler had conducted in his days at St. Peter's. Christler was well aware that he was marrying above his own social and economic station. But he was a man of some reputation, having served a term in the Montana legislature. He also had some powerful friends, including Thomas J. Walsh, a newly elected U.S. senator who was at the beginning of a long and productive political career. With the senator from Montana as witness, the Christlers said their vows at Anna's home at 186 Genesee Street in Auburn. Christler's rector from his hometown of Waterloo performed the ceremony. Ironically, it was Norton Houser, Christler's replacement and Dr. Brainard's permanent successor, who recorded the marriage in the register at nearby St. Peter's. The reverend was thirty-seven and his bride, nearly a spinster at thirty-three, was tall, plain, sad-looking, and always dressed in black. In retrospect, she seemed a fitting offspring of her late father's, a kind of female grim reaper who might have well been a ghoulish advertisement had she carried one of her father's scythes. It was a strange match, the popular silver-tongued Bishop of All Outdoors and the tall, unattractive, black-clad spinster.

The newlyweds made their home a half mile south of Havre on the Beaver Creek Highway at Christler's Hill Top Farm. Meanwhile, the reverend's following grew. As he had done in Auburn, Christler won the respect of the workingmen who toiled on the railroad and in the little towns along the hi-line. He joined their fraternal organizations—the Masons, the Elks, the Eagles, the Knights of Pythias, and the Independent Order of Foresters. He talked their talk, his congregation hung on his every word, and his services were in demand for weddings, baptisms, and funerals. Everywhere he went children hung on his coattails. He endeared himself to the people of Havre, promoting the community by encouraging displays at the depot showing local crop yields. Novelist Steward Edward White even patterned a character after the reverend from Montana in his 1913 book, *Gold*, giving his handsome, breezy, character the title "bishop of all outdoors."

When Long George Francis, a popular prominent local character convicted of horse stealing, died by his own hand, it was Christler who delivered the eulogy. Francis and Christler, as it later turned out, had a few things in common. Both had experienced controversy—Christler in the social struggle that brought him to Montana, and Francis in his disregard for evolving range laws. Both had many friends and defenders. Francis was a cowboy, well known on the rodeo circuit where he was in demand and won his share of prize money steer roping, bulldogging, and bareback riding. His home on the Milk River west of Havre was a comfortable four-room house, and he had fine horse tack and two special horses he rode at rodeos and fairs. But Francis lived by the old hazy rules of mavericking that held that any unbranded animal was fair game to the first person to put a brand on it. These times were changing, and opinions divided. Some were outraged when Francis was convicted of grand larceny in March of 1917 for the theft of a bay mare. Others saw Francis as a rustler and approved of his conviction. They saw it as a moral victory long in coming. The morning after the verdict, an editorial appeared in the Havre newspaper explaining that rustlers in recent times had taken a toll on the stock raising industry, and that some local ranchers had suffered significantly enough to give up their businesses altogether. The writer believed that men like Francis would get their due: "Others may deserve the same fate," said he, speaking of Francis' jail sentence. "Do not worry, their time may come soon. They will have to take their medicine, too." In retrospect some saw these words as eerily prophetic when Francis met a fate worse than a stint in jail.

Francis had been in hiding since pronouncement of his sentence in 1918. Two years was a long time to be on the lamb, and he was tired of it. On Christmas Eve 1920 he prepared to give himself up, but first he determined to make one last trip to visit his schoolteacher girlfriend near the Canadian border. Loaded with apples and gifts for her and the children, he started out on the journey. It was snowing and cold. Thirty miles northwest of Havre in the middle of nowhere, he wrecked his car and broke his leg in the accident. Fashioning a splint from an apple box, he tried to crawl for help. Exhausted and in pain with little hope of rescue, Francis slit his own throat and bled to death in the snow.

Francis, according to the editorial writer, had lived by distorted moral principles. Many would later believe the same of the Reverend Leonard Christler. The sermon Christler preached at this legendary funeral was also strangely prophetic. The Bishop of All Outdoors said of Francis, "It may not have been with the rose of Heaven upon his cheek, or the fire of Godliness in his eyes that he died, but there was nonetheless the charm of invincibility stamped upon the tragedy." According to Havre author Gary Wilson, Christler believed Francis was not guilty of any crimes, but rather he " ... was framed and betrayed by people who were supposedly his friends and railroaded by the court." Many would later see Christler as a man framed, wronged, and blameless.

The Christlers moved to town by 1920 while the reverend built a grand new home at Hill Top Farm. The couple took up residence in the church rectory in the 800 block of Third Avenue, only a block or so away from St. Mark's. The home was an unpretentious, comfortable worker's cottage, a reflection of the working class parishioners who saw Christler as their champion and hero.

The Christlers' circle of friends included well-respected, prominent citizens. Among them was Judge Frank Carleton, who had been Long George Francis' defense counsel. When Carleton and his pretty, vivacious wife Margaret separated in 1921, there was much talk of infidelity. Rumors flew around Havre as the reverend spent time counseling Margaret. Longtime Havre resident Louise Wigmore recalled, seventy-five years after the fact, that all the teenagers in Havre closely followed the "romance" between the minister and the judge's wife. Like opinions about Long George Francis, opinions about Reverend Christler are still divided. Old-timers will vouch that half the women in Havre were in love with the handsome clergyman. While none will begrudge the good and important works the reverend accomplished, his involvement with Margaret Carlson is still a subject of heated debate.

In the summers, Christler put his silver tongue to work on the Chautauqua circuit and his recommendation helped get Margaret hired as well. By the fall of 1922, it was widely rumored that the two spent time traveling together in the Midwest while Anna Christler remained in Havre. The *Havre Daily Promoter* published a report by the Associated Press confirming that fact. C.E. Booth, official for the Mutual Elwell Chautauqua that employed the two, said Christler and Margaret Carleton had been together in Chicago twice and spent much time in each other's company.

Public opinions varied concerning Anna Christler, the supposedly wronged wife. She seems to have been a contradictory figure who was eminently well respected, but in contradiction to her mild manner, she packed a pistol in her purse. A niece of Senator James W. Wadsworth of New York, Anna was "phlegmatic and reserved," and had no children after eight years of marriage. "She was the type," said the *Tribune*, "who would cast off any suspicions as to her husband's conduct." With no one to look after but herself, Anna spent her time tending the flowers her husband planted around the new church. With all the gossip flying, it would seem that Anna now had a reason to clothe herself in black.

Complaints to the Episcopal Diocese of Montana resulted in an investigation into the minister's moral conduct. Bishop Frederick Faber told the Associated Press,

> I found evidence which made me believe that the accusations were actuated by animosity on the part of persons making them, due to activities of Mr. Christler which had nothing to do with Mrs. Carleton.
>
> Mr. Christler was a big man, physically and mentally, an outdoorsman and he did many things in novel and unusual ways. He had many activities for the benefit of his fellow men which were outside ordinary church activities and many people were to be found who were willing to find fault with him.

Margaret's estranged husband, Judge Carleton, wrote letters to his wife in which he tried repeatedly to make her see the snare into which he believed Christler had lured her. Margaret was a descendant of a well-known and well-respected pioneer Helena family. Her grandfather had come with the first miners to Last Chance Gulch, settled there, and raised his family. But Margaret, considered a beautiful woman, seems to have lived a troubled life. She was divorced from her first husband because, according to the *Great Falls Tribune*, she allegedly attempted to take his life.

In the fall of 1922, neighbors observed Margaret stealthily sneaking around the Christlers' home at all hours of the day and night. Sometimes she got inside and roamed around when the house was empty. Neighbors could see the light she carried, moving from room to room. Margaret was clearly unbalanced, depressed, and headed for a breakdown. The neighbors watched these developments with interest, wondering how the bizarre situation would end.

Margaret attempted suicide, taking an overdose of sleeping powders in her room at the Havre Hotel. Doctors later said that she took three times the dose that would have induced eight hours of sleep. The effects of the powder should have impaired her judgment and left her in a hazy frame of mind. Yet late on the night of October 27, 1922, barely a day after the failed suicide, the reverend was seeing a visiting minister off at the depot. Anna Christler returned home alone and sensed something amiss. She saw a light in the house and cautiously opened the door. Inside she found Margaret, muttering incoherently, still under the influence of the sleeping powders, tearing up a photograph of Leonard. Why Margaret was not under a doctor's supervision so soon after her attempted suicide has never been explained.

Great Falls Leader, *October 28, 1922*

Later that evening, as the Christlers sat in their living room, Margaret burst through the front door announcing that Anna had no place in Leonard's life. After some conversation, the minister got up to prepare for bed and Anna got up to show Margaret out. Anna later told authorities that as she turned her back to Margaret to move to the front door, two shots rang out. When police responded to her call, they found Anna looming in the doorway, waiting for them. The silver-tongued Bishop of All Outdoors lay crumpled dead in the bedroom doorway and pretty, vivacious Margaret, shot through the heart, lay near him. Was she an innocent victim? Was she actually guilty of adultery? Did she pull the trigger? Most at least agreed that she was not completely innocent, and like Long George Francis, did not die with "the rose of Heaven upon her cheek."

The deaths were ruled murder-suicide—with Margaret pulling the trigger. But questions remained. The murder weapon was a gun used in a shooting in 1919 at the Havre Hotel where Margaret Carleton lived at the time of her death. Margaret's ex-husband had been the judge in the case and had acquired the gun after the trial. But could Margaret have pulled the trigger twice, once to kill Christler and once to kill herself? She was still incoherent and weakened from the effects of the sleeping powders. Even in the best of health, she could hardly have concealed or wielded the heavy revolver used in the shootings. Further, diamond rings missing from Margaret's finger were never found. Margaret's mother, Mrs. Joseph Pyle of Butte, succeeded in persuading the court to re-examine the evidence a few days later, but the judge determined that the murder-suicide ruling would stand. Margaret left a thirteen-year-old daughter who had been in Mrs. Pyle's custody at the time of the shooting. The funeral was held at Helena where her mother's family had settled in the 1860s. Margaret Carleton was interred in Forestvale Cemetery in the family plot with her pioneer grandparents.

Christler had funeral services both in Montana and in his native New York. The service in Havre brought throngs of mourners from all over the state to St. Mark's. The *Havre Daily Promoter* noted, "Montana could have lost no man whose going would have left a greater void." In the fifteen years of his work from Glacier National Park to the North Dakota line, Reverend Christler was a friend to those who needed befriending, and he left churches all along the hi-line. "His truest memorial," said the *Promoter*, "is enshrined in the hearts of those whom he served with entire forgetfulness of self." Whatever Christler's shortcomings might have been, his accomplishments were many and his death was a tragedy keenly felt along Montana's remote hi-line.

According to locals, the district attorney pulled some strings, making certain that authorities questioned Mrs. Christler only in the most perfunctory manner, skirting whatever inconsistencies there may have been in her story. She was quickly absolved of any responsibility for her husband's death and prepared to take him back to his hometown for burial. And so Leonard

Christler's childless widow, above suspicion, took the long ride back to her husband's boyhood home of Waterloo, New York, with her hand on her husband's coffin. Meanwhile, Reverend John Arthur, rector of St. Paul's Episcopal Church of Waterloo, grappled with details. Because of the scandal and circumstances under which Reverend Christler died, Bishop Charles Fiske of Syracuse believed a church funeral inappropriate. But after consultation with colleagues who had known Christler, the rector decided otherwise.

The Masons of Waterloo had their own dilemma. They had learned that Christler had been affiliated with the Blue Lodge of Havre, and that the Masons there had been generous to their fallen brother. They determined to accord him all ceremonial honors due a fellow Mason. But before the train pulled into the station at Waterloo, they discovered that Christler had not paid his dues in fifteen years and that he had been suspended. Not wishing to cause further embarrassment, the Masons decided to carry on for the widow's sake as if their brother has been a member in good standing.

Tall, grim, and swathed in black, Mrs. Christler remained faithful to the memory of her husband. She took up residence with her widowed mother in the family mansion on Genesee Street, and was a familiar figure in the pews of Auburn's St. Peter's Episcopal Church. When youngsters whispered about the grim-faced woman dressed in black sitting alone in her pew, they were told "Shhh! That's Mrs. Christler!" in a tone that smacked of scandal.

Anna Christler periodically returned to Havre, so they say, and some reported seeing her tend the flowers at St. Mark's years after the tragedy. Although records in Auburn, New York, list her death as 1940, there is an eerie discrepancy. As late as 1941, the Havre city directory lists Anna Christler in residence in a small house next door to St. Mark's church. And in recent decades when moonlight spills across the church grounds, a shadowy figure has been seen moving between the church and the house next door.

According to locals, the residence a block or so down Third Avenue where the tragedy occurred has seen at least one other suicide. Howdy Beaver wrote about it in Halloween legends in the *Havre Daily News*, October 30, 1997: "A rental house in Havre which was the scene of a murder/suicide years ago and more recently another suicide is impossible to keep rented because of strange feelings the house seems to produce." These reports are unconfirmed. But after the house was divided into three apartments in the 1980s, its sole resident reported hearing ghostly footsteps in the unrented rooms. This may explain why the apartments have been vacant as often as they have been occupied.

And finally, the Christlers' handsome home at Hill Top Farm was never finished, never sold, never lived in except by wild creatures seeking a comfortable, dry place out of the winter cold. It is doubtful that even they found much comfort there. In later years arson brought the home down and left it a blackened ruin unfit for anything. They say that partying teenagers were guilty of accidentally starting the blaze. Today, nothing stands there but a chimney as black as Anna Christler's gowns. Such ruins draw the curious, and this one has a magnetism like that of its long ago builder. It is a ruin, as the Bishop of All Outdoors himself might have said, with "the charm of invincibility stamped upon the tragedy."

Sources

Newspapers of late October 1922 across the state carried the details of the Christler murder as did newspapers in New York, Cincinnati, and San Francisco. Jon Axline included a chapter on Leonard Christler in *Speaking Ill of the Dead: Jerks in Montana History* and helped me collect the haunted threads. He conducted the National Register survey and authored the nomination for the Havre Residential Historic District in which the Third Street house is included. The historical/architectural inventory form for the residence is housed at the State Historic Preservation Office in Helena. The funeral of Long George Francis, and Christler's role in it, is discussed in *Guts, Grits and Gusto: A History of Hill County*. For more information on Long George Francis, see Gary Wilson's *Tall in the Saddle*. The article by Reverend Robert C. Ayers, Rector Emeritus of St. Peter's Church in Auburn, New York, "Though he Married the Scythemaker's Daughter, the Grim Reaper Found him Out: A True Story from Auburn's Past," is an excellent resource for the New York and Anglican side of the story. The article, published in the Anglican online newsletter, can be found at http://anglicansonline.org (February 1, 2004). After interviewing several longtime Havre residents, at least one of whom remembers Leonard Christler firsthand, it is clear he, like Long George Francis, will always have supporters and detractors.

STRANGER AT THE DOOR

Five Sisters of Charity of Leavenworth, Kansas, and lay music teacher Rose Kelly arrived in the booming gold camp of Helena on a wintry day in 1869. The women had traveled by rail to Corinne, Utah, and then by stagecoach to this remote corner of the wilderness. It had been a long and treacherous journey, and at first they were very homesick. Despite their low spirits, they set right to work and on a gentle hilltop, known in the beginning as Church Hill, founded St. Vincent's Academy for girls, the first Catholic institution in Montana. This fulfilled the first of the threefold mission that directed the sisters to teach youth, nurse the sick, and care for orphans. Another group of sisters soon joined the first contingent, and they set about establishing a hospital. With the sisters' hard work and the help of Jesuit priests, the hilltop was soon home to St. John's Hospital, the girls' boarding school and convent, and a boys' day school. Helena's first Catholic church, the Cathedral of the Sacred Hearts of Jesus and Mary, stood on the west side of Ewing Street. The Jesuits' residence, later home to the bishop, was between the church and the hospital. All sat overlooking Vawter Street and Broadway beyond it.

During the 1870s the sisters fulfilled two of their missions, teaching youth and nursing the sick. The sisters did much more than they were asked to do. Behind the wood frame cottage that served as the first hospital was a small house surrounded by a high picket fence. There the sisters cared for the indigent "insane and mentally deranged of the entire territory" under contract with the territorial legislature. Major John Owen, former owner of Fort Owen in the Bitterroot Valley, was one among a dozen such patients the sisters cared for during the 1870s. Major Owen suffered from severe dementia, probably what is today known as Alzheimer's disease. He and his fellow patients moved back and forth between St. John's and the County Hospital from the early 1870s to 1877. Territorial Governor Benjamin Potts

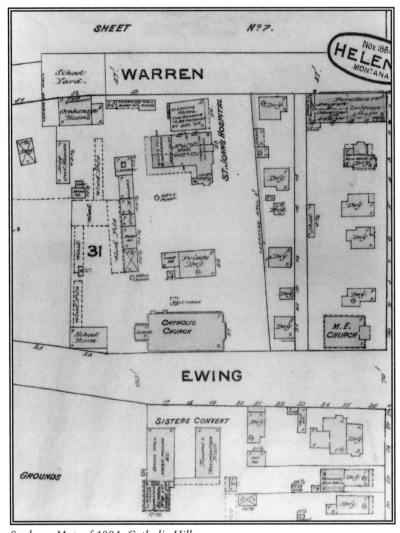

Sanborn Map of 1884, Catholic Hill
COURTESY MONTANA HISTORICAL SOCIETY RESEARCH CENTER

wrote on March 12, 1874, that " … the law is not oblig[ed] to care for the insane at the expense of the Territory, but if I can make an arrangement on reasonable terms, I shall do so." Thus, the institution offering the best price in any given year received the territorial contract. In the years that it fell to the sisters on Catholic Hill, the patients' sometimes violent and dangerous behavior tested their caregivers' resolve. The sisters dealt with these patients as humanely as they could, but, according to common practice and with medical treatment primitive at best, patients suffering from all types of disorders were housed of necessity alongside each other. For safety's sake, restraints were standard care to protect these unfortunate inmates from themselves and others. These patients provided the sisters with hair-raising tales of narrow escapes.

The founding of the state institution at Warm Springs in 1877 freed the sisters of their obligation to care for the territory's indigent mentally ill and allowed the women to fulfill the third part of their mission with the founding of an orphanage on Catholic Hill. The sisters remodeled the asylum and in 1881 took in the first three of many children. The sisters named the home St. Ambrose Orphanage after Ambrose Sullivan, one of the first young residents. The sisters took in both orphans and children placed there by parents who for various reasons were unable to care for the children themselves. St. Ambrose operated on the west end of the hill overlooking Warren Street until the 1890s when the new St. Joseph's Home opened in the Prickly Pear Valley. On Catholic Hill, St. John's Hospital, rebuilt in 1884, was an imposing building overlooking Vawter Street on the north edge of the hillside. At the same time in 1884, substantial brick buildings replaced the old St. Vincent's Academy for Girls and St. Aloysius School for Boys.

In 1905 the Sisters of Charity began the state's first nursing school at St. John's on Catholic Hill. Then, with substantial funds from wealthy Helenans Thomas Cruse and Peter Larson, the Catholic community focused upon the building of the great cathedral that would replace the Cathedral of the Sacred Hearts. Construction began in 1908 and at Christmas in 1914, St. Helena Cathedral was ready to replace the old, quaint Cathedral of the Sacred Hearts. The unused church stood abandoned until it and the vault under the rear of the church, where bishops and priests for the past half-century had been interred, were razed in the 1920s. According to records, most of the remains were accounted for and transferred elsewhere. The only remnant of that earliest period, when the old cathedral graced the hill, is a cornerstone incorporated in a grotto in the yard of Immaculata Hall. The date "1874," with the "4" written backwards, is scratched into the stone.

On Friday October 18, 1935, just before ten o'clock, students at St. Vincent's Academy for Girls on Ewing Street were preparing for bed when the earth began to shake violently. Sisters of Charity Eugenia Donnelly, Helena Fisher, and Maurita Postlewait instructed the girls to dress quickly. Carrying candles, the sisters led the girls down the stairway in pitch darkness.

Feeling their way along, someone shouted, "Don't take the first doorway!" They bypassed it and continued down the stairs to another exit just as they heard the awful rumble of the wall falling, blocking the doorway they fortuitously had bypassed. At first light, it was clear that only Providence could have guided the sisters and the girls safely over live wires, fallen walls, and breaches in the floors.

The 1935 earthquakes destroyed Catholic Hill leaving only the hospital's laundry building and Immaculata Hall, formerly the St. Aloysius School. St. John's Hospital was rebuilt across Ewing Street on the site of the old St. Vincent's Academy. Modern apartments now spread over the area where the original St. John's and the Cathedral of the Sacred Hearts once stood, where black-robed nuns and dark-suited priests once attended to their duties, and the priests of old lay moldering in their crypts.

Today the laundry building is home to an engineering firm. Immaculata Hall houses offices and a private elementary school. Tenants love the historic building and its comfortable, quiet ambiance. In decades past, however, one cleaning crew that came in to sweep the halls and keep the offices tidy claimed to hear the nuns still walking the hallway on the top floor. They said they could hear the footsteps on the wooden floors, moving from one end of the building, down the hallway and back again in endless shifts. Mrs. Gordon Tracy attended the Carroll College School of Nursing in the 1940s when the Sisters of Charity had charge of the classes and the students. At this time Carroll College was for men only, and the nursing program newly associated with Carroll was the first step in integrating women into the student body. But the women were not housed on campus, rather on the top floor of Immaculata Hall. Mrs. Tracy says the nuns walked that hallway all night long, keeping watch over the students to make certain they stayed in their rooms and didn't sneak out. The sisters wore heavy crucifixes and rosaries at their waists, and the students could hear them clank and jingle up and down the hall all night long. Mrs. Tracy says that sometimes in her dreams she still hears the clanking and the footfalls.

In the summer of 2004, Patrick Marsolek conducted a class for ten students who wanted to practice intuitive skills. After a series of exercises to make the students, most of whom did not know each other, comfortable as a group, the class moved from the initial meeting place to Immaculata Hall. Building owner Shauna Thomas graciously opened the vast three-story building and accompanied the class. The idea was to walk through the various floors, take notes on impressions and feelings experienced in the various rooms and hallways, then compare notes with the group. There was no previous discussion of the history of the building.

The outcome was interesting. As the students moved through the rooms off one particular hallway, more than half of them experienced feelings of panic, anger, claustrophobia, fear, or a combination of these associated with one area in one of the rooms. The group gathered at the end of the hallway to compare notes and discovered their similar reactions to the one area. Shauna then offered a revelation. In the late 1980s, she told the group, that wing of Immaculata Hall housed an adolescent treatment center. Shauna said that when she took possession of the property, the room that had elicited such negative reactions had a smaller closet-like room, now removed, that was painted completely black—ceiling, walls, and floor. It had a lock on the outside. The youngsters who needed time out or calming down were placed in lockup in the "black room." The Helena city directories from 1989 to 1991 confirm that the Adolescent Day Treatment, a division of Southwest Mental Health, Inc., was housed in the building. Further, Patrick experienced what he described as "tremors, body or building vibrations" while in this particular area of the hallway. "They may have been earthquake related," says Patrick, "but may have also been connected to the energy of that room."

One young couple that recently lived in an apartment where the old St. John's Hospital building stood heard the usual legends and tales that made the rounds among the residents. Candy and Richard heard that the apartments stood on an old graveyard where many orphans had been buried. While it is true that from 1915 to 1935, the former bishop's residence was used as St. Ann's infant home, these whispered legends about Catholic Hill are of long standing, told and perpetuated by those who know only parts of its real history. Research has shown that probably the only burials on Catholic Hill were those of bishops and priests in the vault of the cathedral. The couple did not know there had been anything on the property except an orphanage nor did they learn about the rest of Catholic Hill's past until long after they had moved out.

They lived in a ground floor apartment in the last few months of 2001 and the beginning of 2002. A young man named Willy lived in a different area of the complex during that same time. Willy had several young children, and he and Richard sometimes had conversations in passing as neighbors often do. One day as they were doing laundry, Willy told Richard that his children had begun to talk about a "really nice guy" who often came to play with them. The man was young, they said, like their dad. He was tall and always wore a black suit. The man came to play with the children and their friends in their room in Willy's upper-level apartment. Willy confessed to Richard that he was growing tired of hearing about this new playmate. Willy wanted to know if Richard had ever met such a guy. Richard had not. Willy was not surprised since neither had anyone else he asked, but he was growing concerned about a stranger playing with his children.

Catholic Hill, circa. 1890, looking south. The back row of buildings, left to right: St. Vincent's, Sacred Hearts Cathedral, bishop's residence, and St. John's Hospital
COURTESY MONTANA HISTORICAL SOCIETY PHOTOGRAPH ARCHIVES PAC 80-27 FOLDER 14

A few weeks later, Richard ran into Willy out in the parking lot taking boxes to his car. Willy seemed to be in a rush. When Richard asked what was wrong, Willy told him that last evening, the kids had come rushing out of their room crying, "Dad, Dad! Come and meet our friend—the really nice guy. He's in our room playing with us!" Willy followed the children into their room, but no one was there. Willy told Richard that he was taking his children and moving out.

Richard and Candy had their own eerie experiences. Candy's mother had passed away recently. Candy had kept her mother's wedding dress and it was hanging in the bedroom closet in the apartment. Several times Candy and Richard both heard pounding coming from inside the closet. They could find no reason for the noise. Stranger yet, the couple had a new baby and they had a monitor set up in the baby's room. At different times when the monitor was on and the baby was sleeping, they could hear someone whispering in the baby's room. Of course, no one was ever there. And there were cold spots in the living room. Candy and Richard noticed that at certain times it would be very hot in the room, but there would be one spot that was so cold you could walk into it and your hair would prickle.

More frightening to Richard was his 4:30 AM visitor. A noise at the front door awakened him as he slept soundly on the living room futon. He watched in horror as the doorknob began to turn. The locked door slowly swung open before his eyes and then slammed shut with a tremendous BANG! Richard jumped out of bed, had to unlock the door to open it, and checked outside. The parking lot was quiet and empty. And yet another time as he was coming into the empty apartment, he turned on the light and saw something about the height of the sofa arm run around the corner of the sofa and disappear into the hallway. Richard came running out to the car and yelled at Candy that someone was in the house. Upon investigation, they could find nothing to explain what he had seen. Richard is quite certain he was not mistaken.

A final incident prompted Richard and Candy to take their baby and move elsewhere. On this particular day, Richard was cleaning the apartment. He pushed the mop back and forth around in circles and back again, thinking about nothing in particular except finishing his chores. The scent of the pine detergent was pungent and not unpleasant as he concentrated on the more stubborn spots. His apartment was going to be nice and clean when he finished, and this was the last step. He worked around the kitchen methodically, one square of linoleum at a time, thinking to himself, "One done, two done, three, and four. Four more squares and I am at the door." Richard made up a little rhyme to make it go more quickly. Rinse and mop. Rinse and mop.

Richard cocked his head and slowly straightened up, aware of some subtle change he could not quite put his finger on. "What is that?" he thought to himself. "What in the hell is that?" An indescribable odor had replaced the pine-scented cleaner that just a moment before had been so strong. This new smell was raunchy, nasty, worse than anything he could imagine, a stench like something rotting. It began to fill the apartment.

Richard turned and through the front door, which stood slightly ajar, he could see the figure of a man standing there in the shadows, silent and unmoving. Richard stood there wondering what he should do. The man on the other side of the door still did not move. Finally Richard strode to the door and opened it a little wider. The man was wearing an odd brown suit. He waited expectantly for Richard to speak first.

"What do you want?" Richard asked, a slight tremor in his voice, now aware that the awful smell emanated from the stranger.

"Can I come in?" the man demanded rather than asked the question.

"Tell me what you want," said Richard, who was nervous before, but now had become frightened.

"Where's Priscilla? I want Priscilla!" The man was agitated, and all the while he averted his gaze, unwilling or unable to make eye contact with Richard. It gave Richard the creeps. Candy's given name, known only to her immediate family, was Priscilla.

"What do you want with my wife?" Richard asked. This whole scenario seemed unreal and Richard was now very much afraid.

"Can I come in?" the man asked once more.

"I can't help you unless you tell me what you want."

"I guess you aren't going to let me in," the man said. Richard now took more notice of the odd and unkempt stranger. His clothing seemed especially peculiar, weirdly out of date, and his white shirt—at least once it had been white—was ripped. Richard could tell from his hands especially that this was an older man, and a very dirty one. Likely crazy, thought Richard, and maybe unpredictable, too. You never know what a crazy person is going to do. Richard took a step back ready to slam and lock the door. To his great relief, however, the man turned to go. Richard shut the door for an instant, and then thought better of it. He stepped outside to see where the man was headed. Richard's apartment was in the middle of a long building with a sidewalk running along its length. The brief seconds it took for Richard to shut the door and open it again was not enough time for the man to round either end of the building, but there was no one anywhere. The man had vanished, and with him went the awful stench that moments before had filled Richard's apartment.

This and the other incidents haunted the young couple. When they learned the history of the hilltop, some of the pieces began to fit. The vault beneath the Cathedral of the Sacred Hearts, according to Church historian Father Lawrence Palladino, received the mortal remains of all the early day priests beginning in 1878 with the death of Father Philip Rappagliosi. A missionary among the Blackfeet, Father Rappagliosi died at thirty-seven of an unknown illness. There were widespread rumors, never proven, that the young priest had been poisoned. Father Rappagliosi was the second priest to die in Montana, and his funeral rites at the Sacred Hearts in Helena were the first solemnized since the organization of the Territory of Montana. Major R. C. Walker wrote the priest's obituary, describing the elaborate funeral rites and his interment beneath the church:

> After the High Mass, at ten o'clock, celebrated by the Rev. Father Imoda, the remains were borne by six pall-bearers, preceded by priests and acolytes, from the sacristy, where they had been watched and viewed by the faithful from early morn, to the front of the main altar, where they were blessed, prayers said, the congregation rising and remaining standing until the ceremonies were concluded. They were then taken from the church, the whole congregation following in solemn procession, to the enduring vault prepared for them under the rear of the church. Here the prayers of the last sad rites were said and the casket containing all that was mortal of the deceased Father was slowly and solemnly consigned to its receptacle built in the rocks of mother earth ... .

The vault beneath the Sacred Hearts was the burial place for clergy until the St. Helena Cathedral replaced the old church in 1914. Resurrection Cemetery became the place of burial for clergy.

Could the dark-suited playmate who entertained Willy's children be the ghost of Father Rappalgiosi or some other early day priest, come to play a ghostly game? At least one other recent resident has seen a spectral man in a suit several times, standing on one of the apartment balconies where there is no outside access. But who was the unkempt stranger, and what did he know of Candy? These questions and the memory of the awful stench the stranger had carried with him especially bothered Richard. And there was one other detail more disturbing than all the others. Having later learned about the house with the high fence and the nineteenth century care of the mentally ill, the man's appearance suggested an unthinkable possibility. This shocking detail about the odd stranger came back to torture Richard. He had noticed that the oddly dressed, unkempt stranger had horrible red, raw chafe marks around his wrists where the man had obviously been tied and restrained.

Sources

Sanborn-Perris Fire Insurance Maps of Helena for the years 1884, 1888, 1890, 1892, 1930, and 1953 provide a good perspective, showing exactly where the institutions were located on Catholic Hill before and after the 1935 earthquakes. There are several histories of the Catholic institutions in Montana and in Helena. These include several histories of the Sisters of Charity of Leavenworth, Kansas, notably *We Came North and Go With Haste into the Mountains*. Father Lawrence Palladino's *Indian and White in the Northwest* recounts the deaths of some of the priests interred at the Sacred Hearts, particularly Father Philip Rappagliosi. Many have been removed to Resurrection Cemetery, and their tombstones can be found today. More from the *Quarries of Last Chance Gulch*, Volume III, includes a section on the devastating 1935 Helena earthquakes. Kyle Hayes, an aquaintance of Richard's, arranged my interview with Candy and Richard.

LATE-NIGHT FRIGHT
AT THE FAIRWEATHER INN

Jaena Dennis gave little thought to ghosts. She was a believer, but she lacked the conviction that comes through firsthand experience. When scouts from the Fox Family Channel visited Virginia City, Montana, in 2000 looking for tales and teenagers to participate in a segment of the series, "Real Scary Stories," Jaena and her friend Chris enthusiastically seized the opportunity. There was little enough excitement in their rural Madison County community. In the gold rush-era town of Virginia City, a sleepy little burg whose winter population on a good day is less than one hundred fifty, they waited in line to share a few stories and answer questions on camera. They filled out some paperwork, and like everyone else interviewed, waited to see what would happen. Jaena and Chris were surprised and thrilled when Fox later notified the two that they had been selected. Jaena was too excited to worry about being scared.

In choosing Virginia City for its Montana segment of "Real Scary Stories," Fox Family picked a place steeped in history, legend, and haunted places. Virginia City is a unique and wonderful little hamlet, snugged into its own niche along Alder Gulch where, in the mid-1860s, one of the greatest western gold rush stampedes brought a diverse and adventurous population to fill its now quiet, still unpaved streets. Raucous miners, ambitious merchants, gamblers, rounders, public women, and families of settlers rubbed elbows along the wooden sidewalks. And it was at Virginia City and Bannack, as well as other local places, that the vigilantes did their work. From December 1863 to March 1864, their kind of justice culminated at the end of a rope at least twenty-four times.

It is little wonder that Virginia City is the haunted capital of Montana. The frenzy of the gold rush worked its way into the hearts and minds of its first residents, and that energy lingers. Descendants of the first pioneers who call Alder Gulch home and newcomers, too, feel the spirit of this important place. They fiercely nurture and protect it, as well they should.

Sightings of those who have gone before are not uncommon for residents and workers who spend time in Virginia City and its sister community, Nevada City, less than two miles away. Nineteenth century goods, from buttons and mining supplies to music machines and cans of snuff, are found in quantities in the false fronted buildings and cabins. Their weathered wood has seen the eras come and go. So intense is the history in Alder Gulch that its energy seeps into every knothole and weathered crack. Even visitors who pause only briefly to soak up colorful gold rush remnants might catch a glimpse of a shadow without a human counterpart. They might find some other evidence of an unearthly visitor as one recent tourist discovered in the Sedman home.

The Sedman House is a beautiful, fully furnished territorial period home in Nevada City. It was one of the first large homes built in the region circa 1873. Oscar Sedman was a Madison County rancher and territorial legislator who met a tragic end. In 1881 during the legislative session in Helena, he suddenly took ill and died of "black measles," the tick-born disease we know today as Rocky Mountain spotted fever. Sedman had the dubious honor of being the first Montana legislator to die during a session. After his unexpected demise, Sedman's official chair in the meeting room, draped in black crepe, was turned backward from his desk in memoriam. Sedman left a wife and four small children. The Sedman House later became the Junction Hotel, and after that, served as a stable. Badly deteriorated, it was disassembled at its original Junction City location about a mile and a half away and put back together in Nevada City in the 1960s. The home, a focal point at the west end of town, is a now filled with period furnishings and its rooms are open to tourists. The historic interior pieces include the desk of vigilante prosecutor Wilbur Fisk Sanders and Colonel Charles Broadwater's bathtub from his private suite at the far-famed Broadwater Hotel near Helena.

The Sedman House especially captivated one eastern tourist. She took a whole roll of film of the antique furnishings. A mirror caught her fancy and she took numerous shots of the lovely old frame. She returned home after her vacation and had the film developed. In several photographs of the mirror, she found the startling reflection of a man in rough clothing, staring out at her. The photographer and her friend had been the only two in the Sedman House that day. Such are the surprises Alder Gulch offers up.

The legendary places of Virginia City, a designated National Historic Landmark, are under both state and private ownership. Tourists find comfortable hospitality, and perhaps a ghost or two, in its several bed-and-breakfasts and the two state-owned hotels, the Nevada City Hotel in Nevada City and Virginia City's Fairweather Inn. Fox producers decided that the inn would be one of the two settings for "Real Scary Stories." The other location, the Elling House, was once home to banker Henry Elling and his family. Today it is a private residence.

The Fairweather Inn has served in its present incarnation since 1946 when Great Falls legislator Charles Bovey remodeled it as a modern hotel. But the oldest inner core, incorporated into the present facility, has a long and colorful history typical of Virginia City's gold rush-era commercial buildings. The present hotel evolved from a log cabin likely built in 1863. By 1865, the site was home to a popular restaurant called the "Young American Eating House." Most Virginia City residents and visitors of that early time enjoyed meals from its kitchen. From 1866 through the 1870s, a meat market under several proprietors occupied the building. By the time Sarah McGarry bought the place in the 1880s, an addition extended thirty or forty feet at the back, but the gold rush relic had fallen vacant, its space used for storage. A dance hall next door on the west side of the building was also vacant, indications that the glory days of Alder Gulch had passed. However, gold dredging operations in the area began in 1890. Conversion and reuse of the building as a saloon around that time brought new life to the property. Frank McKeen bought the saloon business in 1896.

McKeen was one of the colorful characters local folk remember even today. He came to Virginia City from Granite City, Montana, on the heels of the silver panic of 1893 when the Bi-Metallic and Granite Mountain mines closed. Born in Boston on Christmas Day in 1858, McKeen spent time in Leadville, Colorado, before coming to Montana. A confirmed bachelor, McKeen stunned the entire community in 1905 when he, at forty-seven, married beautiful thirty-three-year-old Amanda who stood a head taller than her husband. McKeen was an excellent businessman, always trying new angles to better serve the community. He advertised that his Anaconda Saloon was the "best appointed and best-kept saloon in Madison County." In conjunction with the saloon, McKeen also ran a billiard parlor and the Anaconda Café; by 1918, it was the only short-order restaurant in Virginia City. McKeen boasted that his was the town's oldest established eating-house and offered a private ladies' dining room and meals at all hours, from six in the morning till eight in the evening.

The large front space of the building housed the bar. The dining rooms were behind the bar with the kitchen farther back in a one-story addition.

A second story over the dining rooms included additional tiny hotel rooms. McKeen declared in the *Madisonian Times* that his were "the best furnished rooms in town." Oldtimers say that McKeen had a back entrance for the ladies of "the Brick," a well-known house of ill repute that stood behind the Anaconda Saloon and to the west on Cover Street. Some local historians further believe that patrons rented McKeen's tiny furnished rooms above the dining room by the hour as often as they rented them overnight. While customers may have rented rooms occasionally for such purposes, it seems unlikely that McKeen himself operated an illicit business since he prominently advertised his "furnished rooms" in the *Madisonian Times*. Besides, McKeen was a city alderman, an active hardworking member of the local Eagles lodge, respected and well liked by his fellow citizens. However, prostitution across Montana went underground during World War I and Prohibition. During the 1920s when maps and directories show the building as vacant, such activity in the hotel could have been ongoing.

If the small-statured McKeen had a fault, it was that he was a man whose temper sometimes got the better of him. Virginia City author Dick Pace tells in his book, *Golden Gulch*, how a local miner known as Old Sim came into town to pay his bills and take a bath. Sipping blackberry brandy at the Anaconda Saloon, Old Sim discovered that the floor of McKeen's bar was not nailed down. He could lift it up at one end and rattle the bottles and glassware. Old Sim thought this was great sport, but McKeen didn't see the humor. When Old Sim would not stop, a furious McKeen broke a pool cue over his head. Old Sim persisted in bouncing the bar floor, so McKeen hit him again. With that, brawny Old Sim gathered McKeen in his arms, carried him outside, and dropped him on the boardwalk. Stepping over him, Old Sim remarked that he would have left the bar if McKeen had only asked him nicely. These kinds of situations were not uncommon, and McKeen was always prepared for a bad outcome—he kept his own coffin stored in the basement just in case.

Prohibition substantially changed local business dealings when Montana went dry at the end of 1918. At the first of November before laws prohibiting the sale of alcohol went into effect, McKeen advertised the sale of his stock of liquor in the *Madisonian Times*. "Buy Wine, Rum, and Gin Now," the advertisement read. "This is your last chance. Never again will you be able to buy at the price I am asking." For McKeen and others whose livelihood was tending Montana's numerous lucrative bars, Prohibition was a bitter pill to swallow. With the end of 1918, the Anaconda Saloon was officially no more. The following May, McKeen was helping workmen build a chicken house in the yard of his home on Cover Street. That evening he was stricken with a sudden chill. Influenza set in and a few days later it developed into pneumonia. He died on May 23, 1919, a late casualty of the deadly 1918 flu epidemic. Amanda, bereft, lasted a few years before she took her own life by shooting herself in the head, committing the act in the bathtub of the McKeens' Cover Street home in 1923. The bathtub remains in use in the house.

After the deaths of Frank and Amanda McKeen, the deteriorating Anaconda Hotel passed through a number of owners. In 1935 Humphrey's Gold Corporation acquired the building and constructed an annex next door to the east. The original bar room was dismantled and outfitted with bunk beds to accommodate dredging crews who brought about a brief resurgence in Virginia City's population. Then in 1942, the U.S. government declared gold mining a nonessential industry under the Gold Mine Closing Order. Operations shut down, and the hotel again fell vacant.

Charles and Sue Bovey began buying the dilapidated gold rush era buildings in Virginia City and Nevada City in the 1940s. They purchased the Anaconda Hotel in 1946 and remodeled it, lowering the sixteen-foot bar room ceiling to create a second story over the building's front end. They installed a new façade patterned after the historic Goodrich House in Anaconda, and added a fire escape for the annex fashioned from the metal stairway of a dredge boat. Preservation of the building's precious old parts, construction of new pieces to look old, and the reuse of material like the dredge's stairway are excellent examples of the Bovey legacy. Preservation of the old layers and creation of new ones allow visitors to "read" the different phases of the town's history.

The Boveys named their hotel the Fairweather Inn after Bill Fairweather, the discoverer of gold in Alder Gulch. Fairweather was a colorful and tragic figure, an example of good fortune gone awry. In company with a party of miners on May 26, 1863, Fairweather panned the first gold while his companions bedded down the horses and cooked dinner. It was he who named Alder Gulch for the trees that grew along the banks of the stream. His companions named the area the Fairweather Mining District and the gulch made him rich, but to Fairweather, the gold meant little. It is said that he would ride up and down the streets of Virginia City, scattering his gold nuggets in the streets to see the children and the Chinese, of whom there were a substantial number, scramble for them. He mixed gold dust in his

Parlor of the Fairweather Inn
COURTESY MONTANA HISTORICAL SOCIETY PHOTOGRAPH ARCHIVES 956-240

horse's oats, saying that nothing was too good for Old Antelope, the horse that brought him such good luck. But Fairweather died penniless of too much whiskey and hard living in 1875. He was not yet forty years old. Mrs. Pete Daly of the Daly Ranch cared for him in his last days at nearby Robber's Roost. A diet of gold dust did Fairweather's horse, Old Antelope, no harm. He long outlived his master, enjoying the Ruby Valley pasture of E. F. Johnson into extreme old age. Fairweather lies in Hillside Cemetery, a windswept burial ground overlooking Alder Gulch where an iron fence surrounds his grave. A recent marker credits him with the Alder Gulch discovery.

Guests can enjoy the hospitality of the historic Fairweather Inn during the summer tourist season, but most times of the year, the building stands cold and empty. The hotel lobby, ladies' parlor, office, side hallway, and public restrooms occupy what was once McKeen's spacious bar room. Upstairs, rooms 8, 9, 10, and 11 of the present hotel are McKeen's original hotel rooms. Archaeologist Cathy Bickenheuser, a member of the building preservation crew in 2002 and 2003, says that state employees doing maintenance and preservation work in the unheated, empty building during the off-season found unlocked hotel room doors that locked by themselves. When workers were in the basement, the sounds of someone stomping up and down the halls sometimes disturbed the quiet. Since the 1950s, there have been numerous reports of "bad energy" hovering in the back stairwell. A desk clerk reported that she heard a tremendous racket overhead in Room 10, Sue Bovey's favorite room. When the clerk unlocked the door to the unoccupied guest room, she discovered bedding and towels scattered and furniture overturned. One guest checked into Room 10 late one night, tired from a long day's travel and looking forward to a good night's rest. He went upstairs. Not long after, the guest returned to the desk with his bags packed. He checked out with no explanation. And state workers discovered an unpleasant surprise in Room 12 at the end of the season that they did not find in any of the other rooms: hundreds of dead flies lined the windowsill. Some believe an abundance of these annoying pests are evidence of supernatural activity.

Because of the tales about the Fairweather Inn and the Elling House, Fox Family decided upon these two sites as the locations for filming the segment. The story line was that Jaena and Chris had dared each other to spend three hours in the supposedly haunted locations. Whoever made it to midnight won the dare. The game allowed each participant one candle, one stationary camera, and a lighted night-vision camera to carry around. Each was instructed to explore with the night-vision camera. While Chris experienced what he described as the blood-curdling screech of a cat, he was mostly bored during the three hours he spent in the Elling House. Jaena's experience, however, was just the opposite.

Her "home base" was Room 10, Sue Bovey's favorite room upstairs in the Fairweather Inn. The crew instructed her to explore the rooms freely, especially the basement where staff had previously experienced unexplained events. The game began promptly at nine with Jaena in Room 10. A winter chill, bone-cold as it can be in Virginia City in the dead of winter, had settled into the old building. It was pitch dark except for the candle on the nightstand next to the bed and the flashlight apparatus on the night-vision camera. Jaena was unafraid and unconcerned, not anticipating anything out of the ordinary. She made up her mind to tough out the dark and the cold, figuring those discomforts would be the evening's only challenges. Dressed warmly in long johns and a heavy parka, she was confident that she could win the dare.

She said to herself, "O.K. So I had better get started exploring." Deciding first to take a walk down the upstairs hallway, she opened the door and stepped out of the room. Jaena slowly moved down the hallway, checking out the other rooms. The door to each of the rooms lining the hall stood open, and she could see inside as she passed by each one. She moved past Room 12 and the public restroom, past Rooms 14 and 15. Nothing at all was amiss.

"This is no big deal," she thought to herself. "Even if I do see a ghost, so what? Nothing is going to happen."

As Jaena approached Rooms 16 and 17, she heard something rustling. She stopped, cocked her head to one side, listening. The sound came from the rooms to either side. As a person sometimes knows when she is being followed, Jaena sensed that something was behind her. She whirled around. She saw nothing there, but yet she could feel something. It was weird. She began to feel uneasy and started down the hall back to Room 10. As she took a few steps, she heard the same peculiar rustling noise in the hallway behind her. Glancing back, again she saw nothing, but instinctively Jaena knew that something was there. Whatever it was made a "swishy" sound like someone in wind pants walking right behind her. Swish, swish, swish, swish. Jaena began to move faster, and as she did so, the swishing moved with her, keeping pace. By the time she reached Room 10, Jaena was running, trying to get away. She spun into the room and slammed the door. Swish, swish, Swish, SWISH. She heard it approaching and felt a wave of anger emanate from whatever, whoever, it was. The anger washed over her, and it was very unpleasant. The entity, or spirit, or ghost—Jaena now shivered at the thought—stopped just on the other side of the door. She was breathing hard and was afraid. As she stood there with only a door between her and the anger pulsing through the wood, she tried to collect her thoughts. She did not anticipate what happened next. She felt, with great relief, whatever it was suddenly leave. She knew as surely as she had known that it was there, that it—whatever it was—had left the hallway. Jaena cautiously opened the door. Nothing there, nothing at all, only the dark.

"This is going to be a long night," Jaena thought to herself. "I might as well try the basement now and get it over with. Surely this is enough for one evening and nothing else will happen."

With her camera in one hand and her other hand against the stair rail, Jaena felt her way down the stairs to the first floor, taking one step at a time in the dark. The camera's light cast an eerie circle of illumination, but beyond the circle, Jaena could see absolutely nothing in the blackness. She reached the ground floor and the space that used to be the dining room. "So far, so good," Jaena said to herself. "On to the basement."

Pausing for a moment at the top of the basement stairs, Jaena adjusted the light in her one hand and felt her way along the wall with the other. She took one stair, then another. Suddenly the light blipped out and she could see absolutely nothing.

"Oh my God!" Jaena screamed. She screamed again and again and again, as the sound of her own frenzied screaming fed her panic. Crewmembers rushed in, bringing the comforting circle of light that a moment before had suddenly gone out. They took the camera from Jaena's grip, checked it out, and asked her why she had turned it off.

"Turned it off? Turned it off? I didn't turn it off," she argued. How crazy would that be, to turn the camera off heading down into the basement!

However, the crew showed Jaena that the light had been switched to the OFF position. Later, Jaena tried to reason out what could have happened. There was no way she could have turned it off by mistake. The camera was awkward; she could barely handle it with one hand. To turn the light off, Jaena would have had to hold it with one hand and turn the switch to OFF with the other. She had been midway down the basement stairs, with the camera in one hand and feeling her way with the other. There was simply no way she could have turned it off, but something had to have moved the switch.

Shaken but still game, Jaena was not going to give up. She assured the technicians that she was okay and went back to Room 10. This time, however, she decided that there would be no more exploring. This time, she would stay in Room 10 until the clock struck midnight and the crew came to get her. Jaena sat on the bed, trying not to think about the terrible fright she had just experienced. But whoever, or whatever, it was, had not yet finished. As she sat on the bed, a succession of quick, very loud raps made her jump. Glancing at the nightstand not two feet away where the candle still burned, she heard RAP! RAP! RAP! It seemed to come from the nightstand. Jaena saw the candle shake, or flinch, as if in response to something sharply striking the edge of the stand.

As the end of the eventful evening drew near, Jaena thought about how good it would be to step outside the hotel and have the warmth of her waiting family and friends surround her. It had been a harrowing adventure, but the Fairweather Inn and those who walk its cold, deserted hallway had still one more trick. Sitting there on the bed in Room 10, waiting for midnight, Jaena heard a familiar sound, out of place in the old hotel. From somewhere in the depths of the basement came the unmistakable rumble of a bowling ball.

On reflection, Jaena wonders who the spirits might be that inhabit the Fairweather Inn. She has no doubt that they are there. She felt very vulnerable on that cold, dark winter night, seeing herself as an intruder disturbing someone's winter sleep. Whoever it was did not want her there and the anger was nearly overwhelming. Jaena is also convinced that the "swishing" spirit was a woman. Perhaps it was a lady of the evening, come to fetch her fee. Perhaps it was Amanda, checking up on her husband, in long silk skirts and stiff petticoats that swished when she walked. Or maybe it was Sue Bovey, who liked to occasionally dress in Victorian period clothing. Room 10, after all, had been her favorite. Asked if Jaena would repeat the experience given the chance she emphatically replies, "No! Definitely not! It was not a friendly spirit in there that night. It was angry, and what followed me down that hallway made me feel unsafe."

As for the bowling ball, it turns out that such an oddity may not be out of character at the Fairweather Inn. The historic Sanborn-Perris Fire Insurance Maps of Virginia City clearly show that Frank McKeen offered his patrons a variety of options. Food, drink, furnished rooms, billiards, pool, and one other entertainment. In 1904 the basement is clearly labeled "bowling alley."

Sources

Sanborn-Perris Fire Insurance Maps and building curator John Ellingsen of Virginia City supplied much of the building information. Additional sources include Dick Pace's *Golden Gulch;* Frank McKeen's obituary in the *Madisonian Times,* May 23, 1919; Amanda McKeen's obituary in the *Madisonian Times,* March 30, 1923. See also the MHS Library Research Center vertical file on Bill Fairweather. For more ghost stories about places in Virginia City, including the McKeen House, the Nevada City Hotel and the Elling House, see the author's *Spirit Tailings: Ghost Tales from Virginia City, Butte and Helena.*

SPIRITED VICTORIAN CHARMER

It was moving-in day. For the past six months, contractor Mark Estep had put his heart and soul into restoring the house. He, his wife Susan, and their four-year-old son, Drew, were now ready to settle into what reporter Mea Andrews of the *Missoulian* dubbed in 1986 a "spirited Victorian charmer." The house was so wonderful, so beautiful, so very old-fashioned and roomy, the Esteps could hardly believe how the home had evolved from the shell that it had been months before. After years of decay, and several recent owners, each of whom left contributions to its present incarnation, the Esteps had come along and vowed to the neighbors to complete in six months the work others had begun more than a decade before. It had been a long road paved with hard work, expense, and setbacks, but now, right on target, the house was ready for a family.

The family's pets—two dogs and three cats—clamored in with the furniture to check out their new abode. The Esteps' black cat, Jack, stalked about tentatively. He planted himself in the entryway, craning his neck upward as if to get the full effect of the open turret. It added a grand openness, soaring unrestricted several stories up to the peak of its pointed roof. Jack then did something the Esteps had never heard him do before. He opened his mouth and out came the most piercing yowl they had ever heard. It reverberated through the house, bouncing first to the top of the turret, then off the walls, echoing eerily through the rooms upstairs and down. The cat let the sound flow. It came from somewhere deep within his sleek little body, like a singer's high note that comes, not from the throat, but from the diaphragm. Mark and Susan considered the possibilities and decided Jack was obviously enjoying himself. When he had finished with his concert, he sauntered off looking smug, as if to say, "This place is all right!" It was a perfect christening for the Esteps' new home.

Jack's behavior was perfect for several reasons. This was no ordinary house, but one with a nationally recognized haunted reputation. And it was not just any haunted house, with a benign spook or cold spots or slamming doors. This was a house that for years was a blight on the neighborhood, that cast such a dark shadow over the homeowners on the block that they tried to have it razed.

The house had a normal beginning. For the better part of its first fifty years, 319 South Fifth Street West on Missoula's Southside was a quiet, respectable member of a quiet, tree-lined neighborhood near the historic campus of The University of Montana. William J. and Sarah Kendall, along with their sons Robert and Francis, bought the lot in 1899 from the Missoula Land Company. The Kendalls operated the Northwest Milling and Lumber Company and built the house on speculation using the best of their materials. From its rubblestone foundation, sturdy frame walls, and intersecting gables to the top of its round turret, the Kendalls made sure the home would long stand. Family members lived there a few years, taking their time to finish the inside to perfection. It was indeed a showplace, with leaded windows, stained glass, beautiful interior wood finishing, and a spacious yard with an apple tree. A two-story stable and carriage house opened onto the alley at the rear.

In 1902 Elizabeth Scheuch (pronounced "Shoy") purchased the house. Mrs. Scheuch's husband, the late Frederick H. Scheuch, was U. S. consul to Barcelona, Spain, from 1873 to 1893. Her husband had passed away and she came to Missoula to join her son Frederick C., a professor at the university. Professor Scheuch was one of the first instructors hired at the newly created state university. He had grown up abroad, attended the best schools in Germany and Spain, and served as his father's secretary. With a recent engineering degree from Purdue University in hand and experience teaching college French, the university hired Professor Scheuch first to teach mechanical engineering. In 1898 he married Jimmie Straughn and shifted his teaching from engineering to French and German. He and Jimmie eventually had two children, Natalia and Straughn, who grew up in the Southside neighborhood. The Scheuch household included the family of four, the elder Mrs. Scheuch, and a household maid.

Professor Scheuch was a revered professor and a familiar figure around campus. Known fondly as "Prof," he had an active and distinguished career and long served as the university's vice president. He stepped in as interim president many times—1908, 1912, 1915-1917, 1921, and 1935—during his lengthy tenure. Scheuch's many campus activities and contributions included helping to found the student newspaper, *Montana Kaimin*. The Professor was also an active member of Sigma Chi fraternity and helped found the University of Montana's chapter.

As the children entered high school, Jimmie Scheuch suffered heart-related health problems. At the insistence of her doctors, she spent much time recovering in Texas. In 1919, the Scheuchs' daughter Natalia was at home with her father and grandmother while her older brother Straughn attended the Kentucky Military Institute finishing his secondary education. While there he suffered a severe bout of pneumonia in April 1919 at the height of the Spanish Flu epidemic but seemed to recover well.

After graduation and following a visit to his mother in Texas, eighteen-year-old Straughn returned to Missoula to enroll as a freshman at Montana State University (now The University of Montana) in the fall of 1919. He pledged Sigma Chi, his father's fraternity. Straughn was a good marksman, excelling at the rifle range. On February 3, 1920, he was acting as an instructor in rifle practice for the Reserve Officers' Training Corps. Marcus Cook Hall, later demolished, had an indoor firing range where students practiced marksmanship. He was lying on the floor helping students when gases caused by the burned gunpowder overcame him. Officials rushed him to the university hospital. The fire department administered oxygen and Straughn initially recovered, but later that night he took a turn for the worse and died.

Doctors determined that the young man's heart had been weakened from his recent illness and the choking gases were too much of a strain. Captain A. C. Cron, commandant of the university's reserve program, said that in all his army experience, this was the first time he had ever seen anyone overcome by powder fumes. Only fifty-one rounds of .22-caliber had been fired over a ninety-minute period, and all the windows in the building were open. The sudden and rather bizarre death of the professor's son—tall, handsome, well liked, and active on campus—was a tragedy that touched the entire academic community.

After Straughn's death, Jimmie Scheuch recovered her health and assumed her place in the household, caring for her aging mother-in-law. Faculty and their wives knew Jimmie as a gracious hostess with a flair for warm hospitality. The Scheuchs frequently welcomed friends into their lovely home on South Fifth Street West.

By 1934 daughter Natalia had long ago married and the Scheuchs' household was pleasantly quiet. On a warm July evening as a gentle breeze ruffled the leaves of the backyard apple tree, the elderly Mrs. Scheuch, who had been enjoying relatively good health, died quite suddenly; she was eighty-five. Less than a year later, in April of 1935, the professor was still mourning the loss of his mother when Jimmie died, also quite suddenly. Both she and her husband had suffered bouts of influenza, and the professor was still at St. Patrick's Hospital, bedridden with pleurisy. Jimmie had been fine the previous afternoon, visiting her husband as usual. But in the wee hours of the following morning, she had a heart attack. The doctor came promptly and thought she would soon recover, but within an hour a second attack quickly claimed Jimmie's life.

Professor Scheuch retired from teaching in June 1936 and sold the long-time family home on South Fifth Street West. He moved to Battle Creek, Michigan, and remarried, but returned frequently to visit the campus he loved. The university bestowed upon him the title "President Emeritus," and "Prof" delivered the commencement address in 1938. When he died in 1954, *The Daily Missoulian* eulogized the man, saying that "Prof" was always available for counsel and sought after by students of all circumstance. Throughout his career, he was never too busy to praise his students for their accomplishments. His great enthusiasm for all youth kept him young in spirit and outlook despite the infirmities of old age. As a long-tenured and original member of the university faculty, his passing in many ways marked the end of an era, and in part for this reason, his home is considered historically significant. However, Professor Scheuch's longtime ownership is not why the house is so well known.

Valentine and Caroline Jacky briefly held the title to the Scheuch home from 1937 to 1939, but they never lived in the house. The Zakos family first rented the property from the Jackys and later bought it in 1939. James Zakos was a native of Greece who immigrated to the United States in 1913. After operating a chili parlor in Butte, he married Eleanor Barker in 1922 and the couple made their home in Missoula. Zakos was the longtime owner of Jim's Café, a local fixture. Jim and Eleanor Zakos raised eight children, many of them in the house at 319 South Fifth Street West. The beginning of their occupancy dates to an important time in James Zakos' life. He became a United States citizen in 1937, and was especially proud of this fact. Zakos was a conscientious businessman who brought a zealous work ethic to his small cafe. He spent long hours taking care of his customers.

The Zakos' house was tranquil, at least as tranquil as a home with many children can be until the day in the 1940s when Eleanor Zakos first heard the screams. She, her sister Henriette Lambros, and the Zakos' infant son, Steve, (or in some versions, it was daughter Mary) were in the house. Mrs. Zakos recalled in a 1980 interview with Steve Smith of the *Missoulian* that "The scream started low and kept getting higher and higher until it split the wall. Then it stopped, and then it started again. There were two screams—they were shrieks—and it was a woman's voice." Jim and Eleanor searched for the source of the screams, but they could never discover what caused the bizarre and recurring sound. They called the police, the fire department, electricians, and plumbers but nothing could explain it. It recurred at random times, in the middle of the day or the middle of the night. The screams seemed to emanate from the walls of the house, and the family was terrified in the knowledge that the sounds were always there, waiting to be unleashed, but they never knew what triggered them. The family did not want to move, so the Zakoses had no choice but to live with the awful noise.

Henriette Lambros' husband, John, became ill, and doctors diagnosed a terminal illness. For spiritual comfort, her sister Eleanor introduced her to Reverend Andrew Landin, minister of Light of the World Tabernacle, whose church was a few blocks away from the Zakos' home. Landin, reverend at the Missoula church from about 1954 to 1960, was known for his healing and compassion. After John died in 1956, the sisters told the reverend about the screams. He offered to perform an exorcism in the house to remove what he believed to be an evil spirit, or spirits. The entire family was there, and according to Smith's 1980 account in the *Missoulian,* a childhood friend of Mary's was also present. The girls were in their early teens at the time. Holding hands, everyone moved in a group from room to room while Landin prayed. The friend, Laurice Roark Fritz, remembered little about the exorcism except that, "Us kids had the living crap scared out of us." Eleanor Zakos claimed the ritual was successful, and the family never again heard the screams. But the incident became a nationally publicized event when years later, in 1975, Henriette wrote an article published in the August issue of *Fate* magazine describing the family's unsettling experiences and the exorcism. The beautiful house on South Fifth Street West, with its graceful turret and Victorian charm, thereafter became known as the "House of Screams."

After publication of the article, the Zakos family seemingly enjoyed their home's reputation, and—consciously or unconsciously—promoted its haunted image. As the years went by, the Scheuch's once well-tended Victorian home began to look the part of a house tormented. As Jim and Eleanor

Spirited Victorian Charmer in 1990
COURTESY MONTANA STATE HISTORIC PRESERVATION OFFICE

Zakos grew older and retired, the house deteriorated. Things broken went unrepaired, trash collected in the yard, and spiders spun their webs in the corners of the windows. The family rejected the city's weekly garbage pickup and instead began storing their trash in the carriage house at the back of the lot. The apple tree suffered neglect and the shrubs grew spindly and died. The weeping birch in the front yard was a favorite perch for ravens and crows. On nights when the moon was full and its light spilled over Mount Sentinel behind the house, the tree with huge black birds perched among its weeping branches made a startling picture. Even in daylight, with the yard devoid of anything green, the house looked haunted.

Cats, dozens of them in various stages of sickness and starvation, roamed the premises. Some neighbors always believed the cats explained the screams that the Zakos family originally heard. But as word spread of the exorcism and noises that supposedly reverberated through the very walls of the house, stories about the house multiplied. *Old Mrs. Scheuch was elderly*, they said, *maybe she had been abused*, they said. *Maybe her family was horrible to her*, they said. *Maybe she died and no one cared. Maybe she is screaming for revenge.*

Other stories written in the house itself added to the tales. Most of the Zakos children, hellions according to the neighbors, married and moved away. Daughter Mary moved away also, but after a disastrous marriage and travel in Germany, she returned to live in her parents' home. Mary, a free-lance writer of lurid confession horror stories, had her own demons.

Mary said she sensed a presence in her second-floor bedroom and saw writing on the walls. "It looks like names and phone numbers," she told *Missoulian* reporter Steve Smith. "When I see that writing, it scares me. It's weird. I'm afraid it's some kind of warning." She gave up driving because she feared an accident, but still smoked two packs of cigarettes a day. Four to six hours every day in a first-floor room of the house, Mary pecked away at her electric typewriter cranking out a story a week on her favorite topics: fear, maniacs, manic-depressives, and vampires. One story, on the average, netted her fifty dollars from such magazines as *Secret Romance, True Love, Intimate Story,* and *True Confessions*. These magazines published her stories under pseudonyms. When she wasn't writing, she spent her time watching horror movies on HBO. Mary said herself that her psychiatrist of nine years told her that she was crazy.

Mary also told the *Missoulian* that she embarked upon her chosen career because she was driven to write. Her imagination needed an outlet, she couldn't sleep, and she felt as if she were going to burst. "It was either write or commit suicide," Mary told the reporter.

Then in 1985, in the upstairs bedroom where she saw writing on the walls, Mary took a lethal combination of drugs and died of an overdose. Eleanor Zakos, widowed in 1983, left everything in the house—furniture, her children's personal items, family papers, and the noisy unwanted cats. She moved to a nursing home where she lived another decade. Neighbors set traps for the cats, helping the authorities round them up. Some say there were perhaps twelve or fifteen, but neighbors who helped trap them say the number was closer to thirty.

The deteriorated "spirited Victorian charmer" went on the market. A prospective buyer toured the house with a person who claimed psychic abilities. According to Mea Andrews' subsequent 1986 article, he sensed "perverted violence and sex" and the spirit of a hateful old woman who died there and was not found for a while, reminiscent again of the old tales. But while Elizabeth Scheuch was an old woman, she was not alone when she died, and by all accounts she was a lovely person. Jimmie Scheuch died in the house too, but under the care of a physician. Threads of Straughn's death, long forgotten with the passage of time, became woven into the tales as well as less connected stories of murder, backyard burials, and even a German butcher who put his wife through a sausage mill. It's true that the professor taught German, and that Mary Zakos traveled extensively in Germany. And of course Mary's life was a tragedy lived out within the walls of the house. But these twisted tales seem much more fantastic than the thread of truth that can be found behind them. Like a house children avoid on Halloween because of lurid tales told by older siblings, the house on South Fifth Street West had acquired a history that was not its own.

Attorney Wally Congdon bought the "House of Screams" in 1987. The first of several to contribute to its ultimate preservation, Congdon removed dumpsters full of trash from the house, salvaged floors, and jacked up the carriage house hoping to save it as well. But the structure had to be demolished and, according to neighbors, when the building came down, a huge population of mice poured out to infest the neighborhood. The neighbors by this time had understandably had enough of trash, cats, mice, and salvage. Even Congdon admits that the property was a disaster with only one window unbroken in the entire house. It was an open invitation to vandals and a danger to children. Neighbors tried to have the building razed.

But Congdon persisted. During his ownership, he collected pieces from around the state for later use on the house. He salvaged doors and trim from Missoula's demolished Smith Hotel and the Victorian Building, a chandelier from the Anaconda Hotel, and Honduran teak and holly wood parquet floors still in their century-old boxes from the Chicago International Trade Fair discovered in Philipsburg. Architects John Biddell and Steve Adler redesigned the house to its original appearance, Congdon gave it a new foundation, and Frank Peterson did the reframing. Congdon then sold the house to Tinsley Pfrimmer, a local house painter who had always admired it. Pfrimmer did more than paint. She repointed the foundation, reframed the windows using salvaged pine from a mill near Wallace, Idaho, and did the glazing work. Pfrimmer hired Brynn Holt to replace the roof and act as foreman during much of the exterior restoration.

During the six months he worked there, Brynn lived at the house. He heard the stories about the Zakos family and the exorcism, and the hints at its unsavory, albeit mostly manufactured, history. The only reason he does not claim the house was haunted is for lack of evidence. He does say that it was a creepy place to live, barely a shell of a house at that point with no interior walls. Brynn has restored many historic homes, and such places, he says, always have a feel about them, "These places in progress are always creepy. You can sense the lingering presence of former occupants," he said. This house was no exception and he had one memorable, frightening experience there.

Late one evening he sensed a change in the air. It grew cold around him. His adrenaline and heart rate surged, his skin prickled, his hair stood on end, and he felt a nearness of something, a presence. He jumped up, assumed a defensive posture, and cried out, "Here I am! Bring it on! I am not afraid of you!" As if in response, a horrible ear-piercing scream answered his challenge. The scream had come from the back stairway and it reverberated through the house. Brynn bounded to the stairway, and there on the landing where the steps turned were two black cats. They whirled around from their fracas, blinking at him, and scrambled away. He had never seen them around before, and he never saw them again. He can't say for certain that the bloodcurdling sound came from the cats, but he says the experience was "beyond weird."

When the Esteps bought the house from Pfrimmer in 1998, it was finished outside and structurally sound, but still a shell with no walls, no wiring, no plumbing, and nothing growing in the yard. Mark went to work fulltime on the project, finishing the interior and making it habitable, earning a well-deserved preservation award in the process. Today the home is gorgeous, with an enlarged kitchen and spacious rooms that seem to radiate its owners' enthusiasm. Susan's tasteful decorating is colorful but understated, and reflects her own love for the house and its past. Mark has an office tucked in the former maid's room off the kitchen. Hanging prominently on one wall is the carved nameplate that once hung over Professor Scheuch's office at the university, a poignant reminder of the home's prestigious history.

Houseguests stay in the room where Mary Zakos met her demons. It is difficult to believe that the charming room with its slanted ceiling, window seat, and treetop views ever frightened anyone. Mark says, with a grin, "We always make sure our guests know the story." The Esteps treasure a few pieces of furniture left behind by the Scheuchs, and deep within the house is a special, secret passageway that Drew has claimed as his own. The chandelier Congdon rescued from the Anaconda Hotel hangs over the stairwell, casting its light to the pointed roof of the turret, and the apple tree out back shades a new deck. Today the historic Scheuch Home is a vital component of Missoula's Southside Historic District, listed in the National Register of Historic Places in 1991. It is a fairytale ending to the sad story of the regal Queen Anne style home.

While the Esteps don't entirely discount the notion that spirits can inhabit houses, they don't believe the stories about their own home. They have seen no unexplained shadows, heard no screams in the walls, and felt no cold spots. Jack the cat's peculiar behavior on moving day, for the Estep family, is enough to explain the House of Screams. And if not, Missoula artist Kent Epler crafted a beautiful little house, much like a birdhouse on a pole, that graces the Esteps' yard. In keeping with the Brahmin belief that a spirit house provides a home for spirits of the household, the Esteps take special care of it, just in case.

Sources

The many articles and stories about the House of Screams include the *Missoulian,* March 16, 1980; September 7, 1986; July 7, 1987; and a chapter in Debra Munn's *Big Sky Ghosts,* Volume II. Straughn Scheuch's untimely death is recorded in the *Missoulian* February 3, 1920, with a follow up February 4, 1920. An editorial eulogizing Professor Scheuch and discussing his contributions appeared in the *Missoulian* on January 19, 1954. The *Missoulian* noted Mrs. Scheuch's death on July 5, 1934 and Jimmie Scheuch's death on April 17, 1935. Judy and John Holbrook graciously contributed additional information for this story.

THE ADAMS HOTEL

R aymond Barry is passionate about history and historic architecture. He came to Montana from the West Coast because he was tired of what he calls "insanity in California." Although his roots were there where his family settled in 1902, Raymond grew weary of the commercialism he saw around him at every turn. By the time he was ten, familiar landmarks had fallen to the wrecking ball and very little remained of his childhood neighborhood. It seemed to Raymond that California lacked appreciation of its past and he observed few attempts at preservation of its historic buildings, so in 2000 he decided to look for another place to call home. He found it in The Adams Hotel in the tiny turn-of-the-twentieth-century community of Lavina, nestled in Montana's Golden Valley County some forty miles north of Billings. Although the tiny community has a population of only about one hundred and fifty, it has a large history.

"Old" Lavina was a ranching community that grew at the endpoint of the annual spring and fall roundups. It was there along the Musselshell River where cowboys and stockmen of Montana's vast cattle and sheep ranches gathered at the end of their seasonal drives. By the spring of 1882, Fort Benton businessman and future U.S. Senator T.C. Power observed the swift westward progress of the Northern Pacific and founded the Billings-Benton Stage Line to link the two important communities. Power dispatched Walter Burke and a construction crew to ready the 220-mile stretch of road. They established seventeen stations before the tracks reached Billings in August 1882. At the best crossing place along the Musselshell River, the crew built stables, accommodations, and a saloon. Burke christened the stage stop "Lavina" after his current sweetheart. In 1885 the stage line built a steel bridge across the river, and for the next two decades, Lavina was a hub where freighters and travelers paused to change horses, have a drink or a meal, or get a good night's rest.

Rancher Ludwig C. "Louie" Lehfeldt was an energetic, forceful man with a bushy handlebar mustache and distinctive blue eyes that revealed a forceful personality. Although he was ambitious, Louie was a kindly man who charmed the ladies and was a good provider for his wife, Julia, and their six children. One of the largest stock raisers in the region, Louie owned 38,000 acres in the Musselshell Valley. And he was always looking for sound business opportunities.

The Adams Hotel
COURTESY MONTANA HISTORICAL SOCIETY PHOTOGRAPH ARCHIVES PAC 96-82 MM1

As the Milwaukee Road Company built a line across Montana, the company scouted for places to build its depots. Officials considered the townsite of old Lavina, but sitting nearly on the river, it was not a choice location. John Q. Adams, company vice president, selected a new townsite a mile downstream where a bend in the river provided ample room for expansion. He purchased Louie Lehfeldt's ranch for $100,000 and located new Lavina on part of it. The first train rumbled into the townsite on February 16, 1908. Louie already operated a stage line between Billings and Lavina. A hotel catering to railroad travelers was essential to the new town and so his friend Adams deeded four lots back to him along the tracks opposite the depot.

Architects Link and Haire—designers of the 1910 Montana State Capitol wings—drew the plans for the Colonial Revival style hotel, completed for $20,000 in the fall of 1908. Louie named the white-painted monument with its towered roofline after his friend, John Q. Adams. The Adams' main entrance faced Main Street, but a secondary north entrance faced the railroad tracks and depot. This mirrored the main façade, welcoming passengers as the trains pulled into town. The grand two-story hostelry became the center of local hospitality.

The Adams boasted steam heat, gas lighting, first class service, a fully stocked bar with the finest liquors and cigars, hot baths, and twenty-two rooms. Actually, there were only twenty-one rooms since superstition and protocol demanded that the room numbers skip from 12 to 14; there was no Room 13. Each guest room was beautifully appointed with carpeting, nice furnishings, and a matching china washbowl and pitcher for the convenience of the guests. Pure linen sheets and down comforters promised a good night's rest even in the coldest winter weather. Once settled at the hotel, stage passengers, rail travelers, and other guests enjoyed fine meals prepared in the kitchen at the back. The spacious central dining room was popular among guests, local ranchers, and Lavina residents. A ladies' parlor at the top of the stairs awaited guests who wished to quietly read or catch up on letter writing. There was often dancing in the hotel lobby after dinner.

The hotel opened with a gala dance in the dining room on November 6, 1908. Louie's daughter, Clara, was sixteen. It was a momentous occasion, made even more memorable since it was at this dance that the lovely Clara met C. B. Egge, the man she later married. Clara was a beautiful, captivating, and popular young lady who had many young men coming to call. At this time C. B. was twenty years old and was working hard to improve the homestead he had recently claimed. He also worked at the hotel, bartending for Clara's father. Although this proximity put C. B. at a distinct advantage as her suitor, it was not until 1916 that the couple married. The wedding was held at the gracious Lehfeldt family home in Billings, preserved today as the Josephine Bed and Breakfast. The Egges had four children, enjoyed a long married life, and celebrated their fiftieth wedding anniversary in 1966 in the dining room of the Adams Hotel. C. B. died in 1971 and Clara in 1975.

The homestead boom in the 1910s was a heady time for the little town as it flourished with the activity the Milwaukee Road generated. In 1911 Louie Lehfeldt expanded his accommodations, building the Adams Annex across Main Street. The progressive little town could boast of three telephones in

1913; one of them was at the Adams Livery, one was at the Slayton Mercantile, and the third was at The Adams Hotel. The exchange was located in the hotel lobby; Hilda Lehfeldt—Louie's second daughter—was Lavina's first telephone operator. Like her sister Clara, Hilda met her future husband at the hotel. She and Oscar Zahn were married at the family home in Billings. Their wedding reception was held at The Adams a few days later on April 29, 1916. Oscar Zahn and Clara's husband C. B. Egge not only worked together at the hotel, they were great friends as well as brothers-in-law. Zahn was an artist whose stenciling once adorned several of the upstairs guest rooms.

The hotel did a brisk business as the trains rumbled into the depot and screeched to a halt, unloading the homesteaders that flocked into Montana. Business boomed. The hotel converted to electricity in 1917 and the town incorporated in 1920. Lavina took pride in its nickname, "The White City," a name bestowed on the town by its physician, Dr. Hugh Heaton, in 1911. The buildings along Main Street were at that time all painted fresh white, like The Adams Hotel.

Drought, crop failures, and bank closures prompted an exodus of disappointed, destitute homesteaders during the 1920s. Montana lost population, and The Adams Hotel struggled to survive. Its annex across the street became the Clermont Hotel. Mrs. E.C. Olcott, who kept the Clermont's rooms, served her guests homemade bread and first-class home cooked meals. It was less grand, but more comfortable, easier to heat, and suited a less pretentious clientele than The Adams had a decade before. The Adams began to deteriorate, and few guests climbed the stairway to stay in its once-opulent rooms. By the mid-1920s, the hotel was closed to visitors, but family members and caretakers lived there off and on.

Over the years The Adams saw characters come and go. Among them was Emanuel Dolt whose years of service earned him Louie's permission to keep a room after the hotel closed. Emanuel was a bachelor who came to the United States from Switzerland in 1902. He arrived in Montana in 1910 and took up a homestead twelve miles north of Lavina. He later sold the property and moved to town where he cooked for the hotel, for the Lehfeldts, and for other local families after the hotel closed. He loved art and music, was an accomplished pianist, and everyone in the community knew and loved "Manny." The Lehfeldt grandchildren especially adored him, nicknaming him "Dolty." He always had time for them, listened to their troubles, and treated them with respect. During those lean, uncertain times after the hotel closed, Dolt lived at The Adams in Room 2, watching over the empty, unheated shell of a building that had been so warm and hospitable in times past.

Throughout those winters of the 1920s, Dolt's life was solitary and cold. The Lehfeldt grandchildren had relocated, he had no family, and he missed his aging mother whom he had left in Switzerland. Dolt liked spirits of the liquid kind, and he spent too much time in the cold empty hotel alone in his room with a bottle as his only companion. Perhaps it was the dark quiet of a deep winter freeze that finally got to him, or maybe it was his own carelessness. Whatever the reason, in March of 1927 Dolt passed out in the cold of his room, took pneumonia, and died. On his deathbed he had asked Louie to promise to send his remains back to his mother, but in the end she could not afford passage for the casket. Louie took care of funeral arrangements, and saw to it that "Dolty" was buried in the Lehfeldt family plot in the Lavina Cemetery. Louie had a tombstone of white Carrara marble placed on his grave. Some time later, $100 arrived from Dolt's mother in Switzerland. Although she could not afford the passage to bring her son's remains home, Mrs. Dolt sent what she could, wishing to thank the community for its care and consideration of her son during his illness. She asked that the town of Lavina create a memorial for him. The community purchased an arch to place over the gate to the cemetery. On Memorial Day, Lutheran pastor Reverend Berndt Alstad led a procession of uniformed soldiers, Boy Scouts, Girl Scouts, and school children to the cemetery to dedicate the gate to the memory of Emanuel Dolt. The gate has been taken down to prevent its falling and placed nearby where the plaque can be read today: "Dedicated to the Memory of Emanuel Dolt by his Mother, 1927."

During the Great Depression most of The Adams' rooms remained closed except for those occupied by family members. While the Egge family had moved into the hotel to weather the hard times, at the end of the 1930s it was empty. The American Lutheran Church bought the hotel for $750. Churchgoers converted the bar side to serve as a chapel. In 1960, the German Lutheran Church leased the building and the small congregation continued to worship in the bar-turned-chapel through the 1970s. Then the building became private property. In 2000, after a series of owners, The Adams Hotel was again on the market.

The owners' decision to sell The Adams coincided with Raymond Barry's decision to find a new place to live. He made an appointment with the owner to see the property. He felt drawn to the building and sensed what the outcome would be, so Raymond brought along his friends, Vianna Miles and John Wilmas, instructing them to kick him in the shins and talk him out of it if he began to show too much enthusiasm for the dilapidated old landmark. But as they came in through the bar side entry, Raymond's first impression of the building was very negative. He noted immediately that the bar side was water damaged, littered with debris, and uncared for. His heart fell. Then as he began to look around, he regained his enthusiasm. His companions gave him a few stern looks, so he tried hard to play it cool. The owner led the way into the entry and up the stairs. Once at the top of the steps near the ladies' parlor, they made a quick left turn and then a quick right and headed down a hallway. Raymond was disoriented. Five hallways on the second floor create a labyrinth made even more confusing by clutter and debris scattered here and piled there. Ceilings missing and fallen in, extensive water damage, and uneven flooring added to the messy confusion. Despite all this, Raymond saw potential.

The group proceeded toward Room 1, once the choice suite and most spacious of the hotel's accommodations. The others were ahead of him as Raymond lagged back, trying to take in all the details. The group passed by Room 2 and then Room 1. As Raymond fell behind, bringing up the rear and passing Room 2, he glanced in the door and saw a flicker of movement. He stood still, transfixed, observing his surroundings while his mind raced in all directions considering the future possibilities of the various rooms. He was startled to see a man rise up in the room in front of him. The man wore a white shirt and dark trousers with suspenders. His shirt was collarless, the type that required a celluloid collar as men of the 1920s commonly wore. He had dark curly hair, a slender build, and was of rather small stature. There was nothing small about his presence, however. He rose up menacingly, challenging Raymond as if to say, "What are you doing here? You don't belong. Get out!" The apparition purposefully moved across the hallway in front of Raymond and passed into the wall separating the row of rooms from the ladies' parlor on the other side.

Raymond at this point asked, as casually as he could manage, if the building might be haunted. The answer did not surprise him. Over the years, said the owner, local residents had occasionally reported glimpses of a man inside the empty building. At this the owner was obviously uncomfortable and so Raymond dropped the subject. But to Vianna, standing near him wide-eyed, he mouthed the words, "Did you see it?" She nodded her head and vigorously mouthed back, "Yes!"

A few months later, Raymond placed his down payment on the building and moved in. The work began and is ongoing. His intent is to turn the hotel into a living museum, and though the building is still unheated, Raymond lives there year round. Room 2 was one of the first things he tackled, furnishing it as a children's playroom with antiques appropriate to the time period. Raymond never saw the man again, but when he cleaned Room 2 he noticed that it seemed to attract an unusually large number of flies. He found hundreds of them dead in the windowsills.

About a year and a half after he settled into the old hotel, Raymond was coming into the dining room from the second parlor, what he calls the "music room," on the first floor. Out of the corner of his eye he saw a woman seated with her back to him. She was dressed in a long dark skirt with a high waistband and white blouse. She sat with her knees together. He could see her black boots peeking out from beneath her skirt. Her hair was pulled back into a chignon at the nape of her neck, arranged as if she were about to put on her hat to go out. Her left hand rested on her right knee with her right hand poised on top, very prim and proper. She seemed to be waiting for something. Raymond thought that that this might be Clara Lehfeldt Egge. He had seen pictures of her, dressed in similar attire. So he stood there, trying to memorize all the details. He studied her intently for several minutes so that he could recall her lovely essence, every little fold of her clothing, and her demeanor. Then she disappeared. Unlike the encounter with the man upstairs, this time Raymond felt nothing negative at all. The woman was serene, simply waiting for someone. He had the distinct feeling that she had been trying to find him, to tell him something. What that might be, he had no idea.

Raymond thought about the woman all evening. He was convinced it had been Clara, and that there was something she wanted him to know. And so the next morning Raymond made his way to the Lavina Cemetery to see if he could find the Lehfeldt family plot and Clara's final resting place. He passed through the gate, passed the arch dedicated to the memory of Emanuel Dolt, and found the Lehfeldts to the right and at the back. He was standing in front of Clara's grave, thinking about the incident of the previous afternoon. After a few minutes, he heard a car turn into the cemetery parking lot and saw a green van pull up, not ten feet from where he stood. A man and two women got out and approached him. They walked with purpose toward the spot where Raymond stood. He finally had to step aside. "Are you related to the Egges?" he asked. The woman sized him up. "I am an Egge," she said. She introduced herself as Jean Egge Fretland, Clara's daughter. Her granddaughter and her granddaughter's husband accompanied her. They had come from Miles City to visit the cemetery. Jean and Raymond chatted for a moment, and then he told her what had happened in the hotel the day before, leaving out his opinion as to the woman's identity. He described each detail he could remember. When he got to the placement of the woman's hands on her knee, Jean gasped. "That's Mother!" she said without any hesitation.

Raymond took the three visitors to the hotel where he showed them all around. As they moved from room to room, Jean reminisced and told Raymond much about the history of her family and the Adams Hotel. They went upstairs and Raymond related his first intimidating visit to the rooms, describing the apparition of the man in suspenders. They came back down to the lobby and suddenly Jean said, "I know who it is! Was the man bald or did he have curly hair?" Raymond told her that the man's hair was definitely curly. Jean then said, "It's Manny Dolt." Jean went on to tell Raymond about Dolt and how he died in Room 2, and the pieces all began to fit.

The huge job of rescuing the hotel's interior continues, and Raymond credits Clara with unlocking the key to much of the hotel's history. Clara has made no more appearances, but Raymond is certain that she appeared that afternoon to tell him her daughter would be coming from Miles City, and to make certain Raymond would be there to meet her. Clara's visit prompted Raymond to go to the cemetery. Had he not, he would have missed Jean and the opportunity to learn about Clara's family firsthand.

Raymond believes he has made his peace with Emanuel Dolt. If the Swiss cook is still around, he doesn't show himself nor does he seem to be upset that Raymond has refurbished his old room. Raymond did spend time in Room 2 talking with Emanuel, explaining to him that he does not have to hang around The Adams. "He was upset when he died," says Raymond, "over the fact that his mother couldn't afford to bring him home." That may be why he never left, and floated around the empty rooms in the familiar old hotel.

Since that meeting in the cemetery, Raymond has been instrumental in listing The Adams Hotel in the National Register of Historic Places. He is sure that his purchase of the hotel was fated, and he has come to believe he is connected to it in other ways. The day he first toured the hotel with his friends John and Vianna, he remarked that he thought it would be a hoot if he somehow discovered that one of his relatives had actually stayed at the hotel. Maybe it was not so far fetched since some of his relatives were from Canada, and Lavina was a stopping place for visitors traveling the railroad north to Havre and on across the border. Some time after Raymond moved into the hotel, he obtained records related to other businesses associated with the hotel. In going through these records, he was astounded to discover a man by the name of Art Wylie who had charge of the Adams Livery in 1911. Raymond's mother's maiden name was Wylie.

Recently Raymond had the opportunity to meet Hilda Lehfeldt Zahn's daughter, Nadine, who had also lived at The Adams before it closed. Raymond meant to follow up his meeting by calling her, but he had not yet done so. He knew he needed to make that phone call. With this mission in mind, Raymond prepared to settle down to make the call. First he needed to open the kitchen door to get some air circulating—with a space heater in use he needs to periodically let fresh air into the room. The cold winter air swirled in and with it came a surprise: the scent of gardenias. "How could the smell of gardenias blow in with this frigid air?" Raymond wondered. He sensed that someone was trying to tell him to make that phone call. He picked up the phone and dialed Nadine. She answered and after a few pleasantries, Raymond just had to ask, "Nadine, did your mother have a favorite scent?" But Raymond already knew the answer.

"Why yes," she replied. "I believe it was gardenia."

Sources

Historical context on Lavina can be found in Aldie Gordon, Margaret Lehfeldt, and Mary Morsanny's *Dawn in Golden Valley* and in the National Register of Historic Places nomination form for the Adams Hotel housed at the State Historic Preservation Office, Montana Historical Society, Helena. The *Roundup Record*, April 1, 1927, carried Emanuel Dolt's obituary.

THE MYSTERIOUS DEATH
OF THOMAS WALSH

On a crisp Thursday morning in March 1933, Montana buried a loyal friend, U.S. Senator Thomas J. Walsh. Mourners by the thousands climbed the front steps of the State Capitol to file through the rotunda. There, the open casket afforded a last view of the renowned statesman whose sudden death was proclaimed a "national calamity." Innuendo and political intrigue surrounded Walsh's demise. Events recorded in the *Helena Daily Independent* and some unpublished papers of Helena Judge Lester H. Loble at the Montana Historical Society library raise interesting questions about the circumstances and coincidences surrounding Walsh's death.

The United States and the world at large were in dire trouble in February 1933. Adolf Hitler was a familiar name as headlines documented his rapid and frightening rise to power. The United States was in the throes of a desperate economic depression. As the nation prepared for the upcoming inauguration of Franklin Delano Roosevelt, officials were still reeling from an attempted assassination of the president-elect that had occurred in Miami on February 15. Mayor Anton Cermak of Chicago was among four people wounded in the failed attack on Roosevelt. A woman standing next to the would-be assassin had jostled his elbow, causing the shots to be fired wildly into the crowd.

On Friday, February 24, while his friend Cermak clung to life in a Miami hospital, Senator Thomas Walsh of Montana announced plans to marry Mina Perez Chaumont de Truffin. The wedding was to take place on Monday, February 27, in Havana. Walsh, 73, and his considerably younger bride-to-be, the widow of a wealthy Cuban banker and sugar grower, had known each other for several years. Their families seemed to approve the match.

General Gerardo Machado, the president of Cuba and family friend of the Truffins, issued a special decree waiving the fifteen-day marriage notice required by law. The wedding was abruptly moved up to Saturday, February

25, at the secluded, vine-covered home of the bride in a Havana suburb. President Machado, who was to have been a witness, did not attend because he claimed he had not enough notice to travel to Havana from his country estate. Walsh's explanation to the press for the sudden change in plans would prove hauntingly prophetic. He said: "I have little time left before March 4." At the time, it seemed he referred to the upcoming presidential inauguration planned for that date.

On Sunday, the day after the wedding, President-elect Roosevelt announced his cabinet members, naming Senator Walsh as attorney general. Walsh announced his resignation from the senate, noting that he had known of the appointment for several days. Walsh was to be sworn into office at the presidential inauguration on the coming Saturday, March 4. His appearance at the ceremonies in the Senate Chamber would have marked twenty years to the day since his first appearance there as a newly-elected senator on March 4, 1913.

Public announcement of the appointment came as the newlyweds were en route from Havana to Miami. During the couple's twenty-four-hour stay in Florida, the senator visited Miami's Jackson Memorial Hospital where Mayor Cermak was battling complications from the assassin's bullet. Twice during a short stay in Daytona Beach, Dr. Harry L. Merryday was called to attend to the senator who was suffering from "a mild angina pectoris and intestinal indigestion." The doctor advised Walsh to stay in bed and cancel his trip. Walsh declared that he had to continue to Washington.

As the train bound for the nation's capital approached Wilson, North Carolina, on Thursday morning, March 2, Mrs. Walsh awakened around 7:00 AM to find that her husband had left his berth and was lying unconscious on the floor of their compartment. The porter summoned Dr. Richard Costello, who was a passenger on the train, but by the time the doctor reached the Walshes' suite, the senator was dead. Dr. M.A. Pittman of Wilson signed the death certificate listing the cause of death as "unknown, possibly coronary thrombosis." Dr. Pittman believed the cause of death to be "failure of blood vessels to the heart, apoplexy or some circulation failure." Mrs. Walsh gave her permission for an autopsy, but officials determined it unnecessary. The body was taken from the train at Rocky Mount and embalmed while a federal agent kept watch outside Mrs. Walsh's compartment.

Senator Walsh lay in state on March 6 in the senate chamber, attended by President and Mrs. Roosevelt and other high officials. During the service, Mrs. Walsh herself purportedly suffered a mild heart attack. Newspapers reported that doctors advised her not to accompany her husband's body back to Helena. President Roosevelt gave the senator's daughter use of his private railroad car for the long trip home. Mrs. Walsh remained in Washington.

On Thursday, March 9, as the funeral train sped across Montana from Billings to Helena, farmers in the fields paused and crowds shivering in the early morning cold stood quietly in tribute at every station platform along the way. A huge crowd waited at the Northern Pacific depot in Helena.

Last photo of Senator Thomas Walsh in the hat, left
COURTESY MONTANA HISTORICAL SOCIETY PHOTOGRAPH ARCHIVES 945-507

Public schools were dismissed that morning, and the superintendent requested that all schools take "time to consider the character and greatness of the late senator" when classes resumed. After the public viewing in the capitol rotunda, more than two thousand mourners crowded into St. Helena Cathedral for the final obsequies. The senator was then interred in a modest plot next to his late wife in Resurrection Cemetery. In a strange coincidence, as the Helena services were being conducted for Walsh, similar services were held in Chicago for Mayor Cermak, who had passed away on March 6.

Certainly there were some who did not share the national affection generally accorded Senator Walsh, but his achievements were undeniably far-reaching. The quiet statesman from Montana won greatest recognition as head of the senate committee that exposed fraudulent oil leases in the Teapot Dome scandals of President Warren G. Harding's administration a decade before. Walsh's investigations led to the conviction and imprisonment of Secretary of Interior Albert B. Fall. A few months before Walsh's wedding, Fall had been released from the penitentiary. As the press commented on the ramifications of Walsh's death, the *Baltimore Sun* went so far as to declare that Walsh had been treading on dangerous ground when he undertook those investigations. According to the *Sun*, he "was inviting personal and perhaps even physical, as well as political, destruction" All agreed that as attorney general, Walsh would have made a difference in Roosevelt's administration. The press pronounced his death a national misfortune.

Walsh's longtime friend, Judge Lester Loble, wrote in 1970 that Senator Walsh's son-in-law, Captain Emmit C. Gudger of the United States Navy, believed that a Cuban attendant of Mrs. Walsh's had poisoned his father-in-law. According to Captain Gudger, this woman was loyal to Machado's opposition. Captain Gudger tried to insist that an autopsy be performed and when that was not done, he later tried unsuccessfully to have the body exhumed.

Genevieve Walsh Gudger, the senator's daughter, disagreed with her husband's theory. In a letter to Judge Loble dated November 17, 1970, Mrs. Gudger acknowledged that "feelings were running high" because of the depression and therefore "suspicions were rampant." Mrs. Gudger also went on to say that her father had long suffered from high blood pressure and so the "heart attack was not a great surprise." Nevertheless, Mrs. Gudger did not further argue against the theory that her father might have been poisoned.

Thomas Walsh was the first Montanan appointed to a cabinet position. Marc Racicot, who declined Present George W. Bush's appointment as attorney general, was the second. As attorney general and personal friend of the president's, Walsh would have been in a position of influence in the Roosevelt administration. He could well have been a victim of either domestic or international political intrigue. Julio Morales, a successful lawyer who fled Cuba with the advent of Castro, wrote to Judge Loble that "...rumors were started by both parties, alleging that Senator Walsh had been poisoned by the opposite party." Reports from Havana on the Monday after the wedding indicated that "something approximating a revolution" was in progress after a violent weekend. Could this have had something to do with the rather odd marriage of a prominent American and an equally prominent Cuban who might have represented different political points of view?

It was no secret that Roosevelt was opposed to Machado's government, and Mrs. Walsh herself had recently been touched by a tragedy bred of political associations. The Truffins' adopted daughter, Regina, had just been widowed. Her husband, Clements Vazquez Bello, was president of the Cuban senate under Machado. Touted as Machado's political heir, the opposition assassinated Bello six months before the Walsh wedding. Surely the astute senator realized that there was some risk in marrying this charming woman whose family was so embroiled in dangerous diplomatics.

Montanans heard the rumors too and wondered. Judge Loble reported that a well-known fellow member of the bench stopped him on a Helena street to comment that Walsh had made a poor matrimonial choice. The rumors quieted down, but speculation has continued. As late as 1985, the daughter of another highly esteemed political colleague of Thomas Walsh's remained convinced that the senator was poisoned.

Elin Gudger Parks, daughter of Captain and Mrs. Gudger, remembers the Cuban woman who married her beloved grandfather as high strung and melodramatic. Mrs. Parks, who was about twelve at the time, admits that children remember strange things. She vividly recalls thinking it peculiar when the new Mrs. Walsh refused to sleep without a silver chamber pot under her bed. Although Mrs. Gudger liked her father's new wife, she and family members speculated that perhaps Mina de Truffin mistook Senator Walsh for another very wealthy gentleman with the same last name. The widow was upset to learn that her half of the inheritance consisted of the senator's Washington, D.C., town house. Mina traded the property for portable items in the estate and returned to Cuba. Among the things she took with her was a prized painting by C. M. Russell. The painting apparently remains uncatalogued and is unknown to collectors. It grieves the family to this day that the Russell painting was lost. Mina Walsh soon sold her Havana home to developers who converted it into the famous and still operating Tropicana gambling resort, a highlight of Havana's night life. What became of the lady herself is a mystery.

There is one final twist to this intriguing story. In preparing the move from the senate to the attorney general's office, Walsh's two longtime trusted employees carefully packed and boxed his files, entrusting them to a trucking company. They were to have been delivered to the House of Justice by the time Walsh assumed his new duties. Among these were files in progress concerning the Harding administration and the American aluminum industry, against whom Walsh intended to proceed. These personal files never reached their destination; in fact, they were never seen again.

Sources

Letters and newspaper clippings, housed in the Thomas Walsh vertical file at the MHS Library Research Center, furnished most of the information for this story. Elin Gudger Parks, the Walsh granddaughter, also contributed her personal opinions and confirmed the facts. Walsh's contributions are ably discussed in the late Richard B. Roeder's article, "Thomas Walsh, Helena Lawyer," in *More from the Quarries of Last Chance Gulch*, Volume II.

FIRE IN THE SNOW

Billings lay blanketed under a fast-falling winter snowstorm at 2 AM on Saturday, December 8, 1945. As the town quietly slept under its downy white cover, Northwest Airlines pilot Captain George D. Miller and his co pilot, First Officer Vernon W. Pfannkuck, fought desperately to bring their C-47 army transport plane down safely at the Billings airport. The plane approached from the east but was too high to attempt a landing, and circled the town to make another try. Battling poor visibility, the tower informed Captain Miller on his second attempt that he was now too low and would have to circle again.

Inside the plane, twenty-one overseas veterans bound from Newark, New Jersey, to Seattle for discharge or stateside reassignment were strapped in their seats. All had recent firsthand experience in the horrors of the world war so recently over. That day at the Newark Airport, the men had been jovial, exhilarated with the burden of dangerous service lifted off their shoulders. They were back on American soil, and things were finally right with the world. At last on the stateside leg, the men could think about tomorrow. They could, for the first time in many months, plan for their futures.

Plane number 45-922 took off from Fargo, North Dakota, en route to Billings with a new flight crew. The young veterans had been nodding off to the loud drone of the big engines; a few of the soldiers were asleep. As the pilots struggled frantically, a few of those still awake intuitively cinched their seat belts tighter but were unaware of the trouble in the cockpit. The plane began to lurch. Technician Fifth Grade Emil A. Hasch later recalled, "I was sitting in the last seat near the door and the plane was rocking back and forth as if we were hitting air pockets, but I didn't think anything about it."

The tower observed the plane make its turn to the south toward the rimrocks, a rocky escarpment that sharply descends some four hundred feet to the valley below where downtown Billings lies. The landing lights disappeared from view. On the ground, the roaring of the engines awakened Mr. and Mrs. J. E. Vogel, asleep in their home on Poly Drive. As the pilot gunned the engines in a desperate, last-ditch attempt to pull up the nose of the heavy transport, the landing lights shone eerily in the Vogels' window. A wing caught the trees bordering Poly Drive and tore loose. In another nearby residence on Poly Drive, Mrs. Marion Ruth drew the shades and gathered her three sleepy children in the living room. With her husband still on active duty in the Navy and not yet home from the war, Mrs. Ruth was careful to keep the house closed and her children protected from the cataclysmic event, whatever it might be, that was unfolding in the neighborhood. Sara Ruth, then seven, remembers sitting on the floor of the living room with her younger brother and sister. She could see the shooting flames from the front window, which lit the night with an eerie orange glow.

Later, Technician Hasch remembered, "When we hit the trees, I looked across the aisle at another boy and we both yelled, 'There she goes' at the same time." Neighbors heard a crashing, muffled thud as the plane came down nose first in a snow-drifted field below the rimrocks. Then it was quiet, and the snow continued to fall.

Like the Ruth family, the Vogels could also see the shooting flames from their windows. They immediately reported the accident before they, along with many of their neighbors, donned whatever warm clothing they could find and hurried to the crash site to offer aid. Soon the piercing wail of sirens bounced off the rimrocks. The first police officers to arrive at the field could hear the agonized screams of the injured and dying. Flames leapt upward, illuminating the entire scene in a hot, eerie circle of brightness against the winter landscape. By the light of the flames officers could see the outlines of seven men tossed from the bowels of the inferno into the deep snow. The torn wing lay nearby, broken like a toy, and an engine had broken free of its moorings pinning one of the pilots beneath it.

Ambulances and private citizens rushed the pilots and six other injured survivors along the icy streets to the hospital as the fire department put out the fire. Later that Saturday the *Billings Gazette* reported details of the horrific aftermath. In addition to those thrown clear of the aircraft on impact, "Twelve smoldering black and red charred forms, some with their arms and legs still in sitting positions," were carried from inside the twisted metal. As smoke curled from the wreckage, officials looked for clues and personal items that could help identify remains. Scattered in the snow well outside the area officials had roped off, neighborhood youngsters found three photographs and a box top, labeled "army decoration medal." They turned these in to the authorities.

Although both pilots initially survived the crash, they died in the hospital later that day. Captain Miller and First Officer Pfannkuck heroically managed to crash the plane in a field instead of nearby residential neighborhoods. Captain Miller was a former lieutenant commander in the navy where he flew with the air transport service in the Atlantic during the war. Although

C-47 Transport Plane
COURTESY JAMES A. REA

he had logged 6,883 hours of flight time, his experience likely did not include flight time in snowy weather, particularly at night. Still fresh from the war in Europe, Miller had been released from duty October 15, less than two months prior. He and his co pilot were flying the army transport under contract with Northwest Airlines. The *Billings Gazette* noted that just hours after his death, a telegram from the navy reached his family home in Minneapolis offering Miller the rank of commander if he would return to service.

Seventeen young servicemen, all veterans of the European front, and the two pilots lost their lives in the crash. Four veterans survived. The remains of the pilots and identified victims were returned to their hometowns within a few days, but thirteen bodies awaiting identification were held at an undisclosed location in Billings until the following Thursday. A military honor guard of thirteen army officers and enlisted men arrived from East Base at Great Falls to accompany the thirteen caskets to their final resting places. In the early morning hours before citizens stirred, coincidentally on December 13, the thirteen caskets, each with a flag and full military uniform hermetically sealed inside, were readied for the journey. The *Billings Gazette* reported, "All of the bodies were placed in a special baggage car at the Union Station and headed westward on Northern Pacific train No.1 to points in Oregon and Washington for burial."

The four survivors, two of them with grave injuries, spent several weeks in the hospital in Billings. Technician Hasch and Private First Class Raymond Parkins were released on December 20 and the two other more seriously injured soldiers were later transferred to Great Falls for further treatment and rehabilitation. Several years afterwards, one of the survivors visited Montana and made a point of thanking the doctors, nurses, and the people of Billings for their care and concern.

The official accident report placed the blame on the pilot's "unsafe acts" or "pilot technique," noting that the pilot's descent was too rapid to make the turn for his final approach, particularly with visibility so poor that the crew could not make proper adjustments. There were other contributing factors. Although mechanical problems were not apparent, the report includes no indication that the investigator reviewed maintenance records or personnel qualifications. Nor was there any review of transmitter or receiver performance records. The weather observer at the Billings airport clocked out at midnight. The tower took over weather observations and communicated with the crew, but likely failed to accurately advise them of deteriorating conditions. The tower routinely closed between two and eight in the morning; the crash occurred at 2:13 AM. According to meteorologist James A. Rea's analysis of the accident report, the tower operator was slow to respond, literally asleep at the switch: "A few more minutes of tower diligence would not have killed the tower operator, but it did [kill] the passengers and crew of 45-922." Captain Miller took the blame, and the crash became a statistic. Its victims, however, none of them local, faded nearly into obscurity.

For Bob and Sandra Hawke, however, owners of the Depot Antique Mall in downtown Billings, the 1945 plane crash still has eerie relevance. Their building is a wonderful historic structure in the midst of the original Billings

Townsite Historic District, listed in the National Register of Historic Places. It is situated directly across the street from Union Station. For decades, it was the main plant and headquarters of Sawyer Stores, Inc., a chain of grocery stores that operated in Montana and Wyoming during the mid-twentieth century. On a prominent downtown corner, the plant was convenient to a railroad siding where trains could pull right up to a loading dock. A bakery and coffee roasting facility, bean mill, seed cleaner, creamery, and warehouse made the plant a highly diversified operation. And in the basement, there was an ice plant and a huge refrigerated warehouse for storing large inventories of goods. The plant served as Sawyer Stores' headquarters from its construction in 1928 until 1963. Subsequent uses of the facility include a warehouse, restaurant, dinner theater, saloon, and now an antiques mall.

When the crash occurred in 1945, Billings had not handled a disaster of such magnitude. The two undertaking facilities, the Settergren Funeral Home and Smith's Funeral Home, were not equipped to store nineteen bodies indefinitely, especially those likely to be unidentified for a period of time. The *Billings Gazette* carried an announcement that the Settergren Funeral Home handled arrangements for air transfer of the remains of the two pilots to Minneapolis. What arrangements were made for the other four immediately identified victims are unknown. According to local tradition going back to the time of the crash, the Sawyer basement warehouse became a morgue while identification of thirteen of the victims was pending. Although no documents have come to light to prove this local belief, proximity to the depot and ample refrigerated facilities in the Sawyer Store basement make it likely. The Hawkes, who purchased the building in May 1996, believe that this use of the basement is not just legend but fact, and that the presence of the dead soldiers left their mark on the building. For example, the motion-sensing alarms at the back of the building and in the basement have been tripped several times when the building is locked and empty. Authorities can provide no logical explanation for these occurrences. Bob, who tends to be a skeptic, spends time working in the basement. He admits that some areas near the now-defunct coolers have definite cold spots. Passing through these areas gives him the chills. On one remarkable occasion, while he and another worker were at the checkout counter, a cup and saucer on a shelf behind him came flying off for no apparent reason. Both cup and saucer crashed down next to him. These small incidents, however, pale when compared to the sightings that have contributed to local lore for more than half a century.

During the Christmas holiday of 2002, Sandra was having a leisurely lunch with an acquaintance at the neighborhood Beanery Restaurant. Conversation turned to the antiques shop and her friend asked if she had ever seen the ghost. She admitted she had not, but asked him what he knew about it. He told Sandra that in the early 1980s when the Sawyer building was in its incarnation as a dinner theater, he had been an actor there. The main floor seating area facing the stage was situated directly above the refrigerated vaults in the basement. Just adjacent to the stage, a series of mirrors decorated the long brick wall on the east side. Light and movement reflected in the mirrors added dimension and ambiance to the space. Sandra's friend told her that, as he was performing on stage, he frequently watched the image of a tall, slim soldier in a brown uniform drift across the mirrors. The reflection had no human counterpart. Sandra thought it was a good story, but she didn't give it too much thought.

Bob and Sandra renovated the spacious building to suit their needs for the Depot Antique Mall. They took care to preserve and incorporate the unique features of the old building, including the still-working 1920s freight elevator, the heavy post and beam construction, wood flooring, and two main floor walk-in safes. Although neither has seen the ghost first-hand, they don't doubt that sometimes he is there, watching customers come and go. Two of the Hawkes' employees report they have seen the uniformed serviceman in the same area that Sandra's friend said he saw the image, directly above the basement coolers where the wall of mirrors used to be. The young man appears there, stoically watches them at work, and then fades away. At other times, he has reportedly been more playful, pitting the two employees in a game of cat and mouse. He has ever so softly called out the name of one worker as if her co-worker were calling her for assistance. The ghostly summons sent the one employee quickly up the back stairs to discover that the co-worker was elsewhere in the building. Both staffers say the presence is not at all frightening. Sandra quips, "Isn't it just like a young soldier to lavish his attentions on the two most attractive women available?"

Customers have come to the counter disturbed enough by something in that same area above the refrigerator as well as at the back staircase to express their feelings that there is a "strong presence" in those parts of the building. Occasional visitors, who know nothing of the history of the place and who have had to go to the closed basement for one reason or another, have commented on a "sad feeling" in the vault area. Things often seem to disappear, or show up where they shouldn't. When things are missing or seem out or place, the staff just remarks, "Must be those fly-boys again!"

At night in the basement, when the building is empty, it is not hard to imagine that the energy of the thirteen unfortunate homeward bound veterans, whose young lives ended so tragically, might linger with energy powerful enough to trip a motion-sensor. And perhaps the image of at least one young man left an indelible imprint upon the place where he rested before his final journey home.

Sources

The *Billings Gazette*, especially December 9, 10, and 12, 1945, thoroughly covered the events related to this tragedy. Follow up articles include *Great Falls Tribune*, December 12, 1945 and the *Gazette*, December 31, 1945. Reporter Kathryn Wright, who covered the event, wrote her own reminiscence of the tragedy for the *Gazette* May 5, 1985. James A. Rea of Glasgow, Montana, obtained the official accident report and patiently explained the findings.

Montana's Nessie: Flathead Flossie

S keptics have explained the mysterious creature sighted in Montana's Flathead Lake as an overweight skin-diver, a mother-in-law in a swimsuit, a sturgeon, a superfish, a prehistoric holdover, even a wayward seal. As unlikely as it may seem, however, the USO (unidentified swimming object) may not be a hoax. For well more than a century, reports of some kind of large creature in the third largest body of fresh water west of the Great Lakes have kept residents and tourists on the lookout. And sightings have been numerous.

While most everyone from school age to senior citizen across the world knows about Scotland's Nessie of Loch Ness Lake, similar sightings in other places have not received such worldwide publicity. There are, in fact, many tales about cold, deep, freshwater lakes and sightings of creatures in them. In theory these lakes could support creatures of very large size. Lake Champlain between New York and Vermont in the United States has its "Champ," and in Canada, sightings of "Ogopogo" in Okanagan Lake in British Columbia date back the 1800s. "Manipogo" of Lake Manitoba is another. There have been sightings of a creature in Utah's Bear Lake as well. Even Brigham Young believed in that creature described as an undulating body of light cream color more than thirty feet long.

Montana's version reputedly lurks in the deep waters of Flathead Lake, a body of water that covers some 189 square miles. The lake is twenty-eight miles long, ten miles wide and more than 120 feet deep. Until the mid-1880s, settlement of this remote northwestern region lagged behind the rest of Montana territory because travel there was so difficult. The advent of the Northern Pacific across Montana in 1883 made access more feasible.

Beginning in 1885, steamboats plied the waters of Flathead Lake, carrying goods and passengers between Polson and Demersville, the early settlement that later relocated to become present-day Kalispell. In 1887 settlers and visitors to the Flathead Lake country took the Northern Pacific to Ravalli where stages left three times weekly. The stage carried the earliest passengers to the little steamer *U.S. Grant,* a converted sailboat. Equipped with an upright boiler, "donkey engine," and a screw-type propeller, the *U.S. Grant's* pilot was Captain James C. Kerr, a veteran of the Great Lakes. Captain Kerr skippered Flathead steamers from 1886 until his death at the helm of the *Klondyke* in 1909. It was aboard the *U.S. Grant* that Captain Kerr made the first recorded sighting of a mysterious creature in Flathead Lake. In 1889 he and his startled passengers saw a twenty-foot object swimming directly in the steamer's path. Passengers began to panic and one man aimed his rifle at the object, fired, and missed. The creature disappeared. Thus began the epic of Montana's own lake monster.

Since that first incident shocked those aboard the *U.S. Grant,* two kinds of sightings have produced two different mysteries. One sighting is that of a huge fish and the other is of a serpent-like creature. In the first kind of report, observers seem to describe a type of sturgeon. Old timers recall Indians of the lake country who told of sighting what they called "superfish." Experiences related by both the Salish and Kootenai suggest that historically, sturgeon existed in Flathead Lake. A strong oral tradition in Kootenai songs and stories tells of the fish they called "Long Nose."

There are many reported sightings of sturgeon in Flathead Lake. In an oral interview conducted by his family in 1954, Flathead Lake pioneer Joe Zelezny told of an incident that occurred in 1899 while he spearfished by torchlight. Zelezny's homestead was north of what is today Rollins, Montana in a shallow bay. A carpenter and homesteader, Zelezny often fished at night, taking large numbers of fish for the family table. On this particular evening, he had finished fishing when he saw something unusual. The object was large, maybe ten or twelve feet, log-shaped, and lying in the lake on the bottom of a shallow bay area. Joe told his brother, Henry, to stick the object, handing him the spear. When Henry did so, it came shooting out of the water: "It tore loose … . It looked exactly like a sturgeon. It couldn't have been anything else." According to John Stromnes of the *Missoulian,* Joe Zelezny was an honest homesteader who had no reason to promote the idea of the Flathead monster, and nothing to gain: "So his report," wrote Stromnes, "must be given considerable credence."

In 1915 a school of sturgeon sighted near Plains in the Clark Fork River was reported heading toward the lake. The huge fish were sixty miles downstream from Flathead Lake and moving in that direction. Then in 1920, commercial fishermen working on the lake discovered their nets ripped apart by something they assumed must have been a gigantic fish.

The late C. Leslie Griffith took the superfish legend to a new level claiming to have caught a 181-pound, seven-and-a-half foot white sturgeon on May 28, 1955. Despite sworn testimony that Griffith hauled the superfish onto his boat off the west shore near Cromwell Island, skeptics dispute that there are any sturgeon in Flathead Lake. But no one has been able to disprove his claim. The fish has since been on display at the Polson Flathead Historic Museum.

On September 2, 1960, bathers at the Polson swimming beach reported a "creature with a head like a horse." Within a day or so, the Ziglers had their own experience. The family, who lived on the grounds of the Polson Country Club, heard large waves crashing and went to investigate. There were no boats in the area, but huge waves were breaking over the swimming pier and on the shore. At the end of the pier the Ziglers saw something that appeared to be rubbing against the pilings as if scratching its back. Gilbert Zigler, part time deputy sheriff, city policeman, and summer groundskeeper at the country club, went to get his rifle. As Mrs. Zigler moved closer to the pier to see what it was, it suddenly came out of the water. She said, "It was a horrible looking thing with a head about the size of a horse ... and about a foot of neck showing." Was this sighting a sturgeon? A game warden explained that sturgeon, if that is what it was, could appear mammal-like because "their mouths are on the underside of their frame and they have whisker-like feelers to boot."

The *Flathead Courier* made a standing offer: $25 to anyone who could either take a picture of the big fish and submit it along with the negative or make it possible for the paper to take the photograph. "So," challenged the *Courier*, "keep your cameras loaded and your eyes peeled." Fishermen near Bigfork at the northeastern end of the lake on August 26, 1961, saw something huge circle their boat and speed away when another boat approached. Others reported big fish swimming in schools. But no one snapped a photo.

These superfish sightings are generally thought to be sturgeon, but that, too, is a mystery. If such fish do exist in Montana waters, experts believe that they are likely holdovers of glacial Lake Missoula or from the lower Columbia drainage that entered the lake before there were any dams. Fresh water sturgeon take several decades to reach maturity and can live for over a century. The Kootenai white sturgeon is an isolated population, officially listed as endangered in 1994. The largest Kootenai River sturgeon weighed in at 200 pounds. There are eighteen white sturgeon populations, but only the Kootenai sturgeon were naturally cut off from the lower Columbia River drainage during the last glacial period 10,000 years ago; it is a genetically unique population. There are only thirty miles of white sturgeon habitat in Montana's Kootenai River. Although experts say that Flathead Lake could support a limited population of sturgeon that survived from ages past, and environmental conditions in the Upper Flathead River system are ideal for breeding, no hard proof thus far places white sturgeon in Flathead Lake.

The second type of sighting is no sturgeon. Whatever the creature is, it and its offspring have been seen enough times—at least fifty-three—for it to merit a name of its own. "Flossie" seems to fit well in company with other monsters like Nessie and Champ and a name of its own gives the creature the distinction it deserves. Flossie has been consistently described since the first sighting in 1889: black-brown in color and twenty to forty feet in length (although this depends upon how much of the creature is visible at the time of the sighting). Witnesses describe a snakelike head, a body with vertical humps, and a tail tapered like that of an eel.

In July 1962 a Polson housewife and some California tourists traversing the wooden bridge across the Flathead River stopped midway and jumped out of their cars to get a better view of a black object. It was some 15 feet long, moving upstream through the lake outlet. It undulated in an up and down motion, then quickly gained momentum and moved into the main part of Flathead Lake.

A few months later on September 12, 1962, brothers Ronald and Maynard Nixon had a close encounter with the monster whose photos they had helped fake. They had regarded the sightings as a great joke and helped their mother rig some spectacular trick photos of it for tourists. But what the brothers saw three hundred feet offshore as they drove along the Polson waterfront made them believers. Ronald Nixon said, "It was moving straight away from the shore and fast enough so that the wave at the front was about two feet high. The wake at the back must have been at least twenty-five feet from the front, so the object must have been longer than that.... It couldn't have been a sturgeon. I don't have any idea what it was."

Several businessmen out for some fishing on a mild December day in 1962 also saw the creature. They were trolling in Big Arm Bay for lake trout when they suddenly saw what looked like a log pop up out of the water. It came from nowhere. They stopped the motor and watched it drift, then started it up again to get closer for a better look. As they did so, the thing disappeared as suddenly as it had surfaced leaving quite a wake.

Businessman George Darrow and his wife of Bigfork also saw the creature and long kept quiet for fear of ridicule. They later told of their 1971 experience. George recalled that as they sat on the deck of their west lakeshore home, he "saw two, then three, loops in the water, one hundred yards offshore moving parallel to the shoreline. The object was snakelike, serpent like, and there was about eight to ten feet between loops."

On May 25, 1985, trolling in Yellow Bay, retired army major George Cote and his son Neal saw an object "as long as a telephone pole and twice as large in diameter." As the creature slowly swam with an undulating motion, they could see four to six humps above the water. It then sped away. At a distance of about four hundred meters, it stopped and looked back, then disappeared underwater. They knew that no one would believe them, and so they kept quiet about it. Then in 1987, Cote was driving along old Highway 93 near Lakeside when he saw the creature again. This time the creature was "quivering as it swam" in a forward motion. He saw the entire creature: head, body and tail. Cote decided to come forward, detailing his two sightings in a letter to the Department of Fish, Wildlife and Parks (FWP) in 1990. Cote's descriptions reveal his army training in observation, "I counted six to eight coils of its body on the surface but couldn't see its tail because it was under water."

The Cotes know what they saw, said George in his 1990 letter. The major is a veteran fisherman who had fished the ocean, caught 1,000-pound tuna, and seen sturgeon. "I have been out on Flathead Lake over 300 times in the last 15 years. I know what a submerged log looks like. There is no doubt in my mind that it was a huge creature."

According to a thirty-year veteran FWP fisheries biologist and expert on the Flathead sightings, Laney Hanzel, the thirteen sightings reported in 1993 were the most in any given year. And one of those was the only report of two creatures. On May 24, there were two creatures sighted swimming side by side in Big Arm Bay. One was larger than the other. In six of the 1993 sightings witnesses described baitfish that seemed to be jumping out of the water to escape whatever it was. Hanzel has seen neither monster nor sturgeon but admits observing "several unexplainable large sized holes in the nets we pulled from the lake."

Not all sightings lack explanation. One proved to be a horse swimming across the lake and another a flock of birds packed together resembling a twenty-foot log. In the 1940s, Los Angeles resident Frank T. Dwyer reported seeing a seal in the lake. "I know seals," Dwyer insisted. "We stopped ... and saw the seal jump from some large rocks and disappear into the water. A few minutes later it was swimming near the shore. I learned there are not supposed to be seals in Flathead Lake but I know definitely there is one there." There were other similar reports of a large mammal at this same time. Several years before, a seal from a traveling circus had indeed escaped into the lake.

"The Narrows," Flathead Lake
COURTESY MONTANA HISTORICAL SOCIETY 957-737

Mark Henckel reported in the *Billings Gazette,* September 6, 1998, that according to Jim Vashro, then regional fisheries manager for Fish, Wildlife and Parks, of seventy-eight sightings on record from 1889 to 1994, twenty-five were of a superfish creature and fifty-three reported an eel-like object up to sixty-feet long with humps and smooth skin. Credible witnesses include life-long residents and tourists. The most likely places to catch a glimpse of Flossie seem to be in the vicinities of Skidoo Bay, Polson Bay, The Narrows, and along the west shore road.

What is it that so many people have seen? Many believe that there is definitely something to the sightings. Even Dorothy Johnson, renowned Montana author who hailed from Whitefish, believed there was something in the lake. In a letter to then editor of the *Flathead Courier* Paul Fugleberg, Johnson wrote:

> "I don't think the monster should be done with tongue in cheek. You have eyewitness accounts by people who were scared and didn't think it was funny. I remember hearing about *something* in Flathead Lake more than forty years ago, so don't give the Polson Chamber of Commerce credit for dreaming it up ... ."

Fugleberg, historian of Flathead Lake sightings, catalogued some seventy of them. He insists, "There's something out there."

Visitor Services Bureau Chief Ken Soderberg of Montana State Parks related an incident that FWP Maintenance Supervisor Merle Phillips shared with him a few years ago. Phillips and his crew were called to Wild Horse Island to dispose of a dead horse that was, as Soderberg puts it, "making a bit of a stink." While sometimes in such a situation the men will resort to dynamite, a nearby cabin made that solution unwise. The horse was stiff as a board and too big to load on the boat, so they built a raft of inflated inner tubes and boards intending to haul it across to shore. They lashed the horse to the boards, legs sticking straight up in the air, but they slightly miscalculated the weight of the horse. Once in the water, it partially submerged.

The boat moved slowly, dragging the raft with its unusual cargo. Boats passing by gave the FWP crew double takes as they saw what was tethered to the raft. Finally one boat turned around, pulled alongside the FWP craft and the driver asked, "Hey, what are you guys doing?"

Phillips replied in all seriousness, "Mister, I would advise you to stay back from this official boat."

The driver was taken aback, "Well, how come? What are you doing?"

Phillips realized he had to come up with an answer. The look on the fellow's face was priceless when he heard Phillips' response, "We're trolling for the Flathead Lake monster!"

Sources

The following sources include details about the history of navigation on Flathead Lake and Captain Kerr's obituary: *Daily Inter Lake*, April 29, 1909; *Great Falls Tribune*, December 2, 1962; and *Great Falls Tribune*, January 6, 1935. For the many accounts of the "monster" of the lake, see *Flathead Courier*, September 8, 1960; *Great Falls Tribune*, March 31, 1963; and *Billings Gazette*, September 6, 1998. John Fraley, "This Is Not Just Another Fish Story" in *Montana Outdoors* (November-December 1991), recounts the Cotes' experiences. The definitive work is Paul Fugleberg's 1992 booklet, *Montana Nessie of Flathead Lake*.

LAURA'S CANARIES

L ouis Reeder looked for opportunity where he thought he could find it. What better place than the booming gold camps of Montana Territory? Reeder didn't mind a challenge, and he welcomed hard work. So the young bachelor took stock of his skills, left his family in Bucks County, Pennsylvania, and came west to seek his fortune.

Reeder arrived in Helena after a long and arduous trip. It was 1867, and the gold camp was a lively and colorful town. Unkempt miners and shifty-eyed gamblers lounged in the saloons, working men and white-aproned shopkeepers milled about the false-fronted log stores, and Sunday auctioneers competed with black-robed Jesuit priests. Oxen and mule teams kept the earthen floor of the gulch constantly churned. Pathways darted here and there in every direction off the gulch, ending in mining claims against the steep hillsides. And everywhere he looked Reeder saw construction. That is what interested him, as he had come west to ply his trade as a mason.

Reeder had no trouble securing work. Lewis and Clark County needed a substantial courthouse and Reeder knew how to build it. He hired on and made a tidy sum, secured more work, saved his money, and by the 1870s he had begun to accumulate a fair amount of property.

Then Reeder had an idea. He himself had experienced the primitive living conditions the miners, whose little shacks and cabins straggled along Last Chance Gulch, had endured. Reeder determined to use his skills to build a series of tiny quarters offering miners something better than a leaky, miserable sod roof and badly chinked walls that let the murderous winter wind whistle through on cold winter nights.

Reeder bought an odd-shaped piece of property on a steep hillside. A few buildings and shacks dotted the lots, and so he used those to begin his project, incorporating them into his little complex. Year by year the complex grew, and Reeder added onto it as he could. Eventually there were more than thirty one-room apartments that stretched along the steep incline. Reeder's little alley had units of stone, log, and brick crafted in the rowhouse form he knew from the East. But, he also tried his hand at adapting the false front idea into some of his buildings. The result was a well-built group of cozy little dwellings, just right for a miner who didn't need much room.

Reeder had been in Helena for a number of years when one morning he was working on the chimney of a house he owned on West Main Street. The house had been moved from its original location to another corner nearby, a tedious job accomplished in those days by setting the building on logs and rolling it along. The chimney scaffolding was piled with bricks to be used for the repair. When Reeder climbed upon it, the weight was too much and the whole thing collapsed sending him plummeting head first, bricks tumbling down on top of him. He lay at the bottom of the heap, broken like a glass bottle in a trash heap. Friends loaded Reeder in a wagon and delivered him, conscious and in terrible pain, to the Sisters of Charity at St. John's Hospital. He had lost all sensation in his extremities, and when asked about his condition, he acknowledged, "The doctors say that there is no show for me." At evening vespers, on August 27, 1884, Louis Reeder breathed his last. He left a sizable estate to a brother, Houston Reeder, in Pennsylvania. A simple tombstone stands alone in Benton Avenue Cemetery marking his grave.

Through the years Reeder's Alley served its intended purpose, housing mostly single men while a string of red light establishments spread out and mingled with the Chinese population at the foot of Reeder's Alley. Through the 1890s, James Gorman managed the apartments, although the property was still in limbo as Reeder's family members argued over who was legal heir. The case had still not been resolved in 1908, but managers continued to take care of the alley, more or less.

The 1920s brought a few changes to the neighborhood. George Duchesnay brought his second wife to live in one of the small apartments in the stone house at the top of the hill. It was an ancient home, probably housing miners or travelers passing through even before Louis Reeder owned the land. The stone house was divided into four walkup flats each with a door that opened into the dusty alleyway. Its triangular end made an odd wedge-shaped room, and this particular apartment was usually the one that was home to the manager of Reeder's Alley. It was here that George and Laura Duchesnay made their home.

George had a little string of cabins above the stone house that he rented to seasonal tourists and he collected rents from the apartments along the alley. His tenants were a mixed group, all men, most of them retired and living on pensions. Among the several dozen renters in the alley were a hotel cook, a musician, several sheepherders, a few city workers, and a railroad man. George himself worked as a groundman for Montana Power Company. Both Laura and George were born in France, and neither lost the charming speech that characterized their homeland. But it was Laura who lent a special quality to Reeder's Alley.

Word soon got around the neighborhood that the quiet lady with the foreign accent was a gentle friend with a healing touch. She had a quiet manner with wild creatures, especially birds. While Laura was always willing to nurse the wild mountain birds of the forested hills, her greatest love was for the beautiful yellow canaries that filled her tiny, odd-shaped apartment with the sweetest songs. Laura loved her little songbirds. She sometimes allowed them to fly at will in the rafters of the old stone house where they would trill and warble. Laura's heart would soar at the beauty of their voices. Although it was hard for her to part with the beautiful birds, it was a business and she advertised in the city directories of the 1920s, "Canary birds for sale: Excellent singers!" And so they were.

In February 1933 Laura became ill. Her songbirds fell silent when she left her little home and went to St. Peter's Hospital, suffering from an intestinal obstruction. Soon after, Laura died. George mourned his gentle wife and wanted to bring her home one more time. So he fixed a place for her in the tiny apartment and the undertaker brought her back to Reeder's Alley. George unlatched the cages and let Laura's little birds find their favorite perches in the rafters, and the old stone house filled again with their sweet songs. The tiny creatures seemed to know the finality of this last ritual, and so they fluttered around their gentle mistress, and perched in the rafters, singing just as sweetly at midnight as they did on mornings when the sun lit up the tiny room.

After Laura was gone, her canaries went to new homes, George collected his rents, life went on, but there was no joy in Reeder's Alley. On August 17, 1940, George died in the modest home he had shared with Laura. They lie side by side at Forestvale Cemetery. Except for one line author Dick Pace wrote about her in an obscure unpublished article years ago, now tucked away in the Montana Historical Society library's vertical files, all memory of Laura ceased to exist.

By the 1950s Reeder's Alley was home to a number of pensioners. Owners Reed Matthews and Godfrey Sullivan supplied a need for low-rent housing for older folks on a small fixed income. But city planners had slated the "seedy" area, along with all nearby reminders of Chinese occupation and red-light activities, for demolition as part of urban renewal. Reeder's Alley would be gone today but for the efforts of three Helena women who became its saviors in 1961. The four small apartments in the stone house and the alley had become a dumping ground for trash and refuse. But these women, compelled by the age of the unusual collection of quaint rowhouse apartments, couldn't bear to see the bulldozer erase such a colorful testament to Helena's past. Pat Boedecker, Eileen Harper, and Jane Tobin brought new life to Louis Reeder's housing project. They knew nothing about Laura Duchesnay, but they did understand the alley's historical significance.

Unbeknownst to their husbands, the three industrious women took out a loan, bought the stone house, and began cleaning up the property. After they sent their children off to school and their husbands to the office, they worked every day. Between the hours of 10 and 2 they cleaned, took out partitions, and made three of the tiny apartments into one big room. The odd-shaped end became a vestibule. The women opened a gallery and lunchroom. Sullivan offered to sell them the rest of Reeder's Alley, but it was home to twenty-three elderly residents who could not afford to move. Sullivan spent months relocating every tenant. After each one had found a new home, he finalized the sale to the women. Then with the advice and encouragement of Charles Bovey, whose restoration projects in Virginia City transformed a dying town into a tourist destination, the seeds of their vision became firmly planted. Eventually they purchased the rest of the alley and cleaned that up too. The complex stands today because of their efforts.

The women finished the project and after several years passed, they sold the property. The old stone house at the top of Reeder's Alley became a popular restaurant as well as a popular place to work. Michaela Crawford was intrigued by the place and thrilled when management hired her as a waitress in November 2000. Staff members were a diverse group but much like a large family; all of them had been at the Stone House for at least several years, and one veteran had worked there for seven. As her training ended, Michaela was told that there were things she needed to know if she were going to work there.

"This is an old building," said the senior staff member, "We have all experienced things in this place that we can't explain. You may see things, feel things, and hear things that are frightening. Just don't be afraid and know that you aren't alone."

The Stonehouse at Reeder's Alley
COURTESY KATIE BAUMLER

Michaela thought this whole scenario a little strange, but she took it in stride and fell in love with the old stone building. She did indeed have some odd experiences, and it helped to know that she was not the only one. During the two years Michaela worked at the Stonehouse Restaurant, odd sounds that everyone heard spun a common thread among the employees. Various staff reported hearing a disembodied sneeze and sometimes a cough when no one else was near. The startling sounds came out of nowhere. Besides the fact that they couldn't see whomever it was, the sound seemed to come from above their heads. Staff also heard a child's laughter, and that too seemed to come from above. Given the building's history housing miners and pensioners, a child's voice was out of place. Although they rarely discussed these incidents, each staff member knew the others had similar experiences.

Most workers at one time or another had the feeling that someone was close behind them in the darkened building, and Michaela recalls with a shiver that once she could feel someone's breath on the back of her neck when she knew there was no one nearby. And there was one more thing the staff had in common: a fleeting glimpse of a mysterious black shadow that sometimes crossed the corridor. It slithered across the cold floor like a snake. It was always an out-of-the-corner-of-your-eye kind of thing, but distinct enough to make a person fairly certain he had not made it up, especially when others saw it, too. Michaela often wondered what kind of body cast that shadow to make it slide so smoothly across the floor.

While some staff had other individually unique experiences in addition to these things, they didn't usually compare notes. Michaela's several experiences, beyond the familiar shadow crossing the hallway and the disembodied voices, were no exception. The lights, for one thing, had often caused her unease. Late at night after the restaurant closed, when she was getting the tables ready for the next evening, the lights would flicker on and off. Was it the shadowy visitor or just old wiring? Then one night something happened that made Michaela believe the strange events were neither coincidence nor tricks of the imagination.

One of Michaela's responsibilities was to get things ready for the next evening and extinguish the lanterns on each table. Usually she did that first thing after the restaurant closed, to save fuel. But this night had been very busy and she didn't get around to it until her other work was finished. It was after midnight and time to go home. She went into the main dining room to blow out the lanterns. While Michaela did not always feel comfortable in other parts of the building, this room that had once been the three tiny apartments had a good feeling. As she entered the spacious room she noticed that not a single lantern was still burning. Michaela thought someone had done her a good turn and wanted to thank him. She asked the cook. He said he did not do it. She asked the waiters. The waiters swore they did not do it either. But someone did.

On the night before Valentine's Day Michaela had another odd encounter. She was getting the dining rooms ready for a very busy serving the next day. It was midnight, and she was putting the last touches on the tables. A sound above her head startled her. "What in the world was that?" she thought. There it was again: a distinct chirping. "Oh, no!" she thought. "A small bird must have gotten itself locked inside the building. How am I going to get it out?" Michaela followed the sound into the foyer, listening intently. As she stood there, she heard loud chirping and the rush of beating wings as if a whole flock of birds was passing overhead. They brushed across the ceiling from one end to the other moving together in an unmistakable group. Then as quickly as the sound had begun, it was quiet. After that night, Michaela now and again heard birds in the foyer. When she left the employ of the Stonehouse, these incidents were almost forgotten. Almost. She tucked the memories away and told only a few people about these events.

In spring 2002 during a history lesson I was guest teaching at Helena High School, a student suggested that her sister had had some experiences at the Stonehouse Restaurant and believed that it was haunted. Taking Michaela's phone number, I called her and she willingly shared her experiences. While she knew about Louis Reeder and some of the history of Reeder's Alley, neither she nor the staff, property owners, nor anyone else knew about Laura's canaries. It was one of those forgotten details buried in Dick Pace's long-ago article, discovered in the process of researching the historic Reeder's Alley neighborhood. That small discovery had prompted my investigation into the Duchesnays' residency at Reeder's Alley. After Michaela related all her experiences at the Stonehouse, except the part about the birds, I asked her if there was anything else she could think of that had been odd about the Stonehouse. She then thought a moment, and mentioned the birds almost as an afterthought. She had no way of knowing that the restaurant's foyer had once been home to Laura Duchesnay and her yellow canaries.

EPILOGUE

In August of 2002, a few months after the conversation with Michaela, a group assembled in the back yard of the historic Pioneer Cabin below the Stonehouse Restaurant. They had come to the annual fund-raiser at the foot of Reeder's Alley in support of the cabin's preservation. Dozens of guests gathered around the tables for dinner, enjoying the warm summer evening. Conversation at my table turned to the stories I was there to tell, and as dinner got underway, guests at my table begged me to give them a preview of my program. I told them the story about Laura and her canaries, a tale still in progress and not on my formal program for that evening.

An hour later as I was nearly finished with my last story, "The Haunted Cabin," a tale included in *Spirit Tailings* about the cabin where we were enjoying our dinner, the wind suddenly began to blow and thunder rolled overhead. The guests made a run for cover as the sky opened and the driving rain instantly soaked everything. In the mad dash for shelter, several guests breathlessly asked if I had heard them. "Heard what?" I asked, having heard nothing but the wind and the sudden onslaught of spattering raindrops. "The birds! The birds! Didn't you hear them? We couldn't see them, but the chirping and fluttering were so loud we couldn't hear you at all. And they weren't sparrows or crows. These little chirps sounded just like *canaries*!"

The following December of 2002, property owners Darrell and Kathy Gustin donated Reeder's Alley to the State of Montana. The Montana Heritage Commission currently manages and maintains the brick and stone buildings. Strolling up the secluded brick alley toward the historic stone house at the top of the steep incline, it is easy to imagine Laura and her canaries in residence there. Since the discovery of Laura's story, dozens of wide-eyed school children and visitors, poised at the top of the alley, have now delighted in it, assuring the gentle Frenchwoman and her songbirds a prominent place in the neighborhood's colorful history. The trees rustling in the wind and the shadows that creep over the old bricks carry her imprint. And in February, the anniversary of Laura's death, when the ground is cold and the wind is lonely, the spirit of Reeder's Alley moves inside. Phantom songs in the old stone house rekindle the sweetest memories.

Sources

William Campbell's *From the Quarries of Last Chance Gulch* provides rich resources for Helena's earliest history. National Register of Historic Places inventory forms for the Helena Historic District housed at the State Historic Preservation Office in Helena include individual inventory forms for the buildings at Reeder's Alley. The Montana Historical Society Research Center includes vertical files on Louis Reeder, Dick Pace, and Urban Renewal (Helena). Pat Boedecker loaned her personal collection of clippings and provided valuable information for this story. Other resources include Polk Directories, US census records, Forestvale cemetery records, and Montana Historical Society's Photograph Archives.

INDEX